LET DOGS
BE DOGS

Also by the Monks of New Skete

How to Be Your Dog's Best Friend
The Art of Raising a Puppy
In the Spirit of Happiness
I & Dog
Rise Up with a Listening Heart
Divine Canine
Dogs & Devotion
Bless the Dogs

LET DOGS BE DOGS

UNDERSTANDING CANINE NATURE
AND MASTERING THE ART OF LIVING WITH
YOUR DOG

The Monks of New Skete
and Marc Goldberg

Little, Brown and Company

NEW YORK   BOSTON   LONDON

Little, Brown and Company
Hachette Book Group
1290 Avenue of the Americas, New York, NY 10104
littlebrown.com

First Edition: September 2017

Little, Brown and Company is a division of Hachette Book Group, Inc. The Little, Brown name and logo are trademarks of Hachette Book Group, Inc.

The publisher is not responsible for websites (or their content) that are not owned by the publisher.

The Hachette Speakers Bureau provides a wide range of authors for speaking events. To find out more, go to hachettespeakersbureau.com or call (866) 376-6591.

ISBN 978-0-316-38793-4
LCCN 2017939186

10 9 8 7 6 5 4 3 2 1

LSC-C

Printed in the United States of America

Marc Goldberg:
For my children, Samantha, Faye, and William.
Sorry about the leashes at Disney World.

Brother Christopher:
For all the dogs that I've worked with these thirty-six years.
You have given me more than I could ever give in return.

Contents

Authors' Note

There is a corollary between our second training book, *The Art of Raising a Puppy,* and *Let Dogs Be Dogs.* The idea for the puppy book came to me eleven years after our first book was published. I'd been at New Skete for about six years and had begun to see the same things over and over: adolescent canines that were undersocialized and ill-adjusted. I also became aware that there wasn't a comprehensive puppy manual to guide new owners. With our experience raising puppies, I thought we could help. I remember being out driving with the abbot, Father Laurence, and saying, "There's a new book and here's what it is." And he simply replied, "Fine, you write it."

Now, twenty-three years later, I've found myself experiencing feelings similar to those I had leading up to the puppy book.

In the intervening years, I'd turned toward writing that was more spiritual. As I look back, I realize that I needed to fully mine this spiritual vein for *this* new project to happen. One way to describe this book is that it's a training guide wrapped in a spiritual philosophy.

The next step in the journey toward this project was attending Marc Goldberg's workshop. Quite frankly, his work with dogs took my breath away. He and I began to collaborate then on myriad dog-training projects. Marc, who is based in Chicago, came east to the monastery frequently. His outsized personality — and mastery with dogs — ingratiated him with my fellow monks.

Soon, we began to fashion an outline for a weekend dog-training seminar at New Skete that would focus on the art of living with a dog.

Within twenty-four hours of announcing the workshop to a select list of dog owners and dog professionals, every available ticket was sold. The demand was so great that we needed to add another workshop just to handle the overflow. It was at this point that I knew we needed to write a book that would speak directly and effectively to the problems today's dog owners experience. Marc was thinking the same thing, and as we went back and forth together on ever-deepening levels, what began to take shape was a different kind of training book. It would be less concerned with the technical step-by-step instructions characteristic of most dog-training manuals, more foundational in nature, a book that would provide the key to a relationship with a dog regardless of the particular training approach one followed. We envisioned a book that would take into account the real needs of the dog based on its nature and that would then show readers how to use that information to radically improve their dog's behavior. We also believed we could help many people deepen their relationships with their dogs so they could enjoy the friendship more. We could feel something magical occurring.

With Marc, I share a common view about the state of the dog-human relationship, and the overwhelming need for a new way of seeing it. Cumulatively, we've trained tens of thousands of dogs. Marc is a celebrated trainer with thirty years of experience, a past president of the International Association of Canine Professionals (IACP) and inductee into its Members Hall of Fame, and a talented contributor to many canine journals. We know you will be just as thrilled as we are that Marc has joined us to write this book. He brings a fresh voice, an enormous insight into dogs, and some of the best training methods we've ever come across.

Blessings to you in your life with your dog(s).

— Brother Christopher, Prior,
Monks of New Skete

Like so many of you, I read the Monks of New Skete's books and was fascinated with the backstory of monks who breed and train dogs. Their work with dogs was and is so wonderfully sensible, especially in a world where common sense in dog training and dog care is far from common. Yet I never expected to meet the men behind those books.

That changed nearly ten years ago when the Monks of New Skete were inducted into the International Hall of Fame organized by the International Association of Canine Professionals. Brother Christopher traveled to the IACP conference to accept the award, an honor conferred upon such notables as Captain Max von Stephanitz, who originated the German shepherd breed, and Konrad Lorenz, an Austrian ethologist who wrote extensively about dogs and won a Nobel Prize in 1973.

I found it remarkable that this bestselling author, whose books I had devoured, was not only a modest man but also deeply interested in meeting and exchanging ideas with his fellow canine professionals. It was in those first meetings that our friendship began.

The idea to write a book together, however, never would have formulated had I not later seen a television series called *Divine Canine*. The show featured the monks, primarily Brother Christopher, working with interesting clients and their somewhat spoiled dogs. What really struck me while watching Brother Chris work was how similar his movements were to my own. It truly seemed as though I were watching myself train dogs. I knew then that we shared the same dog-training philosophies. Not long after, Brother Christopher and I began a series of conversations about ways to improve our training, especially taking the needs of today's clients and their dogs into account.

The dog universe has changed enormously in the past twenty years, and Brother Christopher and I both believed that we had an important message for today's dog owner, a philosophy that could help both dog lovers and, just as important, dogs be happier. So we brainstormed, we talked, and we outlined.

About that time, I spent a week visiting New Skete and had the chance to help Brother Christopher work with some of the dogs he was training. It was an ideal opportunity to collaborate, to exchange ideas, and simply to get to know each other better. I remember one of the dogs we trained that week was an energetic golden retriever named Annie that was owned by a retired couple. The couple loved Annie dearly, but had brought her to New Skete because she was proving too wild for them, constantly pulling and jumping. They needed help.

In working with Annie those few days, Brother Christopher and I recognized she had a profile similar to that of so many of the dogs we work with: energetic, full of fun, and totally doted on and spoiled by her owners. We laughed as we trained her: Annie was charming yet totally used to having her own way, and we could only imagine the fits she had been giving her owners. That said, both of us were pleased with how quickly Annie began responding to our training. With a little structure and some basic instruction, discipline, and exercise, Annie started to shine as a student. By the time her owners came to pick her up, she was ready to go home and was able and willing to follow a new program.

I vividly remember that concluding interview with amusement. It was a carbon copy of many of the interviews I've had through the years. Before bringing out Annie, Brother Christopher began giving a full report on how she had done, explaining her progress and the various skills she had learned. After about ten minutes, the wife broke in and demanded, *"Where's Annie?"* Brother Christopher replied that she was in the kennel, but before they saw her he needed to coach them on how to follow up on the training. That kept the woman quiet for another ten minutes, after which she said again, *"Where's Annie?"* Brother Christopher explained that there were still a number of points that had to be covered, but it was becoming evident that the woman was losing her patience. I smiled as Brother Christopher picked up the pace, trying to keep the couple's attention while providing them with important information that they were going to need to continue at home. Finally, after another five minutes, the woman shook her head and practically yelled, *"Where's Annie?"*

We had a good laugh together, and Brother Christopher said, "Okay, I get it. I'll get Annie and do the demonstration, but then I'll spend as much time as we need working together." Then the husband broke in and said with a smile, "I think what you're seeing is that we both love the dog, but I'm the one who is going to have to keep up the training. My wife simply wants to love Annie without Annie knocking her over."

Well, Brother Christopher did his best with the couple, and fortunately Annie did quite well in the return session. The husband listened attentively to Brother Christopher's coaching, and by the time they left, he seemed to be handling Annie nicely. But it was also clear that his wife wasn't interested in the technical details of the training. She simply wanted to be able to love Annie and have Annie behave. She just didn't understand how her own behavior impacted Annie's.

After the session I couldn't resist teasing Brother Christopher. I looked at him and said, *"Where's Annie???"* and we burst out laughing. We both knew that we've had many clients with a similar profile. But the episode with Annie triggered a serious conversation in which we acknowledged the need for a new type of dog book, one that would lay a foundation for understanding dogs as they are and would help owners understand and use certain basic principles, regardless of what type of formal obedience training they practiced. After all, your behavior will always have an impact on your dog.

— Marc Goldberg,
ChicagoDogTrainer.com

LET DOGS
BE DOGS

1

The Promise

In a fractured world of broken relationships dogs can teach us the meaning of devotion and fidelity. — Dogs & Devotion

There is an art to living with a dog that combines grace and elegance with understanding and realism, that fosters compassion and a spiritual connection without doting and pampering. Such an art is based on respect for the true nature of the dog and the vital role we have in helping the dog to fulfill its highest potential. What's even more remarkable is that, as we nurture this relationship, we become increasingly sensitive to the wondrous interconnectedness of life and, for the lucky ones who believe, more connected to a universal spirit.

Unfortunately, too many dog owners today don't experience the gifts that this type of relationship offers. Instead, they carry dogs in purses and lavish them with outrageous gifts like Gucci collars and mink booties. They place demands on their dogs for comfort and emotional support, forcing the dogs to become agents of therapy rather than recognizing them as sovereign beings with needs of their own. They spend less and less time with their dogs. The leisure time today's dog owners have is often devoted to events and activities deemed more important than creating a healthy relationship with their pets. Owners feel forced to isolate and marginalize dogs that can't be trusted around other dogs or people. There is no relief in sight. Puppy mills churn out dogs by the tens of thousands, shelters fill with dogs that are victims of not only physical neglect but also ineffective training methods that have hoodwinked a swath of the dog world. Too many of today's basic obedience classes are dumbed down and truncated, more concerned with being politically correct than with offering dog owners effective solutions.

Something needs to be done, and that's why we've written this book.

Let Dogs Be Dogs is a bit of a departure from the Monks of New Skete's previous training volumes, *How to Be Your Dog's Best Friend* and *The Art of Raising a Puppy*. It is also different in the way it is presented. Throughout this volume, you will occasionally hear from both Marc and Brother Christopher in their own voices. These vignettes are intended to make the experience of reading this book as personal as possible, as if you were sitting across from us as we share anecdotes from our decades of experience in both working and living with dogs.

MARC GOLDBERG   I grew up with dogs, and my first was a sheltie pup that I raised named Gus. In some sense, Gus also raised me from the age of eleven to twenty-nine. During those eighteen years, Gus taught me so much. He taught me to value the relationship first.

Perhaps the first serious lesson Gus taught me was that merely being your dog's pal is not enough to qualify you as a "best friend." To be your dog's best friend, the first thing you must do is teach him how to be safe. Gus, untrained, ran into the street and was hit by a car in his fifth month of life. Luckily, it wasn't his last. When Gus's broken bone healed, my mother enrolled us both in a local dog-training class, and within a few short weeks I was hooked on training — and so was Gus.

We went on to learn and train at the highest levels of obedience, winning a few prizes along the way. Decades later, I still cherish the silver trays and bowls Gus and I won in the obedience ring.

What shines brightest in my memory, however, is the recollection of the day when, as a young teenager, I ran home from school, eager to practice a dog-training routine with Gus in preparation for a dog show that weekend. Since we had already won some ribbons, and I had developed a taste for the winner's circle, I wanted a repeat performance. So when I arrived home, I snapped a leash on Gus and took him outside for a quick training session.

Marc Goldberg and Gus circa 1972. They guided each other through life for nearly eighteen years.

But Gus behaved oddly. I was telling him to heel in order to practice the heeling pattern common at obedience trials. This was a routine that Gus knew well and excelled at, yet on this day, he wouldn't do it. My dog refused to obey the simple heel command that I knew for sure he completely understood. So I corrected Gus for disobeying. And he took that leash correction, in the form of a pop toward me, without protest. Yet Gus still did not obey. Shamefacedly, I admit that I corrected Gus again, and that again he refused.

This was very unusual, and for a long moment it confounded me. Thankfully, I stopped bullying Gus and began to reflect.

"What's different? Every day I come home from school, I play with my dog, and then I train him." That's when it hit me square in the face. I was so eager to practice that when I got home I snapped a leash on Gus without actually acknowledging him, and then I began to make demands, demands that Gus was usually happy to comply with out of friendship. But this time I hadn't greeted or played with Gus. I had simply ordered him around, and he communicated his displeasure with passive resistance.

I sat down on the ground. I invited Gus up into my lap, and then I played with him for a few minutes. I collected myself, stood up, and began the training session again. It went beautifully. That weekend we brought home more silver, which I still have. But the real prize was what I learned.

In these pages, we promise to unveil for you a pathway to a life with your dog that might once have seemed unimaginable. We will explain how to use the time you already spend training—or simply living with your dog—more wisely, and provide specific goals to meet your dog's needs. Much more than a training manual, this book will show you how to have a life with your canine companion in an intentional, purposeful, and satisfying way. Most dog-training books focus on the one hour a day the average dog owner should spend training and exercising her dog. Here, we'll show you not only how to get the most out of that hour but also how to build and strengthen the relationship during the other twenty-three hours.

We identified the central concept of this book as "the art of living with your dog" for good reason. Ask any good artist and he'll tell you his work is drawn not only from inspiration but also from years of education and application. Violinists such as Joshua Bell and Hilary Hahn, for example, demonstrate a remarkable technical proficiency honed by many years of dedicated practice but also a creative, intuitive sense of expression that transcends pure technique. It is what makes listening to them such a delight. They've reached a point at which technique becomes an avenue of freedom and personal expression—an art. A similar dynamic can take place in a relationship with a dog: Technique can become art, where the various movements and commands between human and dog seem to flow effortlessly, in a relaxed rhythm of attention and respect. How different an ordinary walk looks under those circumstances from the more familiar daily drama of dog pulling owner down the street. To witness the harmony and connection between a well-behaved dog and its owner is a thing of beauty, and deeply inspiring.

But there is an important caveat to note here. In a healthy relationship with a dog, training technique needs to be balanced with a sound understanding of the nature of the dog. Too great an emphasis on technique alone can make the relationship seem artificial and stilted, inserting a level of pressure on both dog and owner that causes it to fall short of reaching the level of art. In our technology-driven world it is easy to see how this can happen. Good technique is never an end in itself, but needs to serve the broader relationship, and when that happens you observe the relaxed give-and-take between owner and dog. Ultimately, this involves putting time, understanding, and practice into a well-thought-out plan for daily life with your dog. That is where the magic happens.

At least, that is where it happens in our relationship with our dogs. Admittedly, there are many dog-training books that reflect a number of training methods. Some of these books are quite good. We'd like to think that we've written a few. But there remains the challenge of writing a book that grounds the reader's understanding of the nature of the dog in reality, providing a sure foundation that can then support and complement any particular training method one chooses to follow. The more you understand how you influence your dog's behavior and thinking, the easier it will be for you to move toward an artful relationship with your own dog.

With this book, we seek to help just about every dog owner, from those whose relationship with their dogs is healthy and who want to keep it that way, to the once conscientious owners whose commitment to their canines has begun to lapse, to those owners whose relationship with their dogs is in need of critical care. This book is written especially for those who suspect that there is something missing in the relationship they have with their dog. Here's our promise: When you master the art of living with your dog in an intentional and purposeful way, you can have a beautiful and easy relationship where training occurs organically and the need for psychotropic drugs or quick obedience fixes is rare or nonexistent. What is even more remarkable is this: In the process, you will become more aware of the critical role you play in your dog's life and behavior, and how the quality of your guidance affects his happiness and helps him be a better dog.

Simply put, by considering and prioritizing his needs, you'll become more human. But first, a bit of a reality check. For this ideal to be realized, we need to set out in a clear and orderly way, laying a solid foundation from which to live the dream. Dreams are essential if we are to become fully alive, but unless you have a road map to follow, you risk not fulfilling them. This applies to your relationship with your dog. For your relationship to flourish and grow into something artful, there are certain elements that absolutely need to be present and that go beyond the nonnegotiables any healthy relationship presumes: good exercise, good diet, and conscientious socialization. These are givens. You also need to understand that dogs read your body language in the subtlest of ways, and that you can positively capitalize on this by being transparent with your dog, quietly praising her with genuine warmth and appreciation, for example, when she follows your lead. Or being patient when you are teaching her how to respond to a particular command. Your dog will perceive the sincerity present when it comes from your heart. By being attentive to how your dog is responding to you, you'll become more conscious of yourself and more in control of your emotions, putting yourself in a better position to communicate clearly with her. She will literally help you be a better companion.

Below is a brief outline of the map we will be following.

Your intention. Any potential or current dog owners need to weigh whether they are truly committed to giving their dog the time and attention it needs to become a good companion. In these pages we will provide you with a brief "examination of conscience" to help you discern how serious you are about acquiring or caring for a dog.

Understanding the basic nature of the dog. Part of providing a dog what it needs to be a good companion involves understanding its basic nature, how it evolved, and what lessons you can learn from its historical development. We will touch on the basic drives present in the dog and explain why, being a highly social pack animal, it needs a benevolent leader in order to flourish. We will then show you practical ways to reinforce your dog's perception of you as leader.

Common traps. Sometimes people's expectations of what they hope to get from their dogs stem more from Hollywood's depiction of dogs than from the real world. Further, people can allow the pressures and demands of modern life to curtail the amount of time they devote to cultivating the relationship. We will discuss these traps and provide you with a realistic picture of caring for your dog that respects her nature, builds the relationship, and then sets the stage for providing her the things she really cares about. The commitment to training is imperative, but there is much that isn't covered by training—the critical teachable moments that you can use as they happen, rather than letting them pass.

Whether you take advantage of and benefit from teachable moments depends not only on your determination to do so but also on your awareness of *what they are*. If you don't recognize opportunities when they knock, you will miss many or most of the critical chances you have to show your dog right from wrong. Even children are not born knowing right from wrong or how to fit the societal norms in which they will have to live. Of course, since we *are* human, it comes intuitively to us to remind a small child to say please when he surprises you by demanding something. You don't have to prepare for or even think about that moment with a two-year-old. That's because you just know it's coming. When it does, you have the necessary guidance ready and dispense it as needed. Although a two-year-old may try parental patience from time to time, the child's behavior is rarely a surprise. Simply put, it's a big job to educate a child, whether she's your own, a friend's, or a relative's. But you have serious advantages in that arena. First, you're of the same species. And, second, we have all been children.

That's not the case with dogs. When raising dogs, we unwittingly come to the job with one of three basic approaches:

1. The "he'll figure it out" method, in which we don't offer the dog a lot of information. Of course we love him, so we pet and play with him and care for him. And as he chews or potties on something inappropriate, we scold and hope he figures it out.

2. The "research it as we go" method, in which we try to respond intelligently, but only *after* encountering a problem. This usually involves turning to Google or YouTube, typing words in a box, and sifting through thousands of conflicting suggestions. Often this causes an owner to throw up her hands and revert back to approach number one: he'll figure it out.

3. We plan ahead. We learn what challenges are coming from puppies and adult dogs either through untold years of experience, as the authors have done, or through well-thought-out plans, such as those we will explain in this book. We mentally prepare to partner up with a different species by studying its psychology and its needs. We give our dog what his species requires to function well within the societal norms we have set up for him. This method might be called the "do it right and the dog won't know he's being trained" method. And it's important. The dog, left to his own devices, wouldn't know it's wrong to pee on the curtains and eat the woodwork, because that is exactly what he would do if not otherwise coached.

We remind the two-year-old child to say please when she demands the ice cream we're dishing out. She says please and we hand over the bowl. (Of course, then we have the thank-you lesson to teach.) Ideally, we'll only have to remind a few times, and the point is not only made but set. That's because we intuitively understand how to motivate the child, using the treat as both motivator and reward. In other words, because we are people too, and because we were once children, we know what children care about and thus how to exploit a teachable moment.

But what do dogs care about...really care about on the deepest levels? What do they crave enough that they will sacrifice perfectly good dog behaviors such as eating whatever food they can reach? In this book we will go into great detail about multiple things dogs want and need on a deeply fundamental level. We call these things "resources." In our childhood example, the resource was ice cream. With dogs, food is a resource, but there are many other things that dogs want: for example, affection, exercise, or rest.

If a resource is something a dog needs to be healthy and psychologically well-tuned, then shouldn't we just give it to the dog? Ultimately, yes, we should, and indeed we will. But the *how, when,* and *where* of that giving will determine whether our dog says please and thank you or snarls, "Gimme more."

We will give you very specific advice on how to provide — not deprive but *provide* — resources.

Relationship. In an earlier book, we described the desired relationship to your dog as pack leader, and we'll talk more about that soon. This is the deeply devoted relationship your dog craves from his best friend, and we will show you how to assume that role in a benevolent way. If you're conscious of what you want the relationship to ultimately look like, you can shape it to that effect and then enjoy the outcome.

Food and treats. Will your dog say gimme? Or will he say please and thank you? That all depends on how you set the expectations — so we'll analyze it. In the animal world, food is a primary motivator. Wild canines have to hunt for food, expending enormous energy to find sustenance. We make it easy for our domesticated pets, and so we should. But we do not think of nourishment in the same way our dog does. Learn to use food well and your dog will be not only physically nourished but also psychologically satisfied.

Holly encourages Charlie to sit for his treat. *(Photo by Jim Darow)*

Space. People don't usually think about space until they're hunting for a new home and they look for more (or less) space. Most people only think about space when someone stands too close to them at a party, or when another driver drifts into their lane...or steals their parking spot. But dogs think about space constantly, consciously and otherwise. We can use this to our advantage. An example of using space correctly is to teach a dog to respect a small child (and vice versa). Another is using space to teach dogs not to jump on guests or bolt out an open door.

Time. "What do you want to do?" "I don't know...what do *you* want to do?" Such phrases bounce back and forth between childhood friends and adults alike. In human culture, it's normal to negotiate activities. Negotiating also happens among dogs, as well as between dogs and people. Have you ever had a friend who never seemed to care about what you wanted? Who never took your ideas or needs into account? Who always insisted on *his* plan? In dog-human relationships this can happen in either direction. Some dogs are so insistent on playing ball that you hide the toys; then they claw up the floor looking for the one lost ball under the couch. On the other hand, some dogs just want a walk now and again, yet the owner can't be bothered. If you parcel out the activities a dog needs, your dog will find it easy to give you the tranquility in the home that you need.

Toys. Many dogs love them. But just as children can learn the wrong lesson when you give and give and give, so too can dogs fail to understand that it's "just love" when you stuff the box to overflowing. Some dogs become possessive and confrontational with "their" belongings and the toy store employees who clean and stock the place. (That's you by the way!) But if you use toys as an educational resource, you can teach your dog to respect you and the rules that help you keep your dog safe.

Emotion and affection. These days *the only reason* anyone in Western culture lives with a dog—with the exception of working dogs, such as service dogs, gundogs, and sniffer dogs—is for emotion and affection. But working dogs are well loved too and are among the most contented, well-adjusted dogs you'll ever meet. That's because they have a job to do, and

Growing up with too many toys and not enough responsibilities can accidentally teach puppies an undesirable sense of entitlement.

the relationships they enjoy with their handlers revolve around an enormous level of mutual respect for the rules of the game. Owners of guide dogs for the blind do not randomly pet their dogs and shower them with affection. Instead, they strategically and pointedly reward them on and off—usually in quite small ways—during the workday. When the dog is off duty, the owner removes the harness and the dog becomes a pet with normal hug privileges. Why are those dogs so much happier and less neurotic than dogs that receive a far, far greater amount of overt affection from their owners? We'll talk about that and help you get it right.

At the end of the day, it's not whether you will provide resources for your dog. You will. What makes the difference in your relationship will be the how, when, and where, and we will be extremely detailed in helping you understand that.

BROTHER CHRISTOPHER   Often the most satisfying clients to work with are those who face a real challenge with their dog but don't give up, who are willing to listen and apply themselves to realize their dream. Take Fred. The fact that Fred bought a puppy in the first place was somewhat surprising. In his sixties and single, Fred had worked for most of his adult life as an executive at a national company headquartered in Manhattan. Not one to make impulsive decisions, Fred was much more of a risk-versus-reward type of thinker. He had recently retired from his high-powered job, however, and for the first time since Fred could remember, there was a hole in his life. Then he walked into a pet store and fell in love.

"I didn't know what I was getting into," Fred said to us.

The puppy, a Jack Russell terrier, was named Eddie. Although it's understandable that Fred was smitten, Jack Russells aren't exactly a couch potato breed and can be a handful, especially for someone uneducated about dogs, which Fred was.

Predictably, Fred encountered all sorts of preliminary problems with Eddie, from house soiling to obstreperous behavior to chewing furniture. Fred even had trouble controlling Eddie on leash during walks, enduring the frustration of Eddie pulling him down the sidewalk.

When Fred brought Eddie to the monastery, the puppy was seven and a half months old. Fred had found out about the Monks of New Skete through *The Art of Raising a Puppy*. In reading our book, Fred realized he hadn't fully considered the change that the addition of a puppy would bring to his life, and he hadn't thought through all that goes into the formative training of a puppy. He also hadn't any idea how important the puppy's background was — Eddie could've come from a puppy mill for all Fred knew.

Puppy mills are horrid places, where puppies are bred solely for profit and live in factory-like conditions. They receive minimal human contact during those first formative weeks, they aren't vaccinated, they sleep in their own filth, and then they're placed in a shipping crate or cage, sometimes for as long as a week. That's the puppy you typically buy at a pet store, and that's why we don't recommend purchasing puppies from pet stores.

As challenging as Eddie was in those early months, Fred wasn't about to quit on him. Whatever he saw in Eddie's eyes that day in the pet store had lodged somewhere in Fred's heart.

Eddie's situation wasn't hopeless by any stretch. By following the principles described in our puppy training book — especially putting Eddie on a regular routine of three good walks a day plus making a concerted effort at socializing him with both people and dogs — Fred had made some real progress with Eddie, and that made our job much easier. In no time, we had Eddie walking politely on leash down our road, as well as doing down-stays and recalls with little rebellion. We discovered that Eddie was very toy motivated, so we concluded our training sessions with a vigorous game of fetch that Eddie looked forward to and delighted in. When Fred came back to pick Eddie up and observed him working happily in the demonstration, he was thrilled with the results. During the outtake interview, we presented Fred with a blueprint that expanded on how he could incorporate Eddie more seamlessly into his life.

The list of suggestions we provided was centered foremost on a predictable daily structure that included exercise, simple training methods, and play sessions — all ordinary things but extremely important in stabilizing Eddie's behavior once he returned home. Most important, we coached Fred on how to claim a leadership role in the relationship in order to help Eddie integrate what he'd learned with us. We showed Fred how to use his voice and body language to express confidence and encouragement in working with Eddie, and Fred did his best to follow our lead. He came to understand that real love isn't just that initial spark of attraction; real love is what follows the chemistry. Real love comes from the attention that goes into a lasting and healthy relationship. We promised Fred that if he followed our suggestions, his relationship with Eddie would not only be manageable but also enrich his life.

Our tale of Eddie and Fred has a happy ending. The letter we received a month and a half later said it all: "It isn't just that Eddie has maintained what he learned at New Skete. Far more importantly for me, he actually wants to be with me throughout the day and I've come to experience an entirely new dimension to the relationship than before. I'm spending more quality time with him and he's far calmer now. He's drawn a better part of myself out in the open and I'm so much the better for it. Thank you."

Fred made the transition to retirement in no small measure because of the happy companionship he found with his Jack Russell terrier. Eddie filled something that was missing in Fred's life. Yet it's not only the lonely who can profit from a relationship with a dog. The type of relationship Fred and Eddie found can be experienced by anyone, whether you're young or old, from a big family, or living on your own. Dogs have the power to change your life for the better, but only when they're allowed to be who they truly are, and only when you take a leadership role.

2

Rescuing the True Nature of Your Dog

The more we learn of the dog's evolution—of its behaviors and instincts, of its needs and desires—the more we appreciate the mystery of its nature.
— Bless the Dogs

BROTHER CHRISTOPHER Perhaps living in a community with nine other monks and a dozen or so German shepherds sensitizes us to pack dynamics. A natural pack structure is on display each day among our dogs, and that structure clearly includes the monks as part of the pack. Each of us cares for at least one dog. In my case, I take care of two,* and all of us look to include the dogs we care for in our lives. For me, that means any number of basic things: My dogs sleep in my room. I'm responsible for feeding them, and I take walks with them several times a day. If we go hiking in the woods or on the mountain where New Skete is located, I take my dogs with me for companionship and exercise. One of the greatest joys I have is seeing my dogs frolic in nature, so obviously fascinated with the feast of scents that surrounds them. I groom my dogs at least once a week (more when they're shedding!), and this includes touching them all over, checking for tics, burrs, or any sore spots. I also clean their ears, check their teeth, and trim their nails, all on a regular basis. I'm fortunate in that I can take my dogs to work with me each day at our training kennel. I use them for distraction with the training dogs, and this allows me to connect with my dogs frequently in a natural

---

* As of this writing, my dogs are Daisy and Raisa.

Brother Christopher walks with his dogs along New Skete's private road.

way. In the afternoons, the dogs will sometimes play with one another for a time in an exercise pen.

At dinner, there are often five or so dogs surrounding the dinner table, peacefully holding down-stays behind our chairs, relaxed yet seemingly grateful to be included in the pack of people and dogs present. After dinner and chores, we routinely gather in our recreation room to watch the news or a good television show or movie, or simply to share with one another the events of the day. On any given evening, you'll find a half dozen dogs on down-stays at the feet of their respective monks, chewing on a bone or toy or just relaxing.

Since we're in the business of breeding German shepherds, each of our dogs is part of the breeding program. When a bitch comes into season she'll spend that time in the puppy kennel under the watchful eye of monks and the lay staff who see to the breeding. When a bitch is ready to be bred, we bring the stud over from the monastery and let nature take its course. Usually, the bitches are bred three times during the cycle, and after the litter is born, mothers will stay with their pups until they are weaned.

One of the most vivid illustrations of pack behavior is a mother interacting and playing with her litter of pups. I remember the last time Daisy had a litter of puppies: I brought her and her pups out from the breeding kennel to our spacious front yard, which also serves as a cemetery. This isn't as grim as it sounds: In addition to our monks and nuns, many of our friends wish to be buried at an Orthodox monastery, and the cemetery is a salutary reminder of mortality. The simple wooden crosses keep quiet watch over a peaceful landscape of rolling terrain filled with birds, bushes, trees, and ever-changing colors that follow the seasons. And the puppies certainly don't seem to mind. We let them play in the open sections of the yard, always respectful of the nearby graves, but also secure in the knowledge that our departed brothers and sisters would happily approve.

On this occasion, Daisy played with her little pack of puppies as they crawled and tumbled over one another. At one point, a particularly bold little female strayed from the group toward a nearby cross. Before I could move to head her off, Daisy skillfully intercepted the pup, herding her back to the

An older dog teaches a puppy not to stray from the pack by intercepting her and guiding her back to the litter.

group, where Daisy could keep a mother's eye on all of them at once. Daisy's vigilance freed me simply to observe and enjoy the dogs' antics, and to provide them with outside time. The pups were enchanted with their surroundings, often sniffing the ground and picking up a leaf or a stick. Invariably, once one of them had something, the others wanted it too, and the little pack would swarm and run, several times ending up in a tumbled pile of German shepherd pups.

They were drawn together, and Daisy dutifully orchestrated the symphony, keeping the pack in place. And when that one pup thought about going her own way, Daisy brought her right back with the others. Occasionally, one of the puppies would try to nurse. Because Daisy had already fed them, she would nudge them off, giving a very clear message: not right now. I smile recalling how one pup tried to latch on while Daisy was distracted by the others. By this time the puppies had sharp little teeth, and this guy must have grazed Daisy with a tooth because she nudged him sharply with her nose and then held him down for an instant. The pup gave a tiny cry, but Daisy held him until he relaxed, only a matter of seconds. Then she let him up, licked his face, and sent him back to play with the brood.

In some ways, this is the nature of the pack, and it's a scene I could easily imagine happening in a wolf pack. The dogs are drawn together. If one commits an infraction of some sort, another is bound to give him an instant of clear education, and then they resume whatever they were doing.

Call of the Wild

From a scientific point of view, the evolution of the dog from the wolf reflects a complex and mysterious history that continues to be uncovered. We still don't know absolutely how the process occurred. There are several theories — from the simplistic older view that dogs resulted when humans domesticated wolves, stealing litters and then raising the young pups, to the view of the biologist Raymond Coppinger, who believes the dog was derived from a self-taming group of wolves that capitalized on feeding from human garbage dumps after the last Ice Age.

More recently, a theory has emerged suggesting the dog gradually evolved from more social wolves that recognized the benefits of associating with hunters and gatherers in Europe thirty-two thousand years ago. The wolves, the theory goes, would eat the carcasses left behind by the human hunters while keeping other predators away. This formed a mutually beneficial relationship that evolved over the years.*

Though divergent, these theories of the evolution of the dog acknowledge the same wild progenitor, a fact that is verified by DNA evidence. In 1993, both the Smithsonian Institution and the American Society of Mammalogists classified our beloved domestic dog, or *Canis lupus familiaris,* as a subspecies of *Canis lupus,* the gray wolf.

Whether our relationship with our best friends began as the result of humans domesticating wolves, wolves domesticating themselves, or some combination of these two theories, one thing is for certain: Humans and wolves were drawn to each other by virtue of their intense sociability and curious nature, and slowly but surely, this familiarity resulted in the emergence of the dog. In the illuminating book *How the Dog Became the Dog,* Mark Derr writes that the association between socialized wolves and humans was consensual and mutual, and "in response to the needs and desires of both species, as well as to exigencies of rapidly shifting environmental conditions.... They helped each other out, and they adapted together to a changing world."

In order to fully understand your dog, therefore, and why your dog behaves as he does, it helps to understand his true nature. In the classic study of dog development *Genetics and the Social Behavior of the Dog,* J. P. Scott and John L. Fuller state that dogs are capable of all wolfish behaviors except when humans have changed their physical and learned responses through breeding.

So what wolfish behavior still exists in dogs? In this chapter, we will identify some of those behaviors and then provide an overview of how you can take them into account in relating positively with your dogs.

---

* http://www.newscientist.com/article/dn24581-wolves-turned-into-dogs-by-european
-huntergatherers.html#.VSpwKYeJdUQ

Driving Force

The well-known dog trainer Wendy Volhard notes in her work that, like wolf behavior, dog behavior is rooted in fundamental drives that have been inherited and strengthened over time. These drives include prey, pack, and defense. For our purposes here, the most important of the three is pack drive — behaviors associated with reproduction, being part of a group, or pack, and learning to follow the basic rules or guidelines of the pack.

Put very simply, by being a strong pack leader you will strengthen your dog's pack drive, which in turn will lead to good behavior and a happy relationship.

You can do this easily from day one. For example, whether you have a new puppy or even an older dog you've adopted, you can facilitate bonding by having your dog follow you around the house wherever you go. We call this tethering. Just keep the dog on a leash held in your left hand while you are moving about. When you sit down for a length of time — to work on a computer, for example — help your dog lie down. If he doesn't know that command yet or if he is restless, step on the leash to hold him in place. Don't pin him to the floor. Give him just enough leash to remain comfortably next to you. Your dog may initially put up a fuss over this, but if you are patient and calm he will gradually settle and relax. The basic lesson this teaches is that your dog should follow you. It naturally puts you in the position of pack leader and conditions your dog to stay with you. If you practice this simple exercise for twenty to thirty minutes several times a day, you'll be amazed at how your dog will begin to look at you with newfound respect. Only a pack leader has the right to tell another pack member where to put his body. Remember how Daisy herded her recalcitrant puppy back to the pack? She was merely acting as pack leader. This is a role you too can fulfill for your dog, and it appeals to his natural sense of pack drive.

The other drives will also express themselves in positive ways. A good expression of defense drive is to bark when the doorbell rings, to alert the owner that a visitor has arrived and to let the visitor know that there's a dog in the house. But most people also want to control

Arizona trainer Tawni McBee and Shanti share a relaxing moment. A dog in pack drive is more likely to relax than one exhibiting prey-drive behaviors. *(Photo by Beth Gouwens)*

the amount of barking, i.e., to get the dog to stop barking when told. This will involve successfully switching drives in the midst of the situation; for example, you can teach your dog to go to a dog bed and wait until you release him (pack drive), something he can learn with a reasonable amount of practice. Even quieting a territorial bark on command asks the dog to switch into pack drive.

Pack drive, to fit into the group and to collaborate with a coherent, benign leader, is what people mostly want from their dogs. Here are some characteristics of a dog in proper pack drive: He's attentive and happily follows directions; he rarely barks, except as a way of protecting the pack leader or the pack as a whole; he's calm and doesn't react negatively to stimuli he encounters, such as dogs, other animals, or people.

Yet many pet owners find that their dogs pull and lunge on the leash, or growl at other dogs or at people, expressing a defense drive. Or maybe your own dog can barely go for a walk because he reacts by jumping hard at every bird, rabbit, squirrel, and cat that he sees because he's constantly flipping into a state of prey drive.

What you really want is for your dog to enjoy the walk calmly by your side, either ignoring or politely acknowledging the presence of people, dogs, and other animals. In other words, you would like your dog, for the duration of the walk, to choose pack drive over either defense or prey drive. And he can. Some dogs gravitate to this desired state of mind naturally, either due to breed tendencies or their individual personality, or because they've been taught by their owner that calm, cooperative behavior is the only acceptable activity while on a neighborhood leash walk. Some dogs choose the behavior you want all on their own. Most have to be taught to select behavior that you desire, however, and this means you'll need to show your dog how to change his mind-set so he can actually deliver what you want. If your dog charges ahead of you, you might need to practice abruptly changing direction to reinforce your leadership role. Your dog will follow your lead when he realizes it is not optional, and then you can reward his cooperation with warm praise. As your dog experiences the benefits of this — love and encouragement — he naturally starts to pay better attention by walking close to your side, and you can make

Going for a walk is more enjoyable for Illinois trainer Mary Mazzeri and Mia when the dog isn't lunging at every squirrel she sees. *(Photo by Steven Drew)*

this his default choice with more praise and encouragement. Your dog will respond to you if you know how to communicate that you are the leader of the pack, the provider of all things good — the inspiring teacher whom all students naturally want to please.

After all, this is what your dog deserves. In the millennia since dogs and human beings have chosen to associate with each other, we have seen how each species has enriched the other. Dogs have proven themselves so much more than simply "useful." Apart from the myriad ways they have helped human beings throughout history, dogs have at the same time shown a capacity for relationships that has inserted itself in the human imagination, and that is an expression of their true nature. When we meet dogs' natural need for social order, they will meet our needs and make our lives better. This means making an intentional decision on our part to provide for their mental and physical health, both of which are important for good behavior. Dogs require meaningful and structured quality time. Good intentions aren't enough. You can block out time in your calendar if necessary to make sure that you fulfill your good intentions. Otherwise, due to the challenges of contemporary culture, your dog can end up spending far more time alone than ever before. Then when you *do* spend a bit of time with him, you may be tempted to spoil your dog rather than lead and educate. That is the chief reason we're seeing so many behavior problems as dogs become alienated from their basic nature.

Honoring Nature

We have seen what happens when the fundamental nature of the dog is respected...and when it is neglected. One gratifying aspect of our work with clients is when we see a dog that has been conscientiously integrated into the life of its owner. The dog's basic needs have been met: He is not only fed a quality diet and given essential veterinary care but also given regular, structured exercise appropriate to his age and breed. Normally, the exercise takes place at predictable times of the day, and the dog looks forward to it. This helps cement the bond with the owner in a completely natural way. Additionally, the responsible owner makes sure to provide the dog with solid socialization —

with both humans and other dogs—so that the dog can interact positively with his environment. Sometimes this will involve making playdates with friends and their dogs; other times it will involve utilizing a doggy day care. Owners who make the conscious effort to socialize their dogs optimally in puppyhood (or, in cases of adopting an older dog, in the first several months of ownership) reap the long-term benefits. These basic ingredients are nonnegotiable: They lay a foundation for a transformative relationship that makes sense to both person and dog. The dog, even if he hasn't had any formal training, is basically well-adjusted, primed to learn, and he takes to the process in a willing manner. The training builds on a beginning that has already been put into place, and the results are delightful.

By contrast, we work with some clients who expect training to replace their dog's basic need for companionship and attention, and who fail to recognize their own responsibility to provide that. How many times through the years have we heard clients whine, "I never dreamed he would suck up so much of my time!" That's precisely the point: When we love and respect someone, do we ever think of him as "sucking up our time"? The key is using the time you have together wisely, and this goes for your relationship with your dog as well. You can't disregard the fundamental nature of the dog and expect it to flourish. When we try to cram a dog into a modern container that doesn't have ample room to accommodate its basic nature, we're going to witness all sorts of problems. That's what we're seeing plenty of today.

For example, people who are away from home for nine to eleven hours a day working, and who then spend significant time at home engaged in solitary behavior in this online, click-and-scroll world, or who frequently go out with friends after work, will no doubt see certain predictable negative traits develop within their dog: destructiveness, antisocial aggression, hyperactivity—the list can go on and on. To be perfectly frank, bringing a dog into your life means a commitment of time, energy, and money. You don't want owning a dog to be a hardship. It wouldn't be good for you, and certainly wouldn't be fair to the dog. That said, even people who have demanding jobs, but are willing to invest in the relationship, can have a dog that will enrich

Every dog needs contact with nature now and again.

their lives. We will give specific recommendations for those who fall into this category later in the book, but the primary requirement is your intention. Are you willing to provide the dog with what it needs to flourish? Will you honor its nature? Before taking a dog home, consider the dog and your circumstances. The chance of behavioral problems is greatly reduced in homes where people spend quality time with their dogs. And here's the kicker: The payoffs are great! Maybe the greatest gift dogs give us is that they draw us into the kingdom of "now." A dog's natural appreciation of the world that surrounds it is contagious. When the dog spots the squirrel, so do we. When the dog sniffs the flowers, we may notice the flowers for the first time. From our dogs, we catch the joy of the moment.

The Importance of Leadership

Fortunately, the list of ingredients for a happy relationship with your dog is pretty simple. There are the basics, of course: good food, plenty of water, exercise and play, lots of praise and bonding, teaching moments where you show your dog what it is and is not allowed to do, and ample time to rest and relax. Supply your dog with those essentials and you'll be well on your way to having a contented dog.

Part of a successful relationship with your dog also includes an understanding of obedience exercises, and we have covered these at length in our other books. Taking the time to teach your dog the basic obedience exercises is a key factor in being able to include your dog optimally in your life. Above all else, these exercises help teach the dog to look to you for guidance. They also require a certain amount of consistency and discipline. Now, we realize the word *discipline* evokes all sorts of emotional responses from people, from positive to negative, so it is vital that we understand the word in the manner we are using it. As we wrote in *How to Be Your Dog's Best Friend*, *discipline* shares a similar etymological path with *disciple*, "one who follows." The Latin root for *disciple* is *discere*, which means "to learn." Discipline in this context is not punishment. Indeed, it is a part of good teacher-student relationships: It clarifies for the dog what you are expecting from him. Further, it is consonant with how canines in the wild communicate with one another in order to maintain pack harmony. Often the pack leader is able to stop unwanted behavior in the pack with a sharp growl and/or penetrating stare. The message is unmistakable: Stop what you're doing…now! Not surprisingly, the same dynamic has its place in the human-dog relationship.

Trust us, there will be times in your relationship with your dog when it will be necessary to correct him, to stop him from exhibiting inappropriate behavior. A correction can take many forms. Think of correction as a way to interrupt a behavior that makes the behavior less likely to recur. This is part of your responsibility as pack leader to keep your dog safe. For example, it is incumbent upon you to teach your dog to come when you call him regardless of distractions. Otherwise, every squirrel he sees can become a race toward a busy street or out an open door. But there is a right, sensible, fair way to approach correction. First, your dog must understand what you're asking of him. Part of this clarity is consistency. If you want your dog to come unfailingly, for instance, you have to follow a logical progression. Initially you'll teach him the recall at leash length (six feet), then extend it to greater distances using a longer lead (twenty to thirty feet). By associating something positive with obeying the command (such as a high-value treat), you create the motivation for your dog to really learn the command. You can then repeat the exercise in the face of distractions, using longer and longer lines attached to the collar. But you always need to enforce the command. You can never let the dog get the message that it is okay not to come when you call. Eventually, as you get better and better compliance in the face of distractions, you can begin to reverse the process by slowly shortening the line a bit each week.

The same kind of consistency helps with regard to other common problems. If you don't want your dog jumping on the couch, but sometimes you get busy and allow him to, the message you're sending him is that he might as well take the chance. It would not be fair to correct your dog for a behavior about which you don't faithfully educate him.

Second, you must reinforce the rule under all and ever more distracting conditions so that your dog learns his responsibilities one

Valerie Ann Erwin, a New York trainer, teaching off-leash behavior with a long lead and a watchful eye.

step at a time. Most owners successfully teach their dogs to sit upon request. So they believe the dog knows "sit." But try issuing that command immediately after the doorbell rings. You're likely to find that, under that circumstance, your dog doesn't know the sit command at all. The command probably won't even register.

The solution is not to jump immediately to correction for a situation that you've never practiced. Instead, work on the sit command at various times. Yes, sometimes it's fine to hold out a treat as you do so, but mix it up: Sometimes there is a treat, sometimes not. Practice in your living room during commercials if you're watching TV, but don't forget to repeat these exercises in other locations where sight, scent, and sound might distract your dog. Once your dog truly understands "sit" under all conditions, it is inevitable that you will encounter a situation in which your dog hears the command but sends you the following message: "Get back to me later on that sit thing. I'm very busy right now." What you do next determines whether your dog learns that the exercise is not optional or whether he learns that crime pays. How best to correct your dog in this circumstance will depend on various factors, including the temperament of the dog, the age of the dog, and the nature of the infraction he has committed — minor, moderate, or major. There is a vast difference between a dog that has failed to sit on command and a dog that has lunged aggressively at a passerby. One infraction might merit a simple upward leash pop and a strong verbal no,* while the other might require something slightly more dramatic such as an abrupt about-turn.**

The critical point is not whether to use discipline. What's important is that you discipline consistently and fairly so that your dog (and you) may profit by it. Too many owners ignore their dog's troubling behavior only to explode in a fit of pique when their patience is finally at an end. Remember that you really do need to teach your dog every step of what he is to do before you can hold him fully accountable.

---

* A quick "in and out" motion with the left hand on the leash that is reminiscent of the way one snaps a towel at someone at the local pool. Its purpose is less punitive than attention-getting.
** Turning abruptly 180 degrees as you allow the dog to hit the end of the leash. The suddenness of the correction redirects the dog's focus on you as you walk in the other direction.

BROTHER CHRISTOPHER It's only from an appropriate philosophical perspective — that of respecting the true nature of the dog, its need for companionship and direction — that obedience training fulfills its true promise. Training is never meant to mask the dog's true nature but to let it blossom. For that to happen effectively, it's crucial to understand the dog as dog, as *Canis familiaris*, a pack animal that is oriented to follow and to cooperate with intelligent leadership. We don't have to apologize for exercising positive leadership. Our dogs will thank us for it, for in such a dynamic the dog understands what is being asked and is clear about how to respond.

The dog that is leaderless is not a happy dog. Rather, it tends to exhibit neurotic, aggressive, or destructive behaviors. When an owner is ineffective, or insufficiently confident in her leadership skills, a dog might step up and try to fill the role himself (exhibiting aggressive or bossy behavior) or might emotionally shut down. Moodiness becomes anxiety, whining, or compulsive behaviors — all the way up to near states of hysteria when the dog is under stress.

Leader of the Pack

For as far back as we can remember, at least as far back as our first dog-training manual published in 1978, the term *pack leader* has been part of the Monks of New Skete's lexicon and culture. We coined that term to help readers better understand their importance to the dog. In our 1991 *The Art of Raising a Puppy*, we discussed the term and its connotations at length. Throughout the following pages you might notice our use of such phrases as "benevolent leader," "good boss," "great parent," and "great teacher." All of these are interchangeable with the term *pack leader.*

If you watch any group of dogs, you will note a couple of things: First, they are naturally drawn together. Second, they sometimes have common desires. We call the objects of said desires *resources.* These resources include food, space, and activity, among others. Third, the division of resources does not always follow a simple pecking order. Dogs are not chickens, and although they are intended for group living, they are also created for a more complex social order. For instance, if two dogs have just completed a long play session on a very hot afternoon and there's one bowl of water, you can bet that the more dominant (you might even call it *insistent*) dog will control the resource. If, however, the two dogs have returned from a short walk on a cool evening, the less dominant dog might have a better than even chance of getting first shot at the bowl. The obvious reason may appear to be that the dominant dog doesn't care, but your dog's reasoning is far subtler than that. It's not only level of desire that drives the sharing of resources among members of the pack. The dominant wolf might be first to enjoy feasting on the prey, but if at all possible he makes sure that the other wolves get their fair share so they stay healthy and strong to assist in the next hunt.

Yet in the dog universe, *dominance* is a word that sometimes causes emotions to run high.

Given the opportunity, dogs form packs. That's an immutable fact. In order for the pack to be stable — a pack that can function to the benefit of all members without constant scuffles — there needs to exist, at least among several of the dogs, a healthy respect for the pack leader.

Dogs want to be led. When a dog follows its pack leader, it is exhibiting an instinctive trait that's some hundred thousand years in the making. Dogs are especially in tune with social hierarchies, and when they understand their place in the pack, they function and are in tune with the world around them at a level they cannot achieve alone. When we, as dog owners, assume the role of leader, we help our dogs reach their highest potential.

Yet there are those in the dog world who would tell us the dog is a domesticated animal, far from its wolf roots and no longer pack-oriented. Such people make this argument to undermine both the concept of pack structure and the need for pack leadership. This is a political movement designed to label mainstream dog trainers as harsh. Adherents suggest the term *pack animals* serves as an excuse to force dogs into compliance in the name of pack leadership. This is not an accurate assessment of what pack structure among dogs really is. Yes, at times there is dominance. Yes, at other times there is submission. But mostly what dogs do is coexist, communicate their needs to one another, and negotiate who gets resources. They do this not according to a simple, slavish devotion but out of a complex expression of who needs or wants the resource the most. As is the case in a wolf pack, the top dog usually gets to say who gets what. In denying that the dog is a pack animal, naysayers discredit all training based not only on dominance but also on leadership. While we do not believe that you need to dominate your dog to live well with him, we do know you must lead him to attain harmony in your relationship.

MARC   Some years ago I visited Cesar Millan's first dog psychology center in Los Angeles and witnessed something remarkable. There, pit bulls, Rottweilers, German shepherds, and terriers of various sorts all lived alongside one another in an open environment, and did so along with pugs, Chihuahuas, a Chinese crested, and mixed breeds.

The dogs behaved much like a school of fish, grouping together as one on this open multi-acre property, and flowing as a unit. They parted like the Red Sea as I walked through the pack, honoring Cesar's request for no touch, no talk, no eye contact.

The atmosphere at Cesar's center is quite peaceful. No squabbles. No scuffles. No barking. Many of the dogs there not only are challenging breeds but also have been rehabilitated after suffering from various forms of aggression, including dog aggression. Over the course of that visit, I saw the reality of the pack with my own eyes, and the experience was unforgettable. The care and handling by Cesar and his staff is first-rate and the dogs respond by maintaining peace and order.

To have such a varied and diverse group of dogs living successfully together requires a much stronger, more effective human pack leader than does, say, a group of three Labrador retrievers. Many, if not most, owners, and even some trainers, are not up to the task of managing an actual pack of dogs. But it can be done, as knowledgeable professionals working in doggy day care can attest. Granted, most trainers and owners today aren't required to manage a large group of dogs as an actual pack. Nevertheless, it is a beautiful sight to behold when dogs manifest this instinct naturally in play and social interaction. It is as if a part of the dog comes to life. Even if you don't live with numerous dogs, you are still your dog's pack, his family unit. In fact, the fewer of you there are, the more important each individual becomes.

BROTHER CHRISTOPHER   Here's a confession that surprises many people. Probably 60 percent of the learning experience we have accumulated and use in the boarding and training facility here at New Skete comes from highly structured, managed animal husbandry. Ranching was, after all, how the monastery supported itself before it went to the dogs, and we've always been deeply connected with animals. From 1966 to 1969, the monks ran a full-scale farm at New Skete, which included tending chickens, pheasants, horses, Herefords, Holsteins, and sheep. These animals were a central part of our world, so when the idea of breeding German shepherds was raised, the monks gravitated to an approach that integrated the dogs into their routine. Without knowing it, those early New Skete monks were emulating the Nuer, a deeply religious tribe near the Nile River in Egypt. The Nuer raise cattle for their livelihood but do so in such a way that the cows are part of the fabric of their lives. I think we were able to accomplish this at New Skete in large part because each of the monks accepted a leadership role in caring for their dogs. That is how love expresses itself. Yes, the dogs served and continue to serve a financial function for the monastery, but their physical and spiritual importance to the community far outweighs the financial advantage they offer the monks. The heart of the monastery is largely structured around them. In this sense, our training philosophy doesn't come from training at all, at least not what you would label "traditional dog training," but from honoring their canine nature. And it has proven to be a most powerful and effective form of dog training. When you live with dogs in a way that makes sense to them and encourages them to collaborate within the pack, nature and the divine force that guides it do the rest.

This can only happen, though, when both your dog and you assume the roles you were meant to play. For you, this means being a benevolent leader.

At well-run doggy day care centers all over the country, groups of dogs run and play all day, every day, and when new members come into the pack they're quickly surrounded, sniffed over, and accepted by the existing pack members. This group greeting usually causes even the boldest of new dogs to assume a cautious and even submissive posture, allowing himself to be sniffed. Once that's over, the new guy is generally invited to play by one or more pack members. Should the new guy begin to show undesired behaviors, such as humping or excessive barking, the pack might become overexcited, a situation that can cause a dogfight. In a good doggy day care, staff will intervene before a situation escalates by using a variety of effective tools: spray water bottles, shaker cans (four to five pennies in a small soda can taped shut), a pet corrector (using air pressure and sound), or even an air horn. Each one of these tools humanely interrupts the undesired behavior and keeps the peace.

Observing dogs in a communal space at a reputable doggy day care is a wonderful way to learn your dog's true nature. We suggest you do it, and we suggest you ask the staff whether they see a pack mentality in the dogs they care for.

MARC   Here's one interesting scenario you might see at doggy day care: Before a staff member can even get to a dog that's misbehaving, one of the

A well-run doggy day care offers good socialization activities for dogs who might otherwise never have a "dog buddy." *(DePaw University, Canine Campus, Geneva, Illinois)*

pack will discipline the guilty party, which generally stops the behavior quite quickly. We see over and over again that, once corrected, the original hooligan discovers his true place in the pack and tempers his wild and mischievous actions. Often this dog then becomes the best member of the dog pack police, helping to enforce rules to prevent trouble.

A human pack leader can gain respect by learning how to interrupt behaviors that are not on the approved list (approaching food in an excited fashion, for instance) and how to redirect the dog to taught behaviors such as sit or calm down. You can practice by setting up situations you are fully prepared to deal with in which you know your dog will act in an undesirable manner. This is far more sensible than waiting for such behaviors to occur spontaneously, when likely you'll be unprepared and your timing will be off. In a setup situation, you have a plan of action and a strategy to teach your dog. For example, try leashing your dog as you bring him into the kitchen to eat his meal. If he gets excited and pulls you toward the feeding area, firmly reverse your direction as you give the leash a tug. Your dog's attention will be redirected toward you, and then you'll be able to put him into a sit. Now try approaching again. Most likely he will go at your pace this time; however, if he tries to bolt for the food again, repeat the process. If you are patient and consistent in repeating the process, your dog will learn quickly. And this will be one more instance in which he recognizes you as pack leader.

As we've seen, wolves have crucial lessons to teach us about the dynamics of pack behavior and leadership, and we ignore these lessons at our peril. Wolves have an essential role to play in the human-dog relationship. The bad rap that wolves have acquired is nothing new. Writing for *National Geographic*, Dr. Brian Hare, director of the Duke Canine Cognition Center, and Vanessa Woods, a research scientist at Duke, chart the history of man's war on wolves from the sixth century BC, when Solon of Athens ordered every wolf killed, to 1930s America, when humans practically wiped the gray wolf off the map of the contiguous forty-eight states.

The writer Barry Lopez says, "Throughout the centuries we have projected on to the wolf the qualities we most despise and fear in ourselves." From fairy tales to horror movies, the wolf has consistently been portrayed as cold-blooded, evil, and otherworldly—the opposite of man's best friend.

Perhaps no one has dispelled those myths better than Jim and Jamie Dutcher. From 1990 to 1996, these documentary filmmakers lived in a tent on the edge of Idaho's Sawtooth Wilderness, where they filmed the social and hierarchical interactions of a pack of gray wolves. We challenge you to watch Jim and Jamie Dutcher's *The Hidden Life of Wolves* and not be moved by the fierce loyalty, intense caring, and unbridled fun that exists within the pack. "You can see a lot of your dog in the wolf, and a lot of wolf in your dog," Jamie Dutcher says. "They are both social animals, and just like elephants, gorillas, and whales, they educate their young, take care of their injured, and live in family groups."*

We have no desire to advocate for the domestication of wolves: That process has already played out over millennia and resulted in the domestic dog. Wolves should be left in the wild. But because of the wide prejudice against wolves, some people have sought to de-emphasize the connection between dogs and wolves, to discount the lessons we can learn from them and the reality that the dog is a pack animal with very sophisticated communication skills. Let us be perfectly clear: If you accept the overwhelming body of scientific evidence that your dog is a pack animal, then you can solve just about any behavioral problem—whether your pack consists of a compound filled with pit bulls and fox terriers or whether it's just one Labrador retriever.

A dog's pack mentality allows him to not only survive but also flourish side by side with humans. Could the pack nature of dogs be a simple explanation for why they love us?

Dogs, like human beings, experience fulfillment based on the quality of their relationships, and this happens most naturally within the context of their pack. From an evolutionary point of view, dogs have long seen the benefits of associating with human beings. One of the most wondrous qualities of the dog is its ability to include its close

---

* National Geographic Live! Jim & Jamie Dutcher: *The Hidden Life of Wolves*

human companions as part of its pack. The ways this can happen are manifold. Whether a household consists of one dog living with an individual owner, multiple dogs living with a married couple, or one or several dogs living in a family with children, the dogs in that household naturally identify their immediate companions (both human and canine) as their pack. When the pack leader shows all other pack members that their role is follower, their behavior is calmer and more stable; their relationship with the pack leader and other pack members deepens.

The Balance of Life

Keeping the dog's life in balance according to its basic nature is the centerpiece of living artfully with your dog. Once a dog is with us at New Skete or Marc's farm, its schedule is quickly meshed with those of the existing pack. There are defined moments when we work, periods when the dogs rest in the crate or on tether, and specific times when we play. "Work, rest, and play" is a mantra you will hear over and over from us. This is the structure on which a happy relationship with your dog is built.

Play is supervised and has rules. All good games have rules. Our primary rule for play is that dogs do not fight over resources such as toys or space, and that they adjust their play style so as not to overwhelm any other dog. This does not come naturally to most of our clients' dogs. By getting them gradually acclimated to interacting with a few stable dogs, we show them that they can share and that they can play without overpowering. Once the dogs start to get it, they get it quickly — they become more than willing to play within the pack rules. Learning our rules, however, may require correction.

For example, many of the dogs we train do not like the crate, according to their owners. And it's true: For the first couple of days, we find we must insist that the dog step into the crate and remain quiet there. But, generally, by the third day, visiting dogs are cheerfully hopping into the crate under their own steam. That's because they know there's a possibility they may receive a treat. We also feed in crates, building the concept that this is the dog's private, happy space.

After the dog is acclimated, very often it likes the crate, responding to it as a safe, denlike environment. If, however, the conditioning of the crating is done in an unenlightened way — if the dog is crated for punishment, for instance — the dog might not have a positive association with the crate. Assuming the owner follows good behavioral protocol, getting a young dog adjusted to the crate in a positive way, the dog can really grow to enjoy the security the crate offers. A dog might even retreat to the crate when it feels the need — for example, during a thunderstorm or if the dog simply wants a time-out from human interaction. Though having a crate is not an absolute must for all dogs, we do highly recommend its use, but it's important to remember not to project the human experience to the crate. To us the crate might seem to be a jail cell; to your dog it offers the comfort and safety of her own little apartment — a place for her to rest.

We're not advocating that you keep your dog crated so much that it becomes stir-crazy. For your dog, however, having its own space is not punishment. In fact, it's something that most dogs covet. Put a dog in a new environment — say, a new house or apartment — or bring a full-grown dog home from the pound, and watch the dog become still and peaceful when she finds her own "crate": the confines beneath a couch or a chair, for instance. Dogs, for the most part, are ever vigilant, always highly attuned to their surroundings. This vigilance takes energy and concentration. The crate offers your dog something of a reprieve from the constant barrage of stimuli that living in the moment brings. Believe us, a crate can be of great benefit to the relationship between you and your dog.

A dog that respects — and trusts — your authority to place his body in a crate is also a dog that will not growl at you for moving him off a couch.

In a related vein, we recommend that you walk through the dog's space occasionally. Do it gently, but note his lack of concern as he moves out of your way. The subtle message you're delivering is this: All the space in the world belongs to me, yet I share it with you. We think similarly of toys. We at New Skete have a bunch of dog toys, but they're not scattered all around. We keep them put away in a box. When we want the dogs to enjoy them we pull a few out and distribute them. Here's a trick: Put some of your saliva on one of your dog's toys. This marks it as yours and makes it extra special to your dog. We'll bet that the toy you mark becomes one of the most sought after of the dog toys. If it's good enough to belong to the boss, your dog thinks, then it must be really special.

Simply put, the *play* part of the work, rest, and play equation means that your dog must earn the resources that she covets and that you control. She must follow your guidance and commands.

As should be obvious, finding the balance of life means being conscious of your dog and her needs. Awareness is crucial. For instance, housebreaking errors, chewing, and incessant barking are all undesirable behaviors, but they are typically crimes of opportunity. Eliminate the opportunity by being conscious of your dog and her needs, and you also eliminate the crime. Simply stated, if your dog knows that you are aware of her presence she is less likely to indulge in bad behavior. Once your dog becomes accustomed to sharing this mental connection with you, she will start to forget that being naughty is even an option.

Building the Bond

As the pack leader, it's your job to build the bond between your dog and you. The fruit of this is extraordinary. Once the bond is formed, your dog will go to just about any length to express its devotion to you. There is no limit to its genuine fidelity and companionship. One of the best ways to strengthen your bond with your dog is by basic grooming. Too often today, dogs are sent to groomers for even the smallest of dog-cleaning tasks. You may be missing a real opportunity to connect on a deep level with your dog.

We can't tell you how often we've had dogs come in for training that are totally uncomfortable with any sort of basic grooming. The dogs won't hold still, they'll fight the brush, try to mouth continuously, and won't allow their nails to be cut. What this reveals is that the owner hasn't spent enough hands-on time with the dog. A dog that can't be groomed is a dog that has missed out on discovering the affirming and caring touch of the owner. If you don't groom your

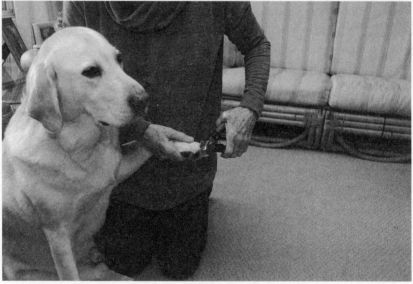

A good pack leader builds a trusting relationship with her dog, who will then permit grooming. You can see that Buddy enjoys brushing more than nail clipping, but he's cooperative for both.

dog, you're going to miss out on a natural exercise that is essential for the overall health of the dog.

Related to regular grooming is canine massage. This is an excellent means of bonding with your dog, and while helping your dog relax, it also lets you check regularly for any health issues like hot spots or tumors so that they can be dealt with promptly. Start by getting your dog in a comfortable position — sitting, standing, lying down — it doesn't really matter so long as the dog isn't forced into holding the position before he is conditioned to it. Be patient. Through massage your dog learns to love the gentle touch of your hand. What we are speaking of here has little in common with deep-tissue human massage and more in common with gentle circular and rubbing motions that progressively move down from the neck to the rest of the dog's body. Not only will your dog learn to love this (and so will you), but at the same time it builds his perception of you as a leader he can trust.

BROTHER CHRISTOPHER   In thinking how my own view of training and living with dogs has expanded into something broader, something more akin to an art, I realize how fortunate I've been to live in a contemplative setting, one that's continually questioning me. In the monastery, nothing's static. There's a continual impulse to strive for excellence, to experiment and to search for what is better... in all aspects of my life. That's what spirituality is about. I've been fortunate to be able to learn from my experiences and to work on making whatever necessary changes reality suggests. And the surprise has been that this process also applies to my work with dogs. I didn't dream that would be the case when I first came to New Skete. Spirituality was about other things, you know? But as time has passed, I've learned that spirituality touches everything in life, dogs included. And what a blessing that's been! Not only have I had the chance to become a student of dogs — something I've found endlessly fascinating — but each dog has taught me so much about myself, about becoming more conscious of the ways I have to grow in order to live more in sync with my stated ideals.

People have asked me when this insight arrived — was it always like this or did it occur at a particular point? Mostly it was something that I grew into, something that was organically part of a process. But if I were to point to a time, I'd say it was the years just before we published *The Art of Raising a Puppy*. I was raising a puppy named Meiko. I had raised several puppies already, but Meiko took me to a different level. He taught me how a pup could naturally grow into a relationship without a lot of pressure, so long as I gave him proper structure. The structure wasn't meant to limit his freedom but to direct it, and Meiko responded beautifully. For example, during the first month, I kept him with me on a tether wherever I went, and after an initial amount of predictable protestation, he quickly caught on and learned to follow me throughout the day. I really didn't have to do that much. I took him for daily walks, played with him, and let him take periodic rests. Also, because we have a breeding program here, Meiko was able to interact daily with all of the other shepherds. I was amazed to see how naturally the older dogs kept him in line, teaching him limits, yet never having to go overboard with him. Meiko was just a quick learner, and found his place naturally in the pack. I took advantage of every opportunity to socialize him in those first months, bringing him to meals and to coffee hours with our congregants after Sunday service, and letting him meet retreatants and guests who came to the monastery. His friendliness became predictable. I didn't have to worry about him. I spent some time every day teaching him simple obedience commands, but it really wasn't all that much work, and it simply helped me

An early photo of Brother Christopher with a New Skete shepherd and Sister Magdalene.

to manage him more naturally. Now, I don't mean to paint a totally idyllic picture — like any pup, Meiko occasionally got into mischief — but I found that simply keeping him within the basic structure I provided him kept those occasions to a minimum. He was a very balanced pup who made raising him a piece of cake.

Here's the thing: It was more than that. I remember one day calling him to me and looking into his eyes affectionately and thinking how lucky I was to have been given this pup to raise. His look back at me took me by surprise: It was as if he were saying as he licked me, "Don't you get it? You're part of this, too." And it occurred to me then that the past eight months had been the most spiritually and emotionally stable months I had experienced since coming to New Skete. Part of what I was seeing in Meiko was a reflection of my own sense of peace, of having found a home and a sense of vocation and purpose. It was as much written on Meiko as it was manifest in me. And it made me deeply grateful. It's a lesson I've never forgotten.

Raising a puppy and having a fulfilling relationship with your dog does demand a certain dedication and commitment. But it's nothing unreasonable, or beyond the scope of any responsible owner. Further, dogs enrich our lives. The better we pay attention to raising and caring for them properly, the more we receive in return. The more you learn about your dog and her true nature, the better position you'll be in to live with her in a way that brings out the best in both of you . . . and the more you'll see the relationship as a true and unique expression of friendship.

3

Beyond Lassie

What is it with the fetish for romanticizing dogs? Dogs do not require such vain attempts at makeover. Their very nature possesses its own dignity, transcending any need of supplement and change. All that is required is our respect and admiration.
—Bless the Dogs

In World War I, on the war-ravaged French countryside, an American soldier named Lee Duncan stumbled upon what he believed was a miracle. A dog kennel had been nearly destroyed by an aerial bomb. Inside the wreckage lay the bodies of a dozen or so German shepherds. Then Duncan, who had grown up as an orphan, saw a mother shepherd nursing five puppies. Only days old, the pups hadn't even opened their eyes. The young soldier took two of the whelps, a male and a female, all he could carry. His fellow soldiers rescued the mother and the other babies. Though Duncan's female puppy would die of pneumonia, the male puppy, along with his soldier-master, would survive the war and then make their way to Duncan's home in California.

The rescue of the shepherd puppy on the French countryside was only the beginning of the story. Duncan named the puppy Rin Tin Tin after a popular French doll. So bright was the fame of the war-born German shepherd that legend has it he received the most votes for Best Actor at the first Academy Awards in 1929. News of his death in 1932 interrupted radio broadcasts across the country.

Though Rin Tin Tin's considerable talent as a performer made him a phenomenon and sold movie tickets by the millions, it was the tale

of his relationship with Lee Duncan that transcended fictional entertainment and ultimately earned him a place in the hearts of the
American people.

For many baby boomers and their children, film and television
dogs like Rin Tin Tin, Lassie, and Benji set the standard for our expectations: a dog that was a loyal companion and that not only could
take care of itself but also would rescue us in times of danger. "What
is it, Lassie? Timmy fell down the well again?" Dogs are capable of
amazing feats of valor, as evidenced by the canine parachute jumpers
our US Army Special Forces employ or the search-and-rescue dogs we
see working in times of natural or man-made disasters. But not even
Rin Tin Tin or Lassie performed in real life as Hollywood depicted
them. While Rin Tin Tin fed the imaginations of moviegoers, he also
had episodes in real life where he snapped and barked at dog show
judges, could be difficult and unruly, bit a number of actors and
costars, and required hours of rigorous training each day with Lee.
None of that was part of the image Hollywood wanted to project.
Similarly, no one ever saw six-month-old Lassie being corrected for
chewing the couch leg, or the arduous training it took to get him to
stop on a mark. (Yes, Lassie was played by a succession of male collies.) Hollywood has never been about reality and so isn't concerned
with what happens behind the curtain during production. Only the
final version on-screen is important. So, of course, all movie and TV
dogs seem to behave perfectly. It didn't matter if it took fourteen takes
and a few bandages to get Rin Tin Tin's scene shot as long as it looked
perfect to the audience.

That said, if you are of a certain age, you most likely remember the
dogs of your childhood as being very much part of your life, fitting
seamlessly into your day-to-day activities. These companions of yes-
teryear didn't seem to need obedience classes, scientific studies, or
formal training. At least that's the way we remember it. Owners didn't
have to be told to spend more time with their dogs or to give them
special activities. We enjoyed a more natural, organic way of interacting and socializing; people tended to socialize with their dogs despite
themselves. In many neighborhoods there were no leash laws. Our
dogs ran out the front door with us on summer mornings, or waited

for the school bus to drop us off on winter afternoons. Dogs were part of the pack of our gang — think *The Little Rascals* or *Scooby-Doo* — part of our family and our neighborhood. It was an environment that naturally programmed the dogs into our lives.

Dogs learned to behave simply by osmosis, or at least that is how we remember things.

That is an important caveat: *or at least that is how we remember things.* While there did seem to be a more natural and integral way of living with dogs in times past, some of our memories of the "good old days" are gilded. Aside from the fact that there were far fewer dogs in the first half of the twentieth century, the percentage of bad behavior among both dogs and dog owners was just as high then, maybe even higher than it is today. Our nostalgia conveniently leaves out some of the more unpleasant realities. Cars ran over unleashed dogs, visits to the vet happened only when something drastic went wrong, and many owners didn't give dogs' nutritional needs a second thought. From today's perspective, such circumstances would constitute owner negligence. So it's fair to say that a certain editing of our memories undoubtedly has taken place, a sanitizing of the stories that accentuates the good elements and minimizes the bad. Put into the blender, our memories create their own romanticism. But that shouldn't obscure an important point: On some fundamental level, we did understand the true nature of our dogs better then, and it is vital to try to recover some wisdom from the past.

This is all the more imperative because times have changed. The boomers have aged and now carry into retirement a litany of pressing concerns and time constraints. Millennials are busy building careers in a competitive environment. Our litigious society has all but banned dogs from the myriad public places where they were once welcomed. So where is the dog in all of this?

A vast new breed of dog owner with less time than ever on his hands has evolved. Today, digital preoccupation holds us hostage. Children and teens sit for hours in front of digital devices playing video games. Even adults spend more time on Facebook and texting than talking face-to-face. We now rely on a world of digital connectedness. People walk down the street using a mobile phone for email, texting, and social media, staying connected with everything but their surroundings. More than one million car accidents a year involve texting. It's not unusual for a group of friends to sit together at a restaurant all using social media rather than looking one another in the eye. The friends sitting together even text each other! People walk their dog (if the dog is lucky) while staring at a rectangle of plastic and black glass. Too many dogs are now either marginalized or, maybe worse, anthropomorphized. Instead of taking dogs along on trips, people board them in kennels or with dog sitters. Dogs spend more time with professional dog walkers or in doggy day care—or, worse yet, alone—than they do with their owners. When dogs are with their owners, they are treated not as pets but as human companions or therapy sponges to soak up their owners' emotional needs.

The paradox here is that with all the supposed advances civilization has made over the past several decades, people are either distancing themselves from their dogs or making them into something they're not. Our society has created a new romanticism, a new alienation from the dog's true nature, that assumes that the dog can take care of itself and spend the bulk of its time alone. Or that the dog is a miniature human being with the same view of reality and needs as humans, as though the only important part of the equation is love. Too often we're blind to the fact that what's really needed is simple canine-human companionship and not some dressed-up version of that relationship. People have lost the natural wisdom that helped keep dogs well behaved and happy and our lives balanced. Because dogs live smack-dab in the here-and-now, where every smell, every sound, every sight deserves and receives their attention, they can help us reconnect to a world that often escapes our notice. Through their example, dogs remind us to engage, to go for a walk, to joyously roll and romp or even to enjoy a quietly shared moment; dogs guide us to become more human. They do this because dogs connect to the world not through their data plan but through the richness of their senses. When we listen to their message we are able to pay greater attention to the reality of now, to ourselves, even if initially it's just for a few hours a day. The good news is that a simple walk with your dog (and with your cell phone put away) can go a long way toward reconnecting you both to this wondrous, real world. We can recover some of the best elements of that earlier era of dog companionship by honoring the spirit that the dog has always possessed and letting it blossom in our company. When we begin to give dogs what *they* need rather than what *we* need, we will have started the journey on the right foot.

But this leaves nagging questions that are brought up to us repeatedly: How do we get beyond the romanticism; how do we transform ideals into reality to attain this spiritual connection with our own dogs? What do dogs need? And how do we give it to them? There's no shame in admitting that the devil is in the details (and we will address this throughout the book). But, before all else, let's take a general overview of how a good relationship evolves and how you can integrate a dog into your life in a way that suits you *both*.

Just about every relationship between an owner and his dog starts with a dream. It doesn't matter whether you're purchasing your first puppy from a breeder or adopting your second or third full-grown dog from an animal shelter. Owners envision a dog that will be an important part of their lives, that will fit into their home and become a *reliant* companion filled with unconditional love. Emotionally, the dream is the same for practically everyone, but it needs to be translated into how a dog truly is, rather than the fantasy version of who we want him to be. We simply cannot overstate this: A relationship that is transformative for both you and your dog builds on an essential foundation of shared time, regular exercise, positive socialization, and dedication on your part to provide the dog with the basic essentials of what it needs. Leadership starts there. All dogs need this from us. With those elements in place, the dream can begin to take flight. The very happiness you will see in your dog each day — walking, hanging out with you, or playing a game of fetch after work — will only encourage you to take things even further. How much richer both of you will be! So root your dream in reality and watch how the process teaches you to live for an hour now and again without Internet.

BROTHER CHRISTOPHER Our own dream began when we experienced firsthand the importance of our first German shepherd, Kyr, in the early years of New Skete. Kyr was a mascot and best friend during the founding of

New Skete, and his "joie de vivre," good nature, and enthusiasm were stabilizing influences for all the monks during those stressful first years. It was only when Kyr passed away that everyone could see what a blessing he had been for us, how he actually inspired us. We never set out to breed German shepherds or train dogs, but the loss of Kyr made such a deep impression on us that we simply had to replace him with another shepherd. That led us to obtain two breeding-quality females, and things developed naturally from there: the idea of each monk caring for a dog, starting a breeding program of German shepherds, training dogs who could live harmoniously with their owners. This has been a grace that none of us could have anticipated. But here we are fifty years later. The strength of the approach we've developed in that time rests in the fact that it's the product of the actual experience we've had of living with dogs — many, many dogs. Without rehashing what we've spoken about in our other books, this experience has taught us that romantic ideas about dogs that are filled with human projection may sell tickets for Hollywood studios and delight and entertain moviegoers, but they fail to offer a realistic portrayal of how we can live with our dogs and allow both species to flourish. Real life is where that occurs. When we think of the early days of New Skete, the primary lesson that jumps out is that the dogs were our best teachers. We listened to what their real needs were and worked energetically to help them live harmoniously with us and with one another. That meant providing effective leadership. Practically speaking, when you have a large group of powerful dogs living under the same roof with a group of ten to fifteen monks, you learn pretty quickly how to manage the dogs as they are, and not as you'd like them to be.

For example, we learned early on how important it is to respect biology. While we might like to have all the dogs be able to play and interact with one another, we discovered quickly that this isn't always possible. In a breeding colony, you have to be very careful with the males you are using as studs. Inevitably they look at one another as competitors, and even if they've been raised together and got along as young dogs, how that changes once they begin to be used consistently for breeding! I will never forget the first dogfight I witnessed between two of our breeding male shepherds. It happened when one was accidentally let into a room where the other was resting. The fight progressed so quickly and so primally. It was only the quick work of two monks that enabled the two dogs to be separated without anyone getting

seriously hurt. But we all understood immediately that we had dodged a bul-
let there. None of us had ever witnessed anything quite like that before —
and it gave us a new respect for the dogs' version of reality as canines.

Though we heartily encourage you to begin your relationship with
your dog dreaming of good things to come, we also believe that a
healthy, modern relationship between owner and dog begins with a
thoughtful understanding of dogs and their behavior, an adherence
to the natural order, and a deeply held love for the dog. This is what
gets beyond romanticism and sentimentality. In real life, it takes more
than the Hollywood version of love to sustain a healthy relationship
between you and your dog. Understanding each other is what keeps
the love affair going strong.

This requires a certain amount of work and study. If a foundation
of knowledge is paramount to a happy relationship with your dog,
let's begin with a very brief overview of how dog training evolved.
Today we are flooded with information about all sorts of dog-training
philosophies. We find some more productive than others. But traced
back to its beginnings, at least in its modern derivation, dog training
draws inspiration from two basic theories of animal behavioral
science.

One is the theory of behaviorism, which is the study of how animals learn. The psychologist B. F. Skinner is perhaps the most famous
proponent of behaviorism. Skinner theorized that animals learn by
experience and through responding to external stimuli. He believed
that good behavior is strengthened when it's reinforced, and bad
behavior diminishes as it's punished. He invented, as you might
remember from your Intro to Psychology course, the Skinner box, in
which, typically, a pigeon or rat was placed. The box included a lever,
a slot for food, and water. If the pigeon or rat touched the lever, a pellet of food would come out of the slot. Skinner devised the experiments and recorded the results. What he learned was that he could
"shape" the animals' actions by rewarding certain behavior — like hitting the lever. There is no question that the general elements of behavior learning theory can be very helpful in the training process.

However, we believe Skinner's form of behaviorism was myopic, and when applied rigidly to a relationship with a dog it risks turning the dog into something that it is not: a behavioral machine. Skinner rejected the view that thoughts, feelings, and emotions are involved in causing behavior. But anyone who has ever lived with a dog would be hard-pressed to deny that dogs have emotions and feelings — feelings that are certainly more complex than those we'd ascribe to pigeons. Something of the dog gets lost in a purely Skinner view of animal behavior.

The other school of thought is ethology, the study of animals in their natural environment. Konrad Lorenz is probably the best-known figure in this field. The recipient of the 1973 Nobel Prize for Physiology or Medicine, Lorenz believed that nearly all animal behavior is innate. He posited that nature and genetics are responsible for the actions of your dog, and he can be interpreted (we believe unfairly) as downplaying the role of training in the life of the dog. Admittedly, much dog training today is based largely on Skinner's theories, and this despite the fact that Skinner was a lab scientist, much more clinical than Lorenz, and, to our knowledge, never trained dogs. By contrast, Lorenz bred, trained, and lived with dogs his whole life. He also wrote extensively about them, including his iconic book *Man Meets Dog,* which we heartily recommend to all dog owners and prospective dog owners. You will, we promise, especially enjoy spending a summer's day with Lorenz and his beloved Susi in his essay (with charming sketches) entitled "Dog Days." Lorenz didn't embrace the romantic ideal of the dog; rather, his inspiration was the reality of the relationships he had with his dogs.

We realize, of course, that many dog owners today don't have the luxury of time that Lorenz may have had. We also know that not all of Lorenz's teaching methods have stood the test of time. But his explanation of the relationship among man, dog, and nature, like a good wine or a classic novel, goes to the very heart of the lesson we are trying to impart in this book.

We believe that the same loving and intentional interaction that Lorenz describes can — and should — exist in the time you do spend with your dog in today's busy world. We also believe the payoff is extraordinary, but it needs to be grounded in reality. Uncritically accepting statements like "Dogs have an innate desire to please" is not helpful and doesn't honor the real nature of the dog. If dogs had a simplistic innate desire to please, then why does your dog have any bad habits at all? Your dog would just always obey and comply out of its desire to please. No, quite understandably, dogs have an innate desire to please themselves, just as we do. However, as we help dogs discover the benefits of cooperating with a conscientious and loving human being, the true nobility of the dog is revealed. That is what we want to draw out. Indeed, the "unconditional" love of the dog is most manifest when the dog is raised in an atmosphere of responsibility, leadership, and companionship. In this context, dogs nurture our sense of self-worth by making us the center of their universe. From them, we learn a dignity that comes from within, not out of some external circumstance. Dogs tell us what's important in life: They don't care what we look like, whether or not our hair is done, or if

When a dog learns to cooperate with a human being, his unconditionally loving nature comes through. Here you can see the devotion between Marc Goldberg and Diablo.

we're clean-shaven. It doesn't matter to a dog what you do for a living, or how much money you have in the bank. From dogs we learn how to connect in spiritual ways with the beauty of the world that surrounds us. In return, all dogs ask for is a walk with some basic rules, a kind word, and a warm bed in the heart of our home... in short, to be included in our lives.

But how? you ask. Well, in addition to establishing a consistent schedule for feeding, walking, playing, and just being with your dog, there is so much more that you can do. If there is love and a willingness to understand your dog's true nature, then there is fertile soil in which a healthy relationship can grow. In a world where humans seem to become more detached and isolated with every technological advancement, dogs remind us of the profound spiritual connection we have with animals and to the good Earth. There are abundant opportunities to prime the relationship and take it beyond sentimental stereotypes — and to become more human in the process.

One obvious way to spend more time with your dog is to include her in your everyday routine. Long walks and exercise in dog-friendly parks are a natural opportunity to build on your relationship with your pet while at the same time offering a reprieve from the daily rat race. Dog owners with families should share the responsibility and the fun. Let everyone spend quality time with the family dog or dogs, either separately, together, or both.

This is eminently doable these days. Taking advantage of the dog-friendly aspects and amenities of the town or city you live in is a great way to share your life with your dog. Chicago offers several dog-friendly beaches and at least eighteen off-leash parks. Las Vegas is also very dog-friendly, with at least twenty-five off-leash parks. Orlando, Seattle, and Austin, Texas, all have made "best dog-friendly cities" lists. In New York City, the great and expansive Central Park is all yours and your dog's with an off-leash allowance, albeit before 9:00 a.m. or after 9:00 p.m. Many city dog owners spend a good amount of time in the park before they head off to work.

Dog owners in big cities more often integrate dogs into their lives as a matter of course. They're used to sharing limited apartment space and having a communal experience. City dogs learn how to follow their owners' lead out of necessity. They must become accustomed to loud noises, cramped elevators, and navigating city traffic, whether vehicular or pedestrian. Both owner and dog must be alert on even the most casual walk. The city experience intensifies the dog and owner bond.

Like graffiti artists, city dogs and their owners use the urban landscape as a canvas, finding ways to artfully coexist. We know of one New York City resident who awakes before dawn and, with his dog, makes his way to a park along the East River. There, dog and owner watch the sun rise each morning over the borough of Queens.

But big-city dwellers don't have a monopoly on the art of living with their dogs. Real rural living, with its wide-open spaces, dense woods, minimal traffic, and nature in all her abundance and splendor, is wonderful for building a happy relationship with your dog — that is, if you don't use the idyllic setting as an excuse to shirk your responsibilities. We monks know a bit about rural living — our monastery sits on top of a mountain. For example, we know plenty of local hunters who take their dogs into the woods regularly for exercise and work, in season and out, and a number of farmers whose dogs accompany them on their daily chores. These are well-adjusted, happy dogs that spend a lot of time with their owners. On the flip side, there is sometimes a temptation in rural locales to let dogs fend too much for themselves. Far too often we've heard stories from the locals about dogs being hit by cars or hurt in other accidents because they were without supervision.

BROTHER CHRISTOPHER A common rural mentality is that the dog can take care of itself — after all, there's an abundance of open space to occupy the dog's time and attention. The dog can make hay with its freedom and will not place any inconvenient demands on the owner's time and attention. The only problem with this attitude is that it plays Russian roulette with the dog's life. I remember a number of years back, for example, a cute mixed-breed puppy that was set out free in its front yard every day. If it wasn't in its yard it was walking along the road, able to explore the local woods or romp in the creek. To some people's eye, it was absolutely idyllic. The dog was totally free. I remember the intense sadness I felt one day when I drove past

its property and there was the dog on the side of the road, a lifeless corpse
that had been hit by a car.

Still, there is nothing as natural as a country or farm dog, and life
with such a dog can occupy the very pinnacle of human-dog
relationships.

Suburbs, too, provide many opportunities to integrate your life
with your dog's. With a profusion of lawns and parks, and with significant dog populations, there are ample possibilities for exercise,
play with children, and safe interaction with other dogs. Responsible
doggy day care facilities are springing up in such locales to give owners who work greater flexibility in meeting their dogs' social needs.
That said, lax leash laws and heavily trafficked roads can become,
without proper training, a dangerous environment for your dog. So
be vigilant and realistic about what your dog's capabilities are.

Regardless of where you live — city, suburbs, or country — there are

A dog that is comfortable in the car can go more places with you . . . but don't let
him drive.

plenty of ways for your dog to spend quality time with you. Years ago, we didn't think twice about loading the dog in the family station wagon. Today it takes a little more thought, planning, and training, but taking your dog along in the car with you can build a sense of camaraderie, a feeling of being together in this adventure called everyday life. We're surprised at the number of dogs that get in the car so infrequently that they see even a short trip as a terrifying or (literally) nauseating ordeal, or that spend the whole ride jumping from back to front, barking at everything they see.

We recall one client who brought her Labrador for training, and when she opened the rear door there were three piles of vomit and bile on the upholstery. This was the reason the woman never took the dog with her in the car. Apparently, the dog would vomit during every trip. Our training of the Lab included helping her associate riding in the car with something she really liked: playing with a favorite toy, for instance. After the ride, we would spend ten minutes playing fetch with her squeaky toy. It was amazing how quickly the dog's attitude changed and her nausea vanished, and how quickly the relationship between the dog and her owner began to improve as a result.

We recommend that you start by taking your dog on short trips, just down the block and back. You might also want to refrain from feeding or giving him water for a few hours beforehand. First, lower the window just a bit so your dog may enjoy the breeze in his snout. Windows should never be left fully open, however. Although it might look cute to see a pooch's head hanging out the window of a car, tongue a red ribbon flapping in the breeze, it's never a safe practice for any animal (or person) to hang out of a moving car. An open window might also prove too tempting of an escape route for some adventurous breeds, and a bug or pebble hitting an eye at sixty miles per hour can do serious damage. Make sure your dog is completely at ease in the vehicle before you attempt any long trips or travel on crowded highways. A canine safety harness, a partition, or a crate are all good options for keeping your dog safe in a moving car. A dog that is easily excited can be a dangerous distraction to a driver. A calm and comfortable dog, however, is a wonderful road-trip companion.

Family vacations to pet-friendly destinations, or just to the seashore or mountains, will go a long way toward integrating your pet into the family. RV parks and campgrounds across the country are investing in dog-friendly features, including leash-free areas and agility courses, according to the *New York Times*.* In our own travels overseas, we have been heartened to see what is recounted so lovingly in Lorenz's book—the integration of dogs into everyday village life. Paris is as famous for its dog-friendliness as it is for its fashion and food. In a park outside the Louvre, with the Eiffel Tower in the background, Parisians meet to let their dogs play and interact. You see dogs on the Metro and sitting at outdoor cafés with their owners. More than the dog-friendly amenities, Paris offers an example of how an intentional relationship with your dog can enhance even the most cosmopolitan existence. For Parisians, a dog adds to the enjoyment of a simple walk, like crusty bread with your soup or chocolate with your coffee. Even chilly old England warms when it comes to its dogs, as the stories of James Herriot and Queen Elizabeth's well-known love for her corgis pointedly attest.

We notice one other important cultural difference between Americans and Europeans. Americans tend to infantilize their dogs. They baby talk to them, they touch them constantly, and they buy them tons of toys. At the same time, Americans leave their dogs alone a lot. Perhaps a sense of guilt for leaving the dogs contributes to Americans spoiling their dogs on occasion. Americans even spoil other people's dogs, stopping them on the street to talk to the dogs as though they were public property. Europeans, by contrast, take their dogs everywhere. Yet if you were to address—or, worse yet, touch—a stranger's dog on the street in Europe, you'd quickly get an earful. It simply isn't done. And, as a result, the European dogs are calmly integrated into public life, able to spend much more time with their owners than most American dogs manage.

MARC   I was in a pub in the Elephant and Castle section of London, and there was a Doberman bitch lounging on the floor of the bar. The barman, who happened to own the pub, noticed my appreciation of the dog's beauty.

---

* http://www.nytimes.com/2015/05/14/business/retirementspecial/retirees-love-their-pets
.html?hp&action=click&pgtype=Homepage&module=mini-moth&region=top-stories
-below&WT.nav=top-stories-below

"You want to see the pups?" he asked in a Cockney accent. He then disappeared through a door behind the bar and reemerged with his arms filled with eight-week-old Doberman pups. I was soon engulfed in a cuddle puddle of puppies. As I walked from the pub that day, I realized that the pub owner had accomplished something truly beautiful: He had seamlessly integrated his dogs into his life. For the price of a pint, a patron would experience his pub, his family, and his dogs all in one visit. It was wonderful.

Zombies, Run!

Another terrific way to make your dog part of your life is to have her join you in your fitness routine. Today, all sorts of running apps fill the market, including one that challenges you to outrun the walking dead. Having a real, living dog along on your run can be equally exciting. A dog makes for a very enthusiastic training companion. Here too, however, dogs need to be indoctrinated into the routine. Start with a long lead and a brisk walking pace. As your dog gets used to the freedom of the run, increase your speed and shorten the lead. Many dogs have a talent for pace and a real runner's determination. It's important to remember, though, that dogs get hot more quickly than you do, and you should bring a water bottle for them and teach them how to drink from it. Though not all dogs are cut out for long distances, many can be perfect running partners: Labs, boxers, and English setters, for instance. Dogs can also enjoy roadwork by accompanying owners on bicycles and even roller skates, though this calls for a high degree of skill and discipline. You don't want to be a novice on Rollerblades with Rover in hot pursuit of a squirrel or another dog. For bicyclists, use a springer attachment to keep your dog at a safe distance from the wheels. Whenever you're on the go, consider bringing your buddy. Playing Frisbee, swimming, hiking, running on a dog-friendly beach—all not only are invigorating but also go a long way toward building a healthy connection between your dog and you.

Perhaps you're lucky enough to be employed by someone who lets you bring your dog to work. Google, Amazon, Ben & Jerry's, and Procter & Gamble are a few of the bigger dog-friendly firms, but there are plenty of small companies that allow—even encourage—canine companionship at work. Some of us work for ourselves. Others work from home. Whatever the situation, if you can bring your dog with you to your workplace, please do. It will provide a natural opportunity to strengthen the bond you share with your dog by significantly increasing her presence in your life each day.

We know from experience dogs aren't all that fond of barriers, especially the ones that keep them apart from their owners. There is nothing as forlorn as the bark of a lonely dog from behind a fence. Sometimes those fences are in yards, but sometimes they encase people's thoughts and feelings. Without realizing it, we can let the pressures of everyday living so dominate our attention that the fundamental needs of our dogs get neglected. Above all, this implies their social needs. For most dogs, the prime need in their lives is a connection with their owners. To think that as a substitute for that connection you can offer an abundance of toys, free rein of the house, or a seemingly unlimited supply of dog food is the height of self-deception and romantic thinking. Such offerings won't impress your dog because they ignore what he most truly values: time with you. Watch out for the fences you erect between you and your dog. You'll both be happier without them. We guarantee it.

Mission of Mercy

Finally, still another sure way to build the relationship between you and your dog—and contribute to the greater good in the process—is to visit someone who is elderly or ill. Although some dogs are a better fit for this than others, and specialized training may be needed, many breeds and mixes have an innate ability to soothe people in physical or mental distress. Dogs can be medicine for the body and soul. One only needs to look at the transforming effect a therapy dog can have. Such dogs can truly work miracles.

MARC   Bobbi was a big white greyhound and a registered therapy dog. We made many visits together to hospitals and nursing homes to comfort the patients. On one of these trips, we visited a hospital for profoundly brain-damaged children. It was there we met Danny.

Eight years old, Danny had sustained a brain injury that had rendered him in a nearly vegetative state. He couldn't sit up by himself, so when I brought Bobbi to see him, a nurse had to prop Danny up. Bobbi nudged the boy's hand, but Danny did not respond. I thought Bobbi would then solicit attention from the nurse instead. But she did not. Bobbi lay down next to the child and rested her head in Danny's lap. Then she promptly fell asleep.

No one dared disturb her, and Bobbi must have slept for a full ten minutes. Then she awakened, stood, and shook herself.

"He's smiling," the nurse said with tears in her eyes.

The nurse had known Danny before the injury. His family lived in her neighborhood. She told me that Danny was the type of child who smiled all the time. Even after the injury, he would smile now and then. Over the past few weeks, however, his condition had worsened and he showed no communicative ability at all.

That is, until Bobbi lay on his lap.

Any well-behaved dog may be a welcome visitor for an elderly or sick friend or relative.

BROTHER CHRISTOPHER Before my mother died, she was an Alzheimer's patient at a health care facility near the monastery. I had the opportunity to bring my dog Zoe to the unit for visits. It never ceased to amaze me how not only my mother but also a number of the other residents responded to Zoe. Somehow Zoe was able to offer a simple comforting presence that elicited real affection. What I think is that Zoe pierced through the ordinary human defenses that some people set up after experiencing phoniness and deceit in their human relationships. Even Alzheimer's patients do this. They learn not always to trust the "face" another individual presents to them. With a dog it is different. Dogs don't lie: What you see is what you get, and for that reason dogs have a unique ability to lift the spirits of patients and touch them in a way that even human visitors do not.

At the risk of anthropomorphizing dogs, it seems fair to say that dogs see the nature of man more clearly than we see the essence of dog.

Many dogs, despite their lack of Hollywood perfection, sense a human need for comfort. And they respond in remarkable ways, enchanting us with their natural gifts. Dogs don't need to live up to the expectations created by Lassie for us to love them. Let dogs be dogs, and at the same time, let us embrace our role in helping them truly become themselves.

4

On a Short Leash: Where Much of Today's Training Fails

Genuine training is about freedom: freedom for both ourselves and our dogs to enjoy each other, enhancing our relationships by allowing their potential to blossom.
— Bless the Dogs

If we repeatedly emphasize the pack nature of the dog, it is because we believe that it is the most natural starting point for understanding your dog and its needs. If you can appreciate your dog's social nature and learn to allow it to work in your favor, you will be well on your way to realizing the dream you had when you first acquired your dog. But realizing that dream also involves concepts such as leadership and pack hierarchy, which, if misunderstood, can lead to owners being too heavy-handed in their treatment of their dogs. The opposite extreme can be equally problematic: If you don't take into account the dog's pack nature and the importance of leadership, you will almost surely find yourself with no effective way of dealing with serious misbehavior. Extremes in dog training ultimately take us into dead ends that fail to serve the overall relationship between you and your dog. What we are advocating here is a middle road that integrates the dog's basic nature into an approach that is positive, respectful, and aware of boundaries. It is your responsibility to your dog to be a trustworthy guide, much like good parents are to their children. At times, you will need to affirm and encourage; at other times, you will need to provide appropriate discipline that teaches your dog limits and the importance of paying attention to you. But in all of this, let us be clear: Our training approach is never an excuse for insensitive treatment, which only creates fear and diminishes the quality of your relationship with your dog.

BROTHER CHRISTOPHER   We've always tried to speak from the fruit of our experience, experience that has not only helped us immeasurably as trainers, but has helped to deepen the relationships we've shared with our dogs. While many people were (and continue to be) appreciative of the guidance and honesty provided in the pages of our books, we are deeply conscious of the fact that ours is a profession in which we continually learn and grow in our understanding of the dog and how to help it live successfully with both humans and other dogs. Over the years, we've refined and deepened our approach, and in the process we've come to see both the advantages and the limitations of a variety of training methods. For example, we've learned from the traditionalist Bill Koehler as well as from the animal behaviorist and trainer Pamela Reid. We've seen what happens when there is too much emphasis placed on physical correction, and we've also seen what happens when bad behavior is ignored in the name of "being humane": The dog learns that it is in control. In both instances, the relationship gets frustrated. What has been of value to so many of our readers is a clear presentation of how reasonable rules and boundaries can be established with a dog, acknowledging that contexts vary. Obviously, setting limits with a ten-week-old puppy is going to be different from doing it with a three-year-old rescue. And over the years, the feedback we've received from ordinary dog owners has been gratifying. Our methods work, and they do so in a way that builds up the relationship.

This is why we're confident in our approach. For more than forty years we've been living in a laboratory where every day we see the effects of our training process. We know what works and what doesn't. We see both the success and frustration of our labor in the dogs themselves. Dogs, as we're fond of saying, don't lie. God kept that ability from them. When we send a client's dog home from the monastery's training program, we send the best dog we can. At the final training demonstration, we can't bribe the dog to act the way we want it to. The training has to have changed the dog fundamentally; otherwise he will quickly revert to the behavior he had when he first came to us. When it comes to dog training, there's talk and then there's results. We deal in the latter. We've accumulated a body of evidence that is grounded in real life. Through the years, we have based our approach on training a single dog at a time. Each dog is unique, and it's from this experience that we've continued to grow and learn from our dogs. The process never gets old. For myself, what's been so enriching, especially about the past fifteen years, has been the opportunity to explore the spiritual dimension present in the human-dog relationship. In a way I wouldn't have anticipated when I first came to the monastery, working with dogs has put me in deeper touch with the mystery that my heart longs for. I feel this especially when I see a concrete transformation take place in both dog and owner, and how their lives are so much better for it. Dogs want to be in close connection with us: We simply have to trust in the principles that allow the relationship to flourish.

Division in the Ranks

The training of dogs has a tumultuous history that affects the dog-owning public to this day. Unfortunately, there is so much dissension among trainers that the industry has a pointed joke, one that has a dark humor to it: The only thing two dog trainers can agree on is that the third doesn't know *anything*. Like so many jokes, this one has a kernel of truth to it. Not that the third dog trainer doesn't know anything, but that you can barely find three trainers who can agree on a coherent approach to creating a harmonious bond between dog and owner.

The divisiveness among dog trainers stems from deep-rooted philosophical differences in approaches. For the moment, let's say that there are three main branches of the dog-training tree. Let's call the first branch compulsion training. The second is treat training, commonly known as "purely positive." And the third is what we would call balanced training because it lies somewhere in the middle, between the other two.

At its worst, compulsion training is harsh, even abusive. The concept involves giving a dog two choices: Perform the exercise in question, such as heel or stay, or suffer the consequences. If you read very old dog-training books, some published in the 1800s to teach owners of hunting dogs, you quickly realize that standard equipment in the trainer's bag was the quirt, a short whip used to punish the recalcitrant dog.

Fortunately, over time, the dog began to be seen more as a family pet than a utilitarian tool. Consequently, training methods softened. Maybe the most famous trainer of the Greatest Generation of the mid-twentieth century was William "Bill" Koehler. His career began by training dogs for the US Army. Later, Koehler became the top dog handler at Disney Studios and was responsible for the performances of the dogs in movies such as *Swiss Family Robinson* and *The Incredible Journey*, among others.

Koehler's book on training dogs became a classic; however, many in the dog world today label his techniques as compulsion. We believe this criticism is shortsighted. Koehler's method is from another era, but its foundation is sound. Rather than quickly jumping to compulsion, he first helps the dog understand and perform the skill he's requiring. He carefully divides each exercise into multiple layers, teaching only one layer at a time. Then as the dog progresses in understanding, Koehler begins to hold the dog accountable for performing successive layers, only increasing the level of difficulty and distraction over time. Ultimately, this is fair to the dog and teaches him to perform a skill set regardless of what's going on around him. In other words, the dog is able to bring the skill set into real-life situations.

Yes, Koehler was a proponent of physical correction, but only when the dog consciously decided to ignore what it had been taught and, moreover, what it *understood*. The movement that labels itself purely positive decries the physical correction part of Koehler's sequence. However, Koehler's approach should be seen in the context of his era. His training was much more thoroughly considered and far kinder to dogs than the methods that preceded it. His love of dogs was unquestioned. He worked with them successfully for fifty years, training dogs to perform sophisticated sequences for film in which they appeared totally natural and relaxed. Seasoned trainers know you can't get such results by punishing a dog into submission.

Partly, what earns Koehler the scorn of modern critics is the terse style in which he wrote *The Koehler Method of Dog Training*. Our friend Mary Mazzeri knew and studied with Bill. She asked him why he wrote his book in such a forceful manner, when in fact she observed him to be a very subtle trainer who was not unduly forceful with dogs. "I expect them to do only ten percent of what I recommend," Bill answered. Further complicating his reputation is the fact that in the ensuing decades, legions of trainers claimed to be using the Koehler system. But analysis of their work shows they either never read his book or chose to employ shortcuts Koehler himself would not have approved of. They lacked the patience Koehler used in his training method. Yes, Koehler corrected dogs, but not before he carefully and sequentially taught them how to perform. Lesser trainers leapt right to hard physical correction without following the obliga-

Brother Marc and two New Skete shepherds, who thrive in the relationship with their pack leader.

tory teaching steps. Too often these hacks labeled their training Koehler-based in an attempt to legitimize themselves.

Koehler may have been a bit controversial, but factor in widespread corruption of his method, and eventually the pendulum would naturally swing away from old-school punishment training. It was in that dawning age of enlightenment, 1978 to be exact, when we first published *How to Be Your Dog's Best Friend*. Seeking a balance of authority and compassion, we tried to present in that first book a holistic view of the dog that emphasized the primacy of the relationship. This has come to be known as balanced training. Good training always serves the friendship, creating a level of trust and dedication that is shared by both dog and owner.

Our first book spoke realistically and candidly about the overall relationship between owner and dog. In any healthy relationship with a dog there has to be an appropriate amount of discipline. Such discipline requires a reliable, clear set of instructions. *How to Be Your Dog's Best Friend* offered guidance on choosing training tools and showed the reader how to use those tools wisely and effectively. It informed owners where to get training if they felt they needed help and gave practical encouragement on how to apply the training lessons in everyday life. It was the book's conviction that every aspect of a dog's life needs to be considered conscientiously.

The golden years of the middle ground lasted into the 1980s. Books like *How Dogs Learn* by Mary R. Burch and Jon S. Bailey (Howell Book House) did an admirable job in delivering a moderate, if technical, middle ground, where positive techniques such as food reinforcement are counterbalanced by mild discipline such as leash correction.

Unfortunately, pendulums rarely stop in the middle ground — that is, at the equilibrium position. Instead, the arm continues its trajectory until it reaches the farthest end of the spectrum. By the 1990s, a new breed of self-labeled purely positive dog trainers began to emerge. The change in dog training was revolutionary.

Rather than correcting for refusal to perform a known command, such as sit, the purely positive, or treat training, philosophy suggests that the dog should be further encouraged with treats to comply. The dog that refuses to sit simply will not receive the treat or will be crated for a time-out until the trainer decides to try again. Time and time again we've met dog owners whose dogs jump on them, their children, and their guests. The owners tell us that after Internet research, i.e., a simple Google search, they find that the recommended solution is to ignore the behavior until it extinguishes itself. Or, worse, the owners are advised to turn their back to the dog to make it clear that they're not responding to the dog's attention-seeking behavior. But anyone with a persistent jumper discovers quickly that some dogs are quite happy to play this game and will repeatedly climb right up your back.

The owner who reads that ignoring bad behavior is the definitive solution, upon finding that it doesn't work for his dog, decides that the dog is somehow "broken" or "untrainable." The dog gets locked away whenever he gets excited or when guests arrive. Some dogs even lose their homes because they're deemed unmanageable. That's a real shame because the solution to this problem, like so many, is actually quite simple. Teach a dog to sit, hold it accountable for the sit even under distracting conditions, and it will get much more attention and family time than a dog that jumps wildly.

By the 1990s and early 2000s, the culture wanted easier and softer ways of training the family pet. Innovators borrowed clickers, markers, and food rewards from the trainers of sea mammals at amusement parks. And, by the way, all of these can be a useful part of a balanced training plan — as long as they are only *part* of the plan. But purely positive training relies solely on these elements. The flaw is that it provides no way to address your dog's bad behavior, especially when he knowingly decides to reward himself by chasing the squirrel rather than focusing on the cookie you're offering him. Ironically, a well-trained dog, one that is used to responding to his owner, can easily learn new tricks with a clicker. So many positive techniques can be usefully employed once a dog understands that obedience is not optional and can be fun as well as rewarding.

We have zero tolerance for people who treat dogs badly. Bullying dogs into submission is not artful dog training. But we believe that once the pendulum started swinging away from hard corrections, it inevitably went too far in the opposite direction. Many positive trainers, certainly not all but many, stipulate that teaching a dog to sit by pulling up on a collar and pushing down on the dog's butt is unacceptable and harsh. And you may not believe this — we nearly didn't — but there are those who argue that denying a dog a treat is punishment-based training. Therefore, they give the treat even if the dog doesn't comply with the desired behavior.

MARC   My client was an elegant woman who lived on Chicago's Michigan Avenue in a swanky apartment situated within one of the city's finest hotels. She very much wanted to walk her French bulldog, Lucy, so they could enjoy the exercise and companionship. The problem was that her little dog attacked the horses that drew carriages giving tours. It almost sounds funny, but Lucy was hard to control and threw all twenty muscular pounds into a screaming frenzy every time she saw a horse, which was often. My client was fearful that Lucy would slip out of her grasp one day and get stomped by a horse or hit by a car on the busy avenue. I was the *sixth* dog trainer this desperate owner had hired to solve the problem.

I taught Lucy to walk on a loose leash and to ignore distractions. I used all manner of distractions in my work with her. I taught her to choose reward rather than humane correction, and we made good progress. One day the client, Lucy, and I headed out for a walk down Michigan Avenue. All went well until we encountered a horse. When Lucy started her shenanigans, I simply executed a rapid about-turn — which, had Lucy been paying attention to me as she had been taught, would have involved her turning with me in a sort of dog and human ballet. But because Lucy was so fixated on the horse, she didn't notice my abrupt 180-degree turn and her screaming lunge toward the horse was suddenly interrupted as Lucy found herself facing a new direction with what seemed to her like no warning.

Rather than be worried about that correction, Lucy knew exactly how to respond because I had taught her loose-leash walking — first with no distractions, then with distractions of increasing intensity. When I turned right back toward the horse, Lucy did just as I expected this time: She looked up at me, made eye contact, and if she were a person, she would have said something like, "The heck with that horse. It's just a trick to take my attention away from me, right?"

The client was not only pleased but also flabbergasted, and although this happened many years ago, I have never forgotten what she said to me.

"I can't believe I paid five dog trainers before you, each of whom did the exact same thing, which didn't work. And you just...well, you showed her she's not allowed to do that!"

"What did those other trainers do?" I asked.

"Every one of them told me to carry food with me and to distract Lucy with treats as we passed horses. And when it didn't work, they yelled at me that I needed to use *better* food that she would like more.

"It got to where I was using provolone cheese and imported prosciutto. Lucy was eating so much that she'd puke it back up...while she was attacking the horses!"

Sometimes it really is kinder to teach a dog, in a compassionate but authoritative way, *You're just not allowed.* To be fair to the dog, however, we always want to start with the easy stuff and work our way slowly up to the big-deal distractions. Life itself is not purely positive. What human doesn't have behavioral limits? It's when you work within these limits that you realize the opportunity to live a full, rich life. The same goes for your dog.

Fortunately, as pendulums tend to swing too far, they also have a way of eventually returning to the middle of their arc. And so it has been with dog training. What we advocate is called balanced training because it includes the careful sequencing of successive behavioral layers, dividing any job into multiple steps, much like Koehler did so many years ago. We do not move on to the second step until the dog understands the first one thoroughly, and demonstrates the ability to comply even with distractions. And those distractions are not added to the mix until the first layer of teaching has been successful. And, yes, without apology we can say that we hold the dog accountable to perform what he has been taught — provided we know beyond a shadow of a doubt that he understands what is being asked of him. If at any point the dog is confused, we help him by showing him again what we're asking. If he refuses, then we correct him in a manner that helps him comply, just like with Lucy and the horse.

But balanced training goes farther in that it also incorporates the best concepts from purely positive training. One of those concepts

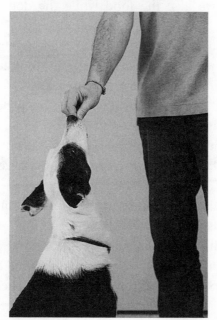

Balanced trainers often use food to teach and reward desired behaviors. Here coauthor and Chicago area trainer Marc Goldberg uses food in a specific manner to ask his dog Tippy to sit. Note the eye contact. After calmly waiting a moment, Marc gives Tippy the food while the dog is still in the sit position. *(Photo by Jill Tabone)*

involves marking a behavior, or giving the dog instant feedback when he's done the right thing. In our case, we do this with verbal praise rather than with a clicker, but the concept is much the same. Also, food is a very powerful motivator for many dogs. Therefore, we use it in multiple ways. An example of food luring is putting food to a dog's nose without releasing it, and then using it like a "nose magnet" to lead the dog where you want him. So, for example, when beginning to teach the come command, we may walk with the dog at our left side, put food to its nose, and say, "Come," then suddenly reverse our direction by walking backward. The dog will invariably turn on a dime, following the food, executing the first steps of the recall exercise. We then stop with the dog now in front of us. We lift the food up slightly, causing the dog to elevate his head, and with little further prompting, the average dog will sit. At that instant we verbally praise — marking the "turn toward me," "come," "sit in front of me" sequence — and we give the food while the dog is in the sitting position.

Once the dog understands, we don't need to use food for each repetition. Sometimes food doesn't appear until after the sit is completed. Other times it doesn't appear at all, with praise as the substitute reward. If the dog decides not to comply because he spots a butterfly, we redirect his attention back to us with a well-timed leash pop. We show the dog the contrast between "what if I do" and "what if I don't." In all respects, this is compassionate, yet it removes the dog's option to outright refuse or quit.

The most obvious limitation of the purely positive dog-training movement affects people whose dogs are not food-motivated. While most dogs are willing to work hard for a treat, some dogs are stressed during the learning process and may not want food at that time. And some dogs "eat to live" rather than "live to eat" — such dogs may have limited or even no interest in food-based training. In these situations, owners are sometimes advised not to feed their dog before a training session. While we believe it is ethical to train before a meal — rather than after — we do not believe it is morally correct to withhold food from a dog simply to render him more susceptible to food-based training. Understand that we don't wish to paint with an overly broad brush. It's only a minority of purely positive trainers who will deprive a dog of needed calories. But food just doesn't work for every dog, and in those cases it is important to use something the dog really cares about to motivate him, such as a favorite toy.

It is a fact that not all food is alike. And to the dog, the relative value of all food is not the same. Some dogs don't have much interest in a pellet of kibble, but they'd do backflips for a dried liver treat. As balanced trainers, we may occasionally use food to show the dog that what he just did is great and that we highly approve. So we keep a variety of high-value treats available; sometimes in desperation, when working with an especially picky dog, we're not above using bits of chicken or beef from our own refrigerator. When no food at all is interesting to a dog, we simply substitute verbal markers and praise. If we find the dog really likes toys more than food, we might tuck a squeaky toy in our pocket to use as a reward after a particularly good performance. But lack of food interest will not get a dog out of his lesson in our form of training.

The reason we have spent so much time talking about the three major branches of the dog-training tree is because, as a dog owner, you'll face a confusing array of choices when you shop around or consult the Internet. The tough trainers will talk a lot about your need to establish dominance. The purely positive crowd will promote clicker and food-based training, which aren't bad but will further stipulate that you must never correct your dog. (They probably won't say *correct* because it doesn't sound harsh enough. They'll substitute *punish* instead.) And in the end, you'll either feel caught in the crossfire or you'll go with whatever method sounds like more fun. Fun and food sound best to most people. Therefore, you're most likely to start with purely positive training. That's what many of our clients do, but eventually they come to us because they need training with more reliable results.

If you have a puppy or a young dog and you'd like to start obedience classes, there is certainly nothing wrong with seeking out a local dog trainer. Just read the reviews and testimonials to make sure the training is not going to be harsher than what you expect. And you can even go to a nearby pet store, many of which offer puppy and training classes. Big-box stores understandably want to avoid controversial techniques, so they tend to steer clear of any training that involves correction. Even so, you're likely to learn some valuable basics on which you can later build. But when you need training that works in the real world — a world in which the squirrel is often going to be more attractive to your dog than the cookie — it's your job as pack leader to show your dog that obeying basic commands is important. Every intelligent dog will eventually wonder, *What happens if I don't come?* And you must correct your dog in a way that not only helps him comply but also motivates him to do better next time and earn a reward.

MARC Larry came to me with his border collie, Maggie. Two prior dog trainers had told Larry he should never walk her off his property because she attacked other dogs whenever she saw them. Both trainers tried to distract Maggie with food in the presence of dogs. The thinking was, if Maggie began to associate other dogs with food, she'd be less reactive. Or maybe she'd forget she wanted to kill the other dogs and would take a snack break instead.

Now, the food-distraction technique may indeed work for dogs that aren't very serious about their aggression. But Maggie wasn't fooling around. In fact, the second trainer was bitten when she, along with her treat, got between Maggie and another dog. I simply taught Maggie the rules of heel. I did so in a way very similar to what the monks describe in *How to Be Your Dog's Best Friend*. Eventually, I added dog distractions, but at a distance where they were minimally troubling to Maggie. Over time, we moved the distractions closer and showed Maggie that the rules applied *no matter what*. In a few weeks, Maggie was able to go for long, uneventful walks with her owner...off their property.

Many trainers today worry that correcting a dog is wrong. Such trainers are more married to their process than they are to actual results. They pronounce a dog like Lucy the horse-attacker or Maggie the dog-attacker as untrainable. We say thank goodness the pendulum has begun to return to the middle ground. Educate a dog on what is required. Show him the reward for compliance. Help him when he is confused. Respect his intelligence when he experiments with refusal by correcting him in a way that doesn't cow him, but helps him understand you're not giving in. Then reward with praise and, yes, sometimes with a treat when he does what you ask.

A good pack leader is not afraid to lead.

5

Change Starts at the Top

Here we are forced to examine our attitudes about everything, including our dogs. We are constantly challenged to become more open to the language dogs use to communicate with us. —The Art of Raising a Puppy

Part of the fascination of working with dogs is that we are always learning new things, becoming more attuned to dogs' true nature. Working with dogs is anything but static. For example, over the years we have honed our view of training. There was a time when we emphasized the repetitive character of obedience, drilling dogs on the basics over and over again. Our axiom was "more is better," and while dogs left our program knowing their obedience exercises cold, we also observed a certain overload, a saturation, a subtle disconnect in the relationship between owner and dog. Our methods needed to evolve to foster a more effective transition into daily life beyond the monastery. By listening to what we observed in the training process, we came to understand that, to a certain degree, less is more, and we began to approach our training process from that vantage. We don't mean to say that we gave any less application to training. We just tried to pay more attention to the dog's emotional state. Over the years, we have seen how this approach has borne fruit. It has aided us in helping countless dogs reach their potential, and has made us better human beings in the process. Changing our minds has meant always being open to learning more, to adopting an attitude of humility, the basic characteristic of the true student. We believe there is no limit to what a human can achieve by being present and spiritually aware. The wonder is, the same can be said for the dog.

Maybe the best way to begin to understand your dog is through what we call inseeing. This is not some New Age concept cooked up by unrealistic monks. Instead, it's based on a genuine understanding of how dogs think and on our experience of listening to and reading a dog's reactions. There are a number of enlightening books that describe the ways that dogs communicate with their bodies, including Brenda Aloff's photographic guide *Canine Body Language: Interpreting the Native Language of the Domestic Dog* and Turid Rugaas's *On Talking Terms with Dogs: Calming Signals*. Armed with this knowledge, and by patiently and faithfully studying the behavior, body language, and ways of communication among dogs, we have become increasingly attuned to what dogs are actually "saying" in the various contexts of daily life. As we have garnered our own experience, more than thirty years working with dogs, our knowledge has grown exponentially. As the founding Monks of New Skete did when they immersed themselves in the athenaeum of dogs, we encourage you to read all you can to build your own foundation of canine knowledge.

If you do, you will find that, since their earliest ancestors, dogs have understood social order and collaborative hunting. A well-ordered pack of wolves can successfully hunt, shelter, raise offspring, and pass on their genes. A pack suffering from disorganization and social strife will not have clear leadership or collaboration, and will eventually die.

Dogs know this on a genetic level. It is why a properly socialized dog is conscious of how to communicate with other dogs using their species' unique and understandable body language. As dog trainers, we have learned to read dogs, recognizing attitude and thoughts and, yes, even emotions by interpreting body language. And that is precisely what allows us to influence dog behavior, using our own body language to clearly show a dog what we want from him. Some call it dog whispering. Whatever you call it, understanding dogs and helping them understand and abide by sensible rules will make both you and your dog happier.

We describe inseeing as the ability to get inside your dog's head, to see the world as it sees the world. We at New Skete have an advantage in this sense, perhaps. Surrounded by German shepherds, and by the

Texas trainer Tod McVicker's Decker terrier, Bindi, helps him connect to nature. *(Photo by Jenny LoBello Photography)*

natural beauty of our setting, we get to observe our dogs living as they were intended to. For instance, a mother disciplining her pups out on the lawn, or an older female shepherd teaching a five-month-old pup the dynamics of hierarchy, is in the true nature of being a dog. One of the hallmarks of a contemplative approach to life is learning to pay attention to life's beauty and complexity manifested in the most ordinary of circumstances.

Brother Thomas, who was the driving force behind New Skete's training program, had this insight into inseeing: "Learning the value of silence is learning to listen to, instead of screaming at, reality: opening your mind enough to find what the end of someone else's sentence sounds like, or listening to a dog until you discover what is needed instead of imposing yourself in the name of training."

BROTHER CHRISTOPHER I came to the community years after Brother Thomas had died, and did so without any plan to be involved with dogs. Although I knew that the community bred German shepherds and trained dogs of all breeds, my reason for coming to New Skete was to be a monk. It was the overtly spiritual and monastic part of our religious life that initially attracted me. It's not that I didn't like dogs. I loved them. Had them all my life. I was happy that dogs were around. I just didn't come to the monastery because of them. My friendship with the dogs developed organically as I worked with them every day.

Novices at the monastery are expected to get involved in a lot of different things, not just in one particular area. When I arrived, I was tasked with practical chores such as mowing the lawn or shoveling snow, cleaning kennels, doing housework. I would also, on occasion, help Brother Job, who had taken over the training program when Brother Thomas died. Things changed quickly for me when Brother Job departed the monastery abruptly in 1982, leaving behind a kennel filled with dogs. That evening we had a meeting. It was Father Laurence, then the abbot, who asked if there was anyone willing to volunteer to take over for Brother Job. As I was the only one who was in a position to do this (all of the other monks were busy with other work), all eyes in the room turned to me. I said I'd be willing to try. For the first eight months, all I did was live, breathe, and sleep dog. I read everything I could get my hands on. I didn't want to feel only a step or two ahead of my clients.

Funny how things happen, though: Through that immersion process I had an experience similar to Brother Thomas's. I discovered, over time, that I was actually very good at training dogs. I had a sort of natural gift and the dogs responded well to me. More important, I was becoming aware of the deeper dimension of our work here. At first, I was too busy learning how to train the dogs to notice it. But as I had the opportunity to work with more and more dogs, I began to feel comfortable. The dogs became my teachers. It was from this perspective that I could make the poet Rilke's concept of inseeing my own. By witnessing the various ways dogs communicate, and by learning to read how subtly they sometimes use their bodies in this regard, I began to appreciate the human-dog relationship on a more intuitive level. I became conscious of what the dogs were really looking for in the relationship — leadership and guidance — and my ability to provide it. This affected not only the relationships I had with my own dogs but also the way I trained. Increasingly, training blended technique with attention to the dog's emotional state.

The good news is you don't have to be a monk to relate to your dog in a way that transcends the species boundary. Listening to your dog takes practice and commitment, yes, but the payoff can be extraordinary. Once we begin to understand dogs beyond what we comprehend by just human communication, our relationship intensifies, our enchantment with them increases, and as it does our understanding of them grows. The more we learn about dogs, the more we know about ourselves. Dogs are absolutely guileless and effortlessly reflect back to us our own emotional temperature, how we are coming across to the world. It is vital that we pay attention to how dogs address us through their body language because it increases our self-knowledge and our ability to interact peacefully with life.

Like rungs on a ladder, with each step we climb higher and see more clearly.

From a practical standpoint, inseeing simply increases your potential to teach and your dog's potential to learn, and it does so dramatically. What begins perhaps as just appreciation gains the depth of insight and knowledge of your dog's true nature. The more sensitive you become to the ways of canine communication, the better able you'll be to respond empathically to what they actually want and

Dogs are drawn together to play. If they seem to understand each other, it's because they usually do.

need. With practice, an unspoken communication begins. In this beautiful stillness, we bridge the gap between species and we're able to experience a relationship of mutuality and trust, one that borders on true friendship.

Dogs speak to us all the time. With a practiced eye, you'll begin to see the subtle changes in your dog's eyes, spanning a spectrum of emotions from joy to fear to curiosity to boredom. You'll begin to understand the positioning of your dog's tail and ears, what she's telling you when she reaches with her paws. You'll know what she's saying by how she carries herself and by her gait as she approaches you. Learning to understand what your dog is telling you is the greatest gift you can give her.

The Challenge

Once we learn to listen to our dogs in the language they speak, their world opens up to us. The first lesson is to understand that you're a human and your dog is a dog. Sounds ridiculous, right? But this sacred communication begins as simply as that. When owners get *lesson one* wrong, bad behavior follows. For instance, one of the most frequent observations we hear from clients about their dogs' naughty behavior involves the human projection of motives onto the dog. Recently, a client with a Brittany spaniel was explaining one of her dog's occasional house-training accidents. "He absolutely knew he had done wrong," she said. "He was irritated that I left him when I went to the store, and so he left a huge pile right in the middle of the living room! I could see it written all over his body. He took one look at me and he slithered away."

As we've often said, dogs live in the present. The Brittany spaniel wasn't feeling guilty about something he had done a half hour before. What the owner saw was the dog's reaction to her disgust at encountering the pile in the living room. When we suggested to our client that the dog was simply interpreting her body language and responding instantaneously to it, she didn't want to believe it. She felt more comfortable attributing human motives to her dog's behavior than honoring the dog's ability to read her body language in a flash. From such a perspective, the dog merited punishment. But even if the owner made the spaniel look at "what he'd done" — or pushed his snout into the pile, which sadly still happens often enough — the dog would not understand why he was being punished.

Dogs are not moral creatures in the way human beings are. They do not commit sins deliberately, as humans are capable of doing. A dog does not possess the psychological mechanics needed for revenge. Scientific experiments conducted in recent years show conclusively that dogs respond with their bodies to cues they pick up from their owners. When an owner projects guilt onto the dog, the owner is being grossly unfair and setting the dog up for real confusion or worse.

"He won't listen to me!" is a refrain we hear over and over. Remember, though, there are always two sides to communication with your dog. Instead of trying to force your dog to understand you, why not try to understand your dog? The ultimate goal is that hallowed middle ground — the shared voice that both dog and owner understand.

Well-behaved dogs can accompany their owners on adventures. Kate Hartson's beloved Ella loved to carry enormous sticks.

So what is your dog asking for? Companionship, stability — not the roller coaster of emotions some owners offer them — and simply to move his body. Dogs are quadrupeds, after all, and are designed to move. Dogs are adaptable, of course, but they're still members of the animal kingdom, and their natural habitat is not a city apartment or a fenced-in backyard. Consigning a dog to the sounds of Dr. Phil or Judge Judy on a television, or walking your dog only until she eliminates, is a form of slow torture. Dogs need to sniff peemail and listen to nature. They need to explore and run. Yet, for so many millennia, they have thrown their lot in with us.

For the Love of Man

A dog's faithfulness can override even her instinct. Why do dogs need us so much that we can profoundly affect their behavior and happiness? Dogs care about what we want from them because, when led properly by the human, they consider us to be more than their pack mates. We provide more than food, shelter, and comfort. In an analogous way, we provide dogs with a sense of meaning, comfort, and purpose. Your dog's faith in you becomes its reason for living.

Dogs do not simply love us. They worship us from the foot of our beds, from the end of a leash. You can see the adoration in a dog's eyes, and the longing she has for you as you touch her. What's interesting is what this devotion provokes in us: not arrogant domination but a desire to give our dogs the best that we are capable of, our best selves.

Trained dogs submit and yield to this worship readily. It satisfies them on a level that humans, with our questioning mentalities, may not fully comprehend. The loyalty of a dog, particularly a trained dog, is absolute. He never questions or has a crisis of faith. He doesn't believe. He knows.

Over and over, we have noticed that after putting a dog through even a basic course of obedience, the dog begins to change behavior that wasn't even addressed in the training. If you do your work keenly, the dog gives up undesirable behaviors without even being commanded.

Dogs know that owners don't like bad behavior. We don't keep it a secret! We grouse and yell at them all the time. What's more, dogs don't want to engage in bad behavior.

When a dog is trained and led by a compassionate authority figure, she naturally begins to look at her humans in a new way. She learns that she is not giving up freedom but gaining a helping partner. She no longer has to make every decision for her life. It's not satisfying to a dog to pull on the leash and be out of control. Yet if that behavior is all she knows, she'll do it over and over. To us, that behavior is a cry for help, the way the dog shows her profound need for leadership. Once the dog has learned to yield her decision-making to a human, a bond between dog and handler is formed that knows no limits of depth.

So why do dogs care about what we want? Why are they willing to do what we ask of them if we can show them clearly what we want? Why will they yield their willpower to ours?

They do it for the love of human beings. They do it because they love us more than they love themselves. They do it because they live as if they are existing among their gods who domesticated and, yes, in some sense created them. We don't mean this in an egotistical way, but rather as a reflection of pack animal science and an indication of the level of devotion dogs hold for us — and the responsibility we have to them because of that devotion.

Is it genetic? The gene succeeds so the gene continues? Probably. But we think it's more than that. We think the dog has a void that only humans can fill. Even those of us who succeed the most with dogs can't love them as profoundly as they love us. We can't. Because we don't need from dogs what they need from us. But we can understand and honor the dog's need for leadership. We can bring a dog to a place where his need for us is paramount yet doesn't destabilize the independent nature of his being.

The ultimate reward is a bond during the dog's lifetime that exceeds any other comfort he can ever know and that fills us in a wondrous way. Dogs have the innate ability to see the best parts of us. Imagine if we actually believed them! The bond we can form with our dogs helps us to be better people. Through a dog's love and devotion, it becomes easier to find your way through life both because you have a companion for the journey and because your companion has an endless supply of faith that you're following the right path.

MARC   My father's parents kept a succession of black English cockers for as long as I can remember. They were all named Taffy. In those days, a dog's life truly was an adventure. The current Taffy would be let out for a morning potty that sometimes lasted until lunchtime.

My grandparents lived in what was then rural West Chester, Pennsylvania, today a center of technology and an exurb of Philadelphia. In my childhood, the town was known best for the Teachers College, a few shops — including my grandfather's furniture store — and miles of cornfields.

Taffy I or Taffy II might run outside for a quick pee and then scratch at the back door to be let in for breakfast. But he might just as easily scamper through the backyard to the end of the street, where the nearby cornfield stretched endlessly. In late summer, the corn was taller than me. My then four-year-old sister and two- and three-year-old cousins still remember how I formed them into my own merry pack. I was six years old and already the pack leader! Without telling the adults, we followed Taffy's route deep into the corn. I became lost almost instantly, since I lacked Taffy's nose and sense of direction. All the rows blended together, and my little-girl pack began to cry. Then we heard the panicky voices of mothers and grandmother calling from far off. Following the sound, and merry no longer, we eventually emerged teary-eyed and drippy-nosed to face the music. As the oldest and self-nominated pack leader, I rightly caught the blame, but in just moments, relief washed over the adults and all was forgiven.

Taffy, on the other hand, never got in trouble over his forays into that field. He was just a dog, following every instinct he possessed to quarter the ground, locate birds and small prey, flush and pounce. Those little cockers never hunted alongside humans because my family didn't hunt. But they hunted nearly every day, for their own pleasure, and very happily indeed.

The funny thing is that none of the Taffys was ever trained to do anything. Yet none of them ran away from home for longer than it took to canvass the neighborhood. None of them ate the furniture. No self-respecting Taffy would ever steal a roast, poop in the house, or bark like a maniac for no reason. They had too much dignity, these dogs. They were allowed to be proper dogs, doing proper dog jobs.

Mind you, we weren't politically correct then. Little did we know that one day we'd neuter all our dogs and fence them in rather than let them run free. Although we now know it is important to be responsible pet owners, we have done so in a way that has left our friends frustrated and unemployed. Back in West Chester during the fifties, sixties, and seventies, most people didn't assign their dog a job. They didn't have to. Dogs ran loose often enough to find their own employment, gainful or otherwise. Taffy chose to hunt rabbits and birds. The terriers terrorized mice and rats in the field. And the German shepherds barked at intruders, real or imagined. But if a shepherd made the mistake of biting the mailman, that dog's owner might spend a month driving every day to the post office to pick up his mail. Inevitably, that dog would find himself on a chain, unemployed and frustrated. Today, most dogs feel just like that German shepherd, without a job, lacking purpose, and, worst of all, wanting freedom.

Next door to my grandparents lived a family who had a huge fenced yard. Eventually a German shepherd appeared, kept behind the fence. Then there were two, and ultimately three or four.

I could never keep track of those dogs because they all looked alike, and they all barked viciously at the sight of any human other than their owners. My grandfather named them Fang. Each of them individually was known as Fang, and as a family, he called them the Fangsers.

The Fangsers never got to roam. In fact, they never left their yard. I simply assumed they were vicious and followed my grandfather's advice never to look directly at them when coming or going. That kept them as settled as possible. Now I realize that the Fangsers were most likely intelligent and active dogs consigned to a life of boredom and frustration. The only job they could assign themselves was to become hyper guardians of their domain, and this is what they did. Unlike the Taffys, the Fangsers were never able to engage in healthy doglike activities. So they substituted viciousness to fill in the gaping holes in their collective psyche.

My mother's family were not dog people. From them I learned appreciation for art but nothing about dogs. To them, keeping animals in the house was an alien idea. Eventually, my father prevailed upon my mother to permit a dog in our home. I believe he must have used Cézanne's breed as an inducement, because this little dog was a miniature poodle, much different from the hardy hunting Taffys his parents owned.

Cézanne drove my mother crazy. From the first day this little curly apricot bundle entered the house, he adopted her as the one he loved above all others. It's a strange thing about my mother: Animals gravitate to her. She has learned to tolerate it, but she's still prone to recoil slightly at their approach. Dogs often avoid those who appear uncomfortable with them, or they may even take advantage. Yet they don't come to my mother aggressively. I have noted many times that dogs seem bent on seducing her affection. Not many have succeeded.

Sadly, little Cézanne was among those destined to fail. If Mother went to the bathroom, the puppy left us and followed her to scratch at the door. When she sat, he only wanted to sit on her lap. If she tied her shoes, his tongue got caught in the knot. Cézanne went back to the breeder, and for several years I kept a small chew toy bearing his tooth marks.

I was no more than seven when the puppy came to us, and only a few weeks older when Cézanne went away. I was not the object of his adoration. But he left a mark on me anyway, and I longed for a puppy of my own. Many children want a puppy, but my dream seemed as impossible as wanting a pony or a baby elephant.

Perhaps it was destiny for me to feel this longing. According to the Chinese calendar, my father was born in the Year of the Dog, as was I. Father loved his dogs then as he does now: passionately and, possibly, with a small touch of insanity.

My parents divorced when I was nine years old.

And because my mother felt bad for me, I was to have a dog. The year was 1969. Lassie was queen of television. At the time, I didn't know Lassie was really king of TV, played by a series of male collies. I did know Lassie was beautiful, noble, intelligent, loving, and loyal.

Mother was not buying into the collie concept. She reminded me that our car was a Volkswagen Beetle, and that with herself, me, and my sister, a grown collie wouldn't fit in the car. She suggested a Shetland sheepdog, telling me they looked much like a small collie. Shelties were not well known in those days, but I was not about to look a gift dog in the mouth. I remember being concerned that the delicately negotiated deal might implode, so I readily assented.

We visited a breeder who showed me several puppies, none quite to my liking. Then she brought out my puppy. From the first second my eyes put that puppy into my brain, I knew he was my dog. At the age of eleven, I'm not sure I had ever known anything as a certainty in quite this way. But I was positive.

My mother had wisely decided to wait in another room while this process took place. The breeder explained to me that the puppy was too young to leave his mother. I would have to wait a few weeks to bring him home.

Today, many people get their puppies at six weeks, and sometimes as early as five weeks, after birth. I now believe there is great value in allowing a puppy to spend those critical extra weeks in the company of his mother and littermates. As he grows within the family unit, a puppy learns many social skills from a good mother.

If he plays too roughly with her, or should he nip her hard, the mother will quickly and fairly discipline the puppy so he understands the limitations placed on his behavior. Similarly, if he should become too rowdy with his brothers and sisters, nipping one of them with too much pressure, the littermate will yip and refuse to play for a few moments. Thus, the puppy acquires social skills by learning to inhibit some of his impulses. Some of those puppies that leave the litter too early find it difficult to adapt their behavior to suit their owner's expectations.

It turns out that impulse control is the most critical part of training your dog. After all, most owners ask trainers to help them stop behaviors such as jumping, nipping, and running away. Solving all these problems requires a dog to stem his own impulse to do something other than what his first instinct tells him to do.

Leaving my new puppy in his home for another few weeks should have been hard for me. But it was not. The deal was struck, and for the moment, that was enough. I don't remember anything about the time I had to wait. It must have passed in a blur. I suppose that as time passes, we have room to store only the most significant details. I named my puppy Gus, and he lived nearly eighteen years. He lived with me, my sister, and my mother until I went to college. Then he lived with my father and stepmother, at whose house I spent time with him often, until his passing.

When Gus first came to me, he followed me everywhere just like a baby duckling follows his mother. I didn't train him, and I rarely even used a leash. Gus followed me, and he came every time I called him. Little did I know that most baby dogs seem to understand their vulnerability to predators and stick close to their mothers. I thought Gus was obedient, and I didn't give it a thought.

But when Gus turned five months old, it was time for my dog to enter the "teenage years" and begin experimenting with independence. Playing outside one day, I called Gus to me and he didn't come. So I chased. He ran. Gus ran into the street, where he was hit by a car. Fortunately, it was a slow-moving Volkswagen like ours and Gus wasn't killed. However, he fractured a front leg. Mother paid for the surgery, and Gus recovered fully.

When he was mended, Mother made an announcement.

"I'm sending you and Gus to obedience school. If you don't train him to come, he'll get killed on that road."

We started obedience classes not long after. Gus and I won all the prizes, and I was smitten with the idea of owning such a smart dog. So I began to read every book on dogs I could find.

The questions that occupied me weren't so much about how to train dogs to do this or that. I already knew how. Rather, I wanted to know why dogs even allow themselves to be trained, and, in fact, why they seem happiest when working closely with a human. After all, dogs are closely related to wolves, and wolves are not considered to be very trainable. What, then, is it about the dog? Why do dogs want to work with us? And why do they love us?

The answers that came to me were shocking and metaphysical, way beyond the manner my normally practical brain works.

It all came back to Gus.

6

Your Training Wheels

One secret of deepening any sort of relationship with our dogs is providing them with leadership they can trust.

You, as a dog owner, are the most critical component of a dog's hierarchy. You are the compassionate authority, the good parent, the benevolent pack leader, even if the pack consists of just you and your dog.

Once you understand how to be your dog's pack leader, the real relationship with your dog begins. As leader, your job is to decide when, where, and how resources of food, space, and time are given. If you do your job well, your dog will not only behave properly, he'll also be happy. Then, once you teach your dog to say please and thank you in order to earn the award of your attention, or the toy, or a treat, you'll eventually be able to pass along most of the responsibility to him. If you exercise your compassionate authority correctly, in time you'll be able to draw back on the micromanagement and hardly have to manage at all.

In this chapter, we'll offer examples of benevolent pack leadership in action and explain why it's so desperately needed.

MARC Recently I met a fourteen-week-old Labrador puppy I nicknamed Piranha. This puppy was a major biter. He had little bite inhibition, as evidenced by the owner's girlfriend, who was covered in scars and scratches. Piranha was detached from humans in that he neither asked for nor accepted any form of affection. He was not housebroken. His play with other dogs was aggressive.

I had the dog for only ten days, but I did some preliminary training with him that was appropriate for a three-and-a-half-month-old puppy. Those ten days were composed of 240 hours, or 14,400 minutes, or 864,000 seconds. For each of those 864,000 seconds, I managed the dog's resources, including how he was permitted to use his mouth, when he ate, and where he eliminated.

Piranha's real name was Frank, and Frank's biggest problem was the biting. He was young, and of course we expect a certain amount of nipping from puppies, but Frank used his razor-sharp baby teeth not only often but also hard. It was important to take control of how he used his mouth. So I showed Frank a treat, and when he began to bite at me for it, I neither removed the treat nor gave it to him. I just closed my fingers around it and bopped him lightly in the nose with that treat. In this manner, Frank learned that he'd have to focus and stop using his mouth inappropriately to release the treat. Consistently practicing this routine helped Frank learn to lick at my fingers for a treat rather than to bite me — an important step in the right direction — and also gave me the opportunity to use the treats as a teaching tool to lure him into the sit and down positions. In this way, I substantially reduced the biting when treats were involved. But some of the behavior remained at other times, such as when I needed to hold his collar for a moment to put on or take off a leash. At those times, Frank might still bite hard in an overexcited state.

So I used an old dog-trainer trick: lemon juice. I kept a handy plastic lemon filled with lemon juice. When Frank started to bite me, I squirted a few drops in his mouth, and then rubbed some on my hand where he bit me. If he started to bite me there again, usually Frank would smell the lemon juice and, remembering the unpleasant taste, stop himself just in time. Over the course of just a few days, the biting diminished to almost nothing.

All I did for Frank was manage his life and his resources long enough for his true nature to come forward. Frank is a dog. A dog is most comfortable in pack drive, which means his nature is to collaborate with the leader so that he receives his share of resources, including food, water, space, playtime, and love.

The result was a puppy that finally began to solicit affection, did not bite, and played appropriately with the other dogs. We also trained Frank to walk nicely on a leash, not to jump, and to come when called. Those skills took only a couple of hours to teach. Frank is an incredibly smart dog. However, he was a puppy completely devoid of respect for authority and, in fact, ignorant of the entire concept. It was living with us, and the structure provided for each of our dogs, that turned Frank around. The dog training was a small bonus.

If love and knowledge of your dog's true nature is the soil of your relationship with her, then providing parental authority, becoming the benevolent pack leader, is the water, the sunlight, and the fertilizer. If you take nothing else from reading this book, please know that controlling resources can be the foundation of a wonderful and intentional life with your dog.

One does not need to be an expert for this technique to work. In fact, it's almost better when it comes naturally.

MARC My friend Evie has five small dogs, each fifteen pounds or less. Though I am very fond of Evie, a recent invitation to her house brought a sense of foreboding. Who wants to be met at the door by an anxiety-ridden pack of jumping, leg-scratching ankle-biters? The dogs had taken control of Evie's home. On earlier visits, I needed to convince the yapping pack that I really was invited and allowed inside. Once, Evie actually used a broom to sweep the little pack of growling dogs away from me.

But on this visit, when Evie opened the door, I found an assortment of five adorable little monkeys all waiting by the threshold. They greeted me with only a bark or two. Rather than charging right for my ankles, they assembled without crowding in front of Evie. As I walked deeper into the house, they parted like the Red Sea and then followed us without so much as a yap or a nip. We went to the back porch, where Evie produced a bag of frozen green beans.

"Treat time," she said. Without a further word from Evie, all five of those dogs lined up in front of her and sat. Evie bent over to give each dog a frozen green bean and each ate his without getting up or bothering the next dog. You would have thought those green beans were pieces of filet mignon being fed to highly trained show dogs.

Though I suspected what had happened, I asked Evie how she accomplished such a miracle.

"They just learned it." She shrugged. "I didn't even have to train them."

The reality is that Evie didn't have to think a lot about training her dogs to behave at the door, to respect guests, and to line up and sit for treats. Evie has a big personality and, by nature, is a take-charge type of person. When she first got the dogs, she tempered much of her strong personality in the hope that they'd like her. Not surprisingly, that personality pivot didn't work for her or for the dogs.

When she reverted back to being "large and in charge" in her own home, a position that comes naturally to Evie, the relationship with her dogs changed for the better. Evie didn't even have to set aside specific training time in any formal way. She administered her lessons organically and on the fly. Now, if we break down specifically what she did, we can highlight several things: She began to use her voice and body language more naturally and effectively, deepening the tone of her voice in situations that demanded more control and focus. When the dogs crowded guests aggressively, Evie began to insert herself between the dog pack and the people, walking into them, blocking them as she moved into the dogs' space. That caused them to yield to their owner because she was claiming their space as her own. Evie became consistent in this. Next, she had the dogs respond to commands they already knew to replace undesirable behavior. Further, she was also able to communicate a sense of confident presence with her body, something she had initially been afraid to do because she thought the dogs wouldn't like her. Actually, the reverse proved to be the case: The dogs already liked her but now they began to respect her right to invite guests into the home. Finally, Evie used the dogs' favorite treat — frozen green beans — to tactical advantage by having them line up in a row and then offering warm praise. This wasn't training in any formal sense — it happened naturally. Without even knowing it — just by being herself — Evie assumed the role of pack leader, and her five little dogs were happy to cede leadership to her.

They weren't perfect. When I sat down, the dogs coiled as if they were going to jump into my lap before I invited them. But Evie just put her hand up, and after a small yet visible battle of wills, they waited and calmed down. But perfection isn't the point. Having dogs who are happy to follow some basic rules is entirely the point. Evie kept the emotion to a minimum as I walked in the house. She doled out those green beans like they were gold nuggets, but required the dogs to relax and sit for the treat. Lap time and emotion with petting and talking was given, but only after an invitation. This controlled approach to sharing resources with her dogs is exactly what makes Evie a terrific dog owner. Even if she doesn't realize it, this is the reason that she enjoys a fulfilling and harmonious relationship with a large number of little dogs in one house.

Some people are afraid that assuming the role as pack leader is going to spoil their relationship with their dog: that the dog is going to resent being subordinate. Nothing could be farther from the truth. Dogs are hardwired for this kind of relationship, and they thrive when given the opportunity to find their rightful place in the pack.

We have a client named Rita whose black Labrador, Scotty, was literally attacking the inside of the front door of her home, leaving claw marks all over the door and frame. It was almost as though Scotty were trying to break free from the house. In a way he was. It wasn't as though Rita mistreated Scotty—at least not from the standpoint of discipline. In fact, Rita was so soft on Scotty that she was reluctant to have him trained. She didn't want to make Scotty do things he didn't want to do.

Now, harsh punishment is not only ignorant but also counterproductive from a training perspective. A smack across the snoot with a rolled-up newspaper might have been an old-time way to respond to your dog's bad behavior, but it has no place in a modern relationship with your dog. Today's inclination toward coddling or ignoring your dog's bad behavior is only a little better and a surefire pathway to more bad behavior and ultimately an unhappy dog. This is especially true when your dog is young. A six-month-old Labradoodle who's pampered and cuddled to the exclusion of learning her place in the pack becomes a sixteen-month-old Labradoodle who barks in your face, claws, and perhaps even growls at you.

Rita not only coddled Scotty but also did little in the way of exercising him or keeping him entertained. Rita rarely walked Scotty because he pulled, and he would destroy the toys she bought for him. Though she lavished him with love and attention, Rita's idea of exercising Scotty amounted to opening the back door to let him out into the fenced-in backyard. It was like dropping her child off at the Little

League field when there wasn't any practice. The child might find something to keep busy, but he would be far better off, and would have much more fun, with a coach teaching him the fundamentals of the game and other kids to play with.

Rita is a mother and grandmother. She's raised a raft of children — there are photographs all over the house. She knew all about Little League practices for her kids. But when she talked about Scotty, she seemed confused and timid. When we asked if her children ever were bored growing up, however, Rita sat bolt upright, her jaw set, her eyes focused. "My children were never bored," she said with conviction. At length she went on to describe a household run with a structured mix of affection, play, and education — all in the right proportion. She would assign each child a chore before he was allowed to go out and play, and she made each chore into something of a game, with play coming as the reward at the end. The result was a family of happy and successful adolescents, teens, and young adults.

Even so-called difficult breeds can happily get along in the presence of a strong pack leader such as trainer Rich Simmons, who works in Pennsylvania.

When we assured Rita that building a healthy relationship with Scotty wasn't all that different from raising a child, she began to understand. She knew when to administer compassionate authority, when to reward, and when to pull back. She began bringing her parenting skills to Scotty, and their relationship changed dramatically.

By definition, the pack is a family, with a pack leader acting as blood or de facto parent. Studies have revealed that dogs have not only the intellect but also the emotions of a small child.* So why wouldn't dogs respond to parenting? The answer is they would. It's really that simple.

One of our clients is a psychiatrist who had an extremely ill-behaved dog. During our usual post-training discussion, we outlined her responsibilities, structure, and rules for her dog—and we talked about how to reinforce those rules. Near the end of the chat, the psychiatrist told us that everything we had just told her was nearly identical to what she tells the parents of her pediatric patients.

When children aren't taught to brush their teeth or to do their homework without continuous prompting from their parents, those same children will try to get away with bad behavior in other areas of life. They do this, the psychiatrist told us, because subconsciously children know they need guidance and rules in their life to be safe. But those rules are invisible, and therefore, kids must test them in order to be sure they're really in place. They are looking for someone to place limits on their behavior so they will feel safe. Do dogs think of it quite the same way? Perhaps not, but the end result of failing to set behavioral limits might just be very similar for kids and dogs.

Try to look at it this way: What would you do if your two-year-old wanted to grab every candy bar off the shelf at Walmart? If you were a good parent, you probably wouldn't permit her to do so. If your four-year-old tried to run into the street, obviously you'd stop him and prevent him from doing it again. If your ten-year-old refused to do his homework, you might take his video game privileges away for the night or dock his allowance. Then you'd help him do his work.

The same restraint should be applied in your relationship with

* http://www.nytimes.com/2013/10/06/opinion/sunday/dogs-are-people-too.html?single= 1&_r=0

your dog. Said another way, a well-behaved dog realizes that his owner is in charge of his food, space, and time. It has been our experience that even dogs that have been written off time and again can be taught good behavior and can earn their way into our hearts and homes when their resources are properly managed.

MARC Not too long ago, I took in a dog that was described to me as a "complete maniac." The dog's name was Lucky. He was anything but lucky. Mine was the sixth foster home in which Lucky had been placed. The first five couldn't cope with him. Most foster families are accustomed to dogs with behavioral challenges, which gives you some idea of how bad Lucky's behavior was. The first thing I did was change Lucky's name to Laddie. One of my favorite authors of dog literature is Albert Payson Terhune. In 1919, Terhune wrote *Lad: A Dog* — a compilation of stories about a rough collie that was a precursor to Lassie. Terhune's book was perhaps the first dog book bestseller.

I might have taken the name from Terhune's collie, but that's the only thing the two dogs had in common. The former Lucky was far from a literary hero. To give you an example of Laddie's behavior, Collie Rescue of Greater Illinois, an organization that helps rescue and place collies in good homes, brought Laddie to a local pet store. They make such trips often to showcase dogs for adoption. But Laddie caused a mini catastrophe that ended when he tried to break the ferrets out of their cage. When he wasn't trying to eat the ferrets, he spun in circles and barked furiously at the other dogs. Not surprisingly, management asked that he be removed.

In his first five foster homes, Laddie was little better. Because he was neutered late in life, his marking instinct was out of control. He would sprinkle all over the house, a dozen times every day. He also tried to fight just about every male dog he met. But none of Laddie's previous owners knew how to be a pack leader. None of them took a leadership role. With me, Laddie's behavior began to change quickly because I immediately showed him what good behavior was and how to earn his resources.

The first thing I needed to get a handle on was Laddie's nose. That nose was trying to sniff all over my house to find the perfect locations for him to lift his leg. The nose, of course, is mobile because the same brain that makes it work also drives four legs. So I put Laddie on a leash right away, and that leash was not to come off for two months unless Laddie was in his crate, where he couldn't get into any trouble. But stopping him from wandering the house willy-nilly was only one piece of the puzzle, because, while it prevented Laddie from finding spots to sprinkle, it didn't stop him from wanting to do it.

The next step was to teach Laddie what I like to call leash manners: Walk at my side; I set the pace and determine what direction we take; and — critically — I decide when and where we stop to sniff. Of course, Laddie wanted to stop every ten seconds and pee on every bush. Plus, he was very used to doing so. Leash manners being a foreign concept to him, the collie would constantly put on the brakes to sniff. However, I never stopped or even broke stride. This meant that every time Laddie tried for an unauthorized lunge at a bush, he received a mild leash correction from my simple forward motion, an unwavering forward motion, leash well gripped in my hand.

At the beginning of the first walk, Laddie treated me much like a post to which he was tied. He gave me little eye contact, remaining preoccupied with his obsessive desire to sniff and mark every few yards. But the lesson quickly started to sink in: "Marc is not stopping. I better not stop, either." As soon as Laddie began to check in with me, looking right at me, acknowledg-

New Skete monks walking dogs at the monastery. Note how the dogs not only aren't pulling but are also psychologically connected to their handlers.

ing that I was in control of the walk, I began to offer him an occasional reward. That reward took two forms. First, I praised him. Second, I led him right to a choice bush at the beginning and end of every walk so he could satisfy himself with a healthy outdoor marking post.

In the house, I prevented Laddie from doing the wrong thing by keeping him tethered to me with a progressively longer leash. But I remained vigilant, and once or twice I caught sight of him just as he was about to hike up his leg. That was certainly a behavior that I wished to interrupt, and I did so with a solid tug on the leash, not hard enough to hurt Laddie but certainly enough to spoil the moment. Eventually, I gained confidence in this dog as his outside walks became ever politer. Laddie came to understand that at the end of the walk he'd have the opportunity to eliminate and also have one or two shots at those special bushes. In the house, Laddie quit obsessively sniffing, so I began to let him drag his fifteen-foot leash around, keeping him within my line of sight. Yes, a few times I had to pick up that leash and pull it, but not a lot and eventually not at all. That's when the leash came off.

The turnaround was remarkable. Laddie became a foster fail, which in dog rescue vernacular is a very good thing. It means I kept Laddie and became his forever home.

For those of you who are still worried that you'll never acquire Evie's natural ability, or Rita's dormant one, or Marc's extensive training knowledge, don't despair. This book is expressly for you. At first, living intentionally with your dog as the pack leader might seem like a challenge. But in short order you can be an expert and make it look easy.

Good parents don't apologize for accepting that role in the lives of their young children. They understand that it is their responsibility to provide guidance and structure, and they are not intimidated by occasional outbursts of resistance and complaining. They know they have the best interest of the child in mind, and with this resolve they grow more relaxed and confident in their role. To use a well-worn analogy, it's just like learning to ride a bike. Before it is easy to pedal on your own it is quite difficult. Then it becomes easier and easier as you build the muscle memory and understanding of how it should feel and how you should react to the circumstances around you.

Consider this book your training wheels.

7

Pack Leader: A Different Paradigm

Every time we take leash in hand it's a new opportunity, a new begin-ning, opening us to a relationship whose dynamism maintains its freshness.

The relationship between Rita and Scotty improved dramatically when Rita adopted the same mind-set with Scotty that she had in rais-ing her children. Her children were never bored. They had to do their homework and complete their chores before they were allowed to play. Bad behavior was simply not tolerated in Rita's home. There was never any question who was in charge. It was Rita.

Because Rita exhibited a clear authority, her home was mostly an orderly and happy one. When she began to use the same parenting tools with Scotty — walking Scotty on a daily basis while holding him accountable for good leash manners, asking him to sit for his treat instead of showering him with dog biscuits, including Scotty in her life on her terms — Rita got the same results: a happy and orderly relationship.

In this chapter, we'll continue to develop for you the concept of being the benevolent pack leader, the foundational role in a success-ful, loving relationship with your dog.

It bears repeating that many people fear that training their dog is going to make the dog dislike them, and so they are reluctant to take on a consistent leadership role. "But I don't want my dog to hate me!"

is a refrain we often hear when we suggest to clients that they take charge. The reverse is true. If you believe as we do that wolves are the antecedents of dogs, then it follows that for dogs to blossom to their full potential we must lead them. This role comes naturally to them, but only if we can coherently show the dog what we expect it to do. Without our instruction, what comes naturally to dogs comes from their DNA and their wild ancestors.

Back to the Pack

Wolves live in a true state of pack dynamics with no human interference. As a consequence, there are few psychologically disturbed wolves. No wildlife biologist we know of will tell you about wolves spinning compulsively, howling constantly without reason, or obsessively chewing inedible objects in the wild.

Indeed, psychological disturbances are rare in the animal world. Poor behavior choices are penalized educationally, and young wolves quickly learn from their elders to make better choices. Good choices are rewarded because they yield good results, such as a place at the dinner table (or the carcass, as the case may be).

For the past twenty years, Rick McIntyre has studied wolves in Yellowstone National Park for the National Park Service. Quoted in the *New York Times*, McIntyre says the main characteristic of a wolf pack leader is a quiet confidence, a quiet self-assurance. "You know what you need to do; you know what's best for your pack," he says. "You lead by example. You're very comfortable with that. You have a calming effect." In the same article, McIntyre goes on to compare the alpha wolf with "an emotionally secure man. A great champion."*

Okay, so humans don't live in a dog-eat-dog world, or a wolf-eat-carcass world, at least not in the literal sense. But you don't need to be constantly bossy to be a great pack leader and certainly you don't need to be aggressive. All you need is to know that your dog

---

* http://www.nytimes.com/2015/06/06/opinion/tapping-your-inner-wolf.html?hpw&rre f=opinion&action=click&pgtype=Homepage&module=well-region&region=bottom -well&WT.nav=bottom-well

views the world in two ways: *either organized and understandable, or chaotic and unstable.*

A dog knows its need for guidance and flourishes when it's given.

The Good Boss

So what makes a good pack leader, exactly? Well, first you have to believe you are a pack leader.

To explain the pack leader dynamic, allow us, in our own words, to offer a few analogies.

Imagine yourself working at a new job. On your first day, you're given the employee handbook. The guide is well written and clearly spells out all the rules. The rules seem fair. The handbook also gives you a complete job description for your role at the company, and all the information you need to succeed in your career.

As you work for the company, you get paid on time. What's more, you notice that your boss gives you feedback on your performance in a constructive way. When you apply the information she's provided, you find you've become even more productive at your job. A series of bonuses follows, along with promotions. With the promotions come new responsibilities and greater privileges.

How do you feel? Confident? Secure? Dare I say, happy?

Okay, now imagine you're working for a different company and for a not-so-good boss. There's no employee handbook. The rules are haphazard at best and change all the time. From day one, you're on your own to figure out how to do your job. You have no idea how to please your boss.

As you work at the company, the feedback you get is erratic. One morning you're an hour late, and the boss doesn't react at all. On another day, you come in just two minutes late, and the boss screams his head off. He'll praise you for making a decision for the company but then arbitrarily discipline you for doing the same thing at another time. Although the pay is good, and sometimes you even get bonuses, you're not sure exactly why, and the pay and bonuses don't give you a sense of purpose or belonging.

Now how do you feel? Nervous? Maybe even rebellious? Makes you want to start chewing the couch, right?

Your dog is not your employee, but some of the successful traits of a good boss are the same in a good pack leader.

Here's another analogy. Remember the substitute teacher you had in fifth grade? Let's call her Mrs. Wilt. She wore a cardigan sweater, had her hair in a bun, and was afraid to exert any authority over the class. How long did it take your classmates to realize they could get away with unruly behavior? So long as you didn't do anything really crazy or dangerous, it seemed in her class you could do what you wanted. It wasn't that Mrs. Wilt was a bad person — she liked kids and, more than anything, she wanted kids to like her. But she didn't know how to be in charge. When things got out of hand, she simply turned her back. As a result, her class was disrupted and unproductive.

What made Mrs. Wilt's teaching style look even worse was when you compared her to Ms. Armstrong, your regular fifth-grade teacher, who was home with a cold. Ms. Armstrong's class always started on time, and the room was filled with energy. She had high expectations for you and prompted you to perform better than you ever thought you could. She knew how to freeze disobedient behavior with a look, but she also seemed to give out praise at precisely the right moments. You loved her class and you learned so much.

As a dog owner, you can be either Mrs. Wilt or Ms. Armstrong. You can take the easy way of over-kindness and ignore the bad behavior that results from it, or you can put in some effort and be a good teacher. Just remember: Great teachers have the happiest, most successful students.

Class Is in Session

Here's how your dog understands the classroom analogy. Pack animals follow a pack hierarchy that the dog experts Jack and Wendy Volhard call pack drive. Each dog happily (mostly) takes its place in the order, which is dictated by the urge to follow and collaborate with the leader or teacher. A vital part of pack drive is the willingness to work as part of a team or, to follow the analogy, as a member of a class. When motivated by pack drive, dogs pay attention to their leader (teacher) and try to comply with every understandable and reasonable request. They remain calm and willing. A dog with a high level of pack drive will be easier to train because he will readily respond to touch and praise, and because he finds training stimulating. Remember those students? They were always first to raise their hands and sat in the front row. But all dogs, even the ones in the back rows passing notes to each other, have some degree of pack drive, so they have the ability to learn in this manner.

Like it or not, by bringing home a dog you have appointed yourself teacher. Or, to be more accurate, by adopting a pack animal you have taken the responsibility of being a pack leader. The pack leader is not always the biggest or strongest member of the group. The leader is the one who controls resources for the rest of the pack. All it takes is mental preparedness, commitment, and an understanding of what to control.

In the classroom, praise and presence are perhaps the most important resources a teacher has. Your posture, effective eye contact, the firm but calm tone of your voice — all go a long way in the process of educating your dog. This doesn't mean you need to be the disciplinarian at all times. The whole point of training your dog is to have more fun with him. But as Rita realized, there's a time for fun and a time for chores.

There is also too much of a good thing.

Praise

If you praise your students all the time for every little thing they do, then the praise eventually falls on deaf ears. In the politically correct world of dog training, dogs are praised so often that it becomes meaningless babble. Don't get us wrong, praise is absolutely necessary in training your dog. But only when praise is appropriately given is it a formidable tool in dog training. An easy way to know if you're using praise inappropriately is if you're using it as a bribe. Dogs see through such ruses very quickly and either disregard the verbal praise entirely or respond to it solely for the treat. Praise should come from you organically, when you are truly grateful for your dog's action and attention.

Believe us, your dog knows when your praise is authentic. Yet there are owners who have trouble accessing that authenticity. We once had a quiet, reserved client who owned a Shar-Pei. Although the Shar-Pei would answer when the man called, the dog would amble over to him in such a lackluster way that the man was embarrassed. We suggested that he be a little more enthusiastic with his command and that he playfully stroke the dog's head and side when she came to him. "But that's just not me," he told us. Though we continued the training, we made little progress. Then, at one training session the man attended, his daughter and granddaughter visited. He met his grandchild in such an animated and playful way that he took us by surprise. When we pointed this out to the man and suggested he use just a portion of this enthusiasm with the Shar-Pei, he was astonished but agreed to try. Almost immediately, the dog began to mirror the man's newfound interest in her. Training became easier, the Shar-Pei was soon bounding back to the owner when called, and the bond between owner and dog began to grow. There was simply more joy in the relationship.

Praise and even play during a training session, used judiciously, are powerful motivators, making good behavior more fun for the dog. Indiana trainer John Rohrig takes a moment to play with Axl.

On the other hand, praise should fit the situation. Just because your dog sits when he's asked doesn't mean you should treat him like he just won an Olympic gold medal. Keep your voice measured, both soft and positive. Praise should be delivered physically as well as verbally. You might want to extend the physical part beyond petting your dog on the head and shoulders—he might appreciate a good scratch on his side or chest more. Although treats may accompany verbal and physical praise, they should not be substituted for it. The way you speak to and pet your dog characterizes the relationship—it's the true connection.

Praise is just one of the many resources for which your dog yearns in appropriate measure, and it's in the control of these resources, and your dog's desire for them, that she learns correct manners. Too often we see dog owners respond to their dog when the dog is being demanding rather than when he's compliant.

For example, we had a client whose dog would stare at the cabinet where the treat jar was kept and then bark at the client. The client found this routine adorable, so he rewarded it by dutifully opening the cabinet, getting out the treat jar, and offering up a cookie. This happened many times per day. The client couldn't see that he was rewarding demanding behavior—and overfeeding the dog.

Dogs inadvertently learn a lesson each time we interact with them, and the only question is whether it is a lesson we intended the dog to learn. So rather than mechanically responding to the dog's command to deliver, we can use the opportunity to our advantage. If your dog wants a treat, ask him to do something for it. It can be as simple as a sit or a down. Or, rather than giving the treat to your dog right away, randomize giving him rewards. Make him wonder, *Is this the time I'll get it?* You can wait until he is off chasing a bird or some other distraction and then whistle him back for the treat he had been craving earlier. When randomized, high-value food treats motivate dogs to obey even in the face of challenging distractions.

The message you're always looking to communicate is this: I have all the good stuff, everything you want and need. Moreover, I'm far more likely to share it with you when you offer me the behavior I ask for in return.

If this all seems deceptively simple, it is. The fact is that your dog will offer good behavior to get the things that it wants.

Mixed Messages

The obvious reason why you need to be clear with your dog is to stay away from unintentional training, which happens when we are unaware of the real message we are sending to our dogs. For example, the dog growls when a person approaches, and the owner soothes, "It's okay, it's okay," in an attempt to mollify the animal. What message is the dog receiving? The boss says it's okay, then it must be okay to growl. We had an adolescent dog brought to us because of his penchant for attacking footwear. After asking the owner a few questions, it was revealed to us that the dog was given a retired loafer to play with when he was a pup. What did the dog's owners expect? We had another case where the owners used an old towel as a tug toy for their puppy yet were baffled when the dog started pulling the laundry off the line in the backyard. Dogs are literal creatures, which makes them terrific students as long as the lessons are clear.

MARC   Claude is a 230-pound brindle mastiff. A giant, friendly, happy dog. He was about four or five when he was brought to us. Claude's owner told us that her dog had always been the rock star of the neighborhood. He loved every human, he loved every dog, and everybody loved him. He especially loved children and would let them ride him like a pony. Claude went to the dog park nearly every day. One day at the park, another dog attacked Claude. The gentle giant didn't even know what to do as the offender bit him multiple times.

The attacker was a miniature poodle that weighed about twenty pounds. Terribly upset, Claude's owner hauled him away.

In the months afterward, whenever Claude and his owner encountered a dog on their travels, Claude would show only mild concern, but the owner was so worried about another attack that she'd drag Claude across the street. So, rather than helping Claude get over the trauma of the poodle attack, the owner was inadvertently reinforcing in Claude the wrong lesson: Dogs are scary, dogs are dangerous, and we need to get away from them. Over the ensuing year, Claude became progressively more aggressive toward other dogs. His owner had unintentionally created a self-fulfilling prophecy. He went from being the rock star of the dog park to its pariah. He couldn't even go for walks because, in the words of his owner, "whenever he sees another dog, he becomes like a lion on the Serengeti. He wants to take them down like gazelles."

Claude trained wonderfully. We began by simply teaching him leash etiquette. In our world, leash manners require a dog to walk by our leg, leash held close to our body but not tight. It is the dog's job to keep the leash loose. To do this he must remain relaxed and pay attention to our pace. He must allow us to pick the speed at which we walk, the direction we're going, when we choose for him to stop, and what we choose for him to sniff. This means that the dog has to concentrate a bit to perform the job correctly. Mind you, once he gets used to it, he can do this while enjoying the walk and the companionship of his owner.

Claude's problem was that he flew into a state of excitement every time he went out for a leash walk. And in that frame of mind, far from calm, he'd become agitated as soon as he saw another dog. Perhaps he was still worried about the incident that had so affected him. But the deeper cause was more likely to have been the attitude of his owner. Rather than guide him through a tricky situation as a good pack leader would do, she panicked more and more until poor, confused giant Claude took matters into his own hands.

But once we taught Claude to remain calm and focused with no other dogs around, we began to walk him with other dogs in sight. Although we did have to reinforce the leash manners Claude had just learned in an isolated situation, his reaction to the other dogs was quite mild compared to earlier precisely because he had leash manners to focus on and because the other dogs were — as a deliberate training strategy — very far away.

So Claude's reaction to other dogs went from lion on the hunt to grumpy old man and, with time and effort, to relatively unconcerned.

Over time, we began to move closer and closer to other dogs. And as soon as Claude realized that (1) the other dogs weren't going to hurt him and (2) he must remain focused and mannerly on the leash, we were actually able to take walks with other dogs. In very little time Claude knew that order had been restored to his world. He learned there was no need for him to be reactive and that poor leash manners simply would not be permitted. In short,

Brother Thomas *(left)* and Brother Christopher *(right)* walking dogs together during a training session, teaching each dog to remain calm around others of its kind.

good leadership calmed Claude enough that he understood panicked aggression was not only no longer tolerated but also completely unnecessary.

Mind you, it's a great deal easier to educate the mind of a 230-pound dog compared to physically wrestling him into submission, so that's what we did. But even if Claude had weighed thirty pounds — and we've worked with many similar dogs in that weight range who had behavioral problems — we still wouldn't want to physically intimidate him. That's because we know that changes in the behavior and the body start with changes in the mind.

In a couple of weeks, Claude was better, the owner was happy, and the neighbors were thrilled — the rock star had returned.

Another example of unintentional training would be trying to comfort your dog during a thunderstorm. An old adage goes, "You get what you pet." Hugging your dog when she's shivering in fear tells her that shivering in fear is the appropriate way for her to feel. In fact, a dog, especially one that doesn't know you well, might interpret a hug as an invasion of space and a dominant move. Frightened by the thunder already, the hug now forces the dog to deal with a dominance issue. Instead, you might want to interrupt and redirect her attention.

Introduced correctly, the crate can become a safe and comfortable resting place for most dogs. Feeding your dog in a crate, at least occasionally, can help him learn to enjoy the space.

You might also encourage her to find a "safe" place in your home — under a couch, in a crate, or on her doggy bed, for example. The encouragement can be accompanied by a tasty treat — so your dog associates the safe place with something she enjoys. This will also distract your friend, which is another way to help her through the storm, so to speak.

Clear communication is perhaps the most important aspect of any relationship, but especially so between dog and owner. You can't expect your dog to interpret nuances. For most dogs, acquiring and occupying space is extremely important. Some dogs will take as much as you give. In the hierarchy of a household (a pack), a dog should be allowed to breach the human's space only when she is invited. Conversely, a dog's personal space should also be clearly defined. When those lines are blurred, the dog is left with little recourse but to defend her space or to encroach on others'. A good pack leader, a great boss or teacher, clearly *explains* and reinforces those boundaries to the dog. Screaming and pulling the dog by the collar does not constitute an explanation. Neither does it help to reinforce the lesson. In our work

Mother dogs teach puppies to get along with one another. Good breeders make sure mothers have the opportunity to teach their offspring early lessons that can pay off for a lifetime.

with German shepherd puppies, we see very early on the mother teaching her pups not to overly dominate one another. She'll discipline a pup that causes too much stress to the other puppies. While she does this in a firm, consistent, and clear manner, she never does it out of anger.

Pet Therapy

As a tribe, dog trainers have strong beliefs, and a good deal of the time we're at odds even with one another. There is one thing, however, that all of us agree on: People are harder to train than dogs. Dogs will change their behavior as soon as it's in their best interest to do so. Humans? Well, that's a different story. We've taught lifetime leash pullers to walk nicely in as little as thirty seconds. We've trained habitual runaways to come happily when called, even off leash, in just a few days. Granted, we are professional trainers, but the truth of the matter is that our principles are not beyond the scope of the interested and informed dog owner.

Yet it took us two hours to persuade the owner of a child-biting St. Bernard not to sleep with her dog. Now, don't put this book down. We know that a lot of you sleep with your dogs, and although it's not always recommended, if that's a nonnegotiable part of your relationship, then God bless. But if your St. Bernard is biting your four-year-old precisely because you're sharing the seat of power with the big fella, we would strongly suggest other sleeping arrangements. The thing is, humans change their views and habits only reluctantly.

BROTHER CHRISTOPHER   Not too long ago, I had a visit from a woman named Margo with an out-of-control two-year-old female German shepherd named Bella. Bella was of working lines not dissimilar to the dogs at New Skete. At the monastery, however, we begin socializing and working with puppies almost immediately so that the pup has everything it needs to cope when the owner takes it home, but Bella had no such advantage. What exacerbated the situation was Margo's behavior with the dog. When Bella would jump and overpower her grandchildren or jump up onto the couch, Margo would begin to shout and grab Bella's collar and yank her away. After several of these episodes, Bella began to bite at Margo's grabbing hand and had more than once drawn blood. A dog biting her owner is a major problem — dogs with a bite history like Bella's find themselves on lists to be euthanized. But Bella worked wonderfully with us. She was thrilled to be in the company of human beings who could explain to her in a clear way what they wanted from her. Dogs find it easy to respect and collaborate with a fair, comprehensible, and predictable leader. A good pack leader lays down rules that are reinforced consistently and in proper measure. One of the deals we made with Bella was that human hands would not be unfairly used for corporal punishment; hands would touch her only to guide or praise her. If corrections were needed, they were measured and delivered impersonally via the leash rather than by grabbing. When we explained this to Margo, she seemed to understand and all was fine, right?

Well, actually, no.

Two weeks later we got a call from Margo saying that Bella had bitten her again, and her husband wanted to get rid of the dog. Margo was very emotional. She admitted that she had reverted to her old habits of grabbing and yanking Bella's collar, and Bella had gone back to reacting the only way she knew how. Though there are dogs that will tolerate physically rough treatment by their owner, Bella wasn't one of them. In spite of the difficult relationship, Margo loved Bella. But she was at her wit's end.

We asked Margo to come in for a refresher lesson. Since training isn't a static process, we offer clients continuing support should they run into difficulties. Truth be told, our final two-hour demonstration at the end of our course provides owners with a lot of information. Sometimes it takes time and reminders to fully digest the material. This was the case with Margo. First, we reiterated the need for her to stop yanking and acting like a WWE wrestler with Bella. We told Margo how to use pressure and the leash to guide her dog. We showed Margo how to read Bella so she could anticipate, interrupt, and redirect her attention.

Luckily, Margo's husband was willing to give Bella one more chance. This time Margo promised to take our instructions to treat Bella in a fair, firm, predictable way. She promised never to grab Bella again. She also promised to follow the leash pressure guidelines we had provided her (and practiced with her), to have Bella walk calmly and politely, and to change direction whenever she sensed Bella trying to lead. Most dogs not only will tolerate a correction with a leash and some form of training collar but also

Building trust and being fair to your dog make for a happy relationship.

will respond with good attitude and better behavior. We're not speaking of yanking on the leash when you get frustrated. That doesn't actually teach anything. But when a dog is forging ahead of you and pulling on the leash hard, you can abruptly and swiftly pivot 180 degrees. If you hustle forward rather than wait for the dog, she will quickly understand that walking by your side will yield a better result for her than lunging ahead. Margo also promised to follow our exercise recommendations, and she began using a ball launcher at her local park to play fetch with Bella. We assured her that this would help enormously in balancing Bella's high energy and make her more relaxed when she was at home.

Happily, Margo kept her word. In an email update that came a month later, Margo called Bella "her best buddy." In the months and years that followed, Bella became an integral part of Margo and her family's life.

How Will I Know?

When introduced to the concept of being a benevolent pack leader, new clients often ask, "How will I know I'm doing it right?"

Well one way, we tell them, is to know when you're doing it wrong.

Here are some easy rules of thumb: You're not being a good pack leader if you find yourself saying, "My dog never listens to me." You're not being a good pack leader if you say, "My dog jumps on people" or "My dog barks all the time" or "My dog pulls on his leash" or "My dog doesn't come when he's called" or "My dog chews up my house" or any of a wide assortment of common complaints. What is missing in these refrains is perspective and a healthy dose of humility. You're not being a good pack leader when you leave yourself out of whatever problem you're encountering and simply blame the dog. A good pack leader is able to be honest enough to judge his own role in a dog's behavior, both good and bad. It takes two to tango. This even includes far more complicated problems such as: "My dog spins in circles" or "My dogs want to kill each other and other dogs" or "My dog is afraid of everything for no reason" or, the granddaddy of them all, "My dog bites me." If you find yourself saying anything like the statements above, then you're probably not being the pack leader you could be.

If you are confident and self-assured in the relationship and provide immediate and consistent leadership, your dog will begin to look to you for direction, signaling that he sees you as the pack leader. Shed all tentativeness. The good pack leader projects a *mind-set,* a spirit that accepts that you know better than your dog what is in his best interest, much like a parent accepts with his young child. This involves possessing a quiet authority and the patience to enforce rules calmly and without drama. When you show your dog these qualities from the start, it will be easy for him to follow you. This is exactly why we recommend several weeks of leashing your dog in the house when you first get your puppy or adopted older dog: Leashing will teach your dog to follow you and naturally accept your leadership. It will also give you the opportunity to provide your dog with the resources he cares about and to be a pack leader he can trust.

Dog "issues" may appear to differ widely. But the solutions are often very similar. Although some dog problems are complicated, such as reforming dogs that fight each other, most problems we experience with people and their dogs have the same origin: the lack of clear leadership.

This has less to do with training the dog and everything to do with the mind-set of the owner. Many excellent books have been written on how to teach your dog to sit or down or heel. These are important skills for your dog to know. But a skill set does not necessarily help your dog to be happy or cooperative when not directly under command. Yet if you can take the simple steps to control your dog's resources and become a true pack leader, you can completely change for the better the way your dog lives his entire life.

If being a good pack leader is so simple, and if it merely comes down to projecting a mind-set and controlling resources — those things a dog wants and needs — then why do so many of us have trouble doing it? Two reasons come to mind. First, many people have no idea what resources their dogs want and need. If you are in this category, read on, because we'll tell you exactly how to use your dog's coveted desires to benefit both of you.

Second, some folks just don't want to exercise any form of authority over their dogs. Yes, here it comes again — they don't want their dog to hate them. But why, in a rhetorical manner, would that be?

Why would anyone buy a dog, a pack animal that thrives on leadership, and give him everything he could possibly *want* except for the one thing he truly *needs*? Even people who exert authority as a matter of course in their lives and careers have trouble assuming a role of leadership with their dogs.

So, for example, when the CEO of a Fortune 500 company comes home, having controlled the resources of a thousand employees for a full day, she immediately turns the decision-making over to her dog. If the dog wants to cuddle, that's what the executive does. If the dog wants to eat—and most dogs constantly do—the executive gives out treats like a department store Santa. When they go for a walk and the dog pulls, the executive lets the dog determine the pace and route. We know why the CEO does this, of course. It's her way of showing the dog that she loves her. Unfortunately, this indulgence produces anxiety in the dog rather than gratitude. We have met some very powerful people in our dog-training careers: doctors, lawyers, actors, and professional athletes. One of our clients manages a very successful hedge fund. All of these people have two things in common, at least from our vantage point: vast personal and professional accomplishments, and their love of dogs. Yet many of them fall into the same trap of selfishly denying the dog the chance to live as she is meant to live.

Of course, this doesn't just happen to the rich and famous. Dogs are great levelers, and many truck drivers, electricians, and teachers have the same problems. After coping with a full day of traffic, bad circuits, or rowdy children, those people also want to come home and just relax with their dog. The problem is that if no one makes decisions for the dog, he'll make decisions both for himself and for the owner. In the world in which we live, it is far too easy for dogs to make the wrong decision.

Our world, as it leaps forward in population and feats of technology, is becoming ever more difficult for dogs to navigate without our help. While it may be entirely natural for humans to project their feelings and motives onto their dogs, this is entirely unfair to the dog. It places unwarranted expectations on the dog and disregards its reality.

Part of the art of living with your dog is to give yourself unselfishly,

Puppies are little sponges, soaking up information about how life works. You want your puppy to respect and love you as the "provider of all things good."

and ungrudgingly, to the dog and its true needs, to honor it for the mysterious and beautiful creature that nature created.

So what does your dog really want? And what does your dog really need? Well, if dogs could talk, the list they would give you would undoubtedly start with hamburger meat and a tennis ball. To put this in more human terms, here's a partial list of the important resources, the "stuff of life," that your dog craves:

- food
- water
- space
- activity
- toys
- scent
- emotion

By strategically timing when and in what proportion you provide and withhold these resources, you ensure a relationship in which your pet considers you "the one who provides all things good." Not a bad title to hold. This type of training doesn't take a lot of effort. It folds naturally into everyday life. Though you must change your mind-set, which by definition is all encompassing, it really doesn't take up much of your time. And the results are just wonderful. No form of dog training is psychologically healthier or more compassionate. Your dog will love you for it.

Living Large?

Before we show you how to control the resources your dog covets, let's first talk about what doesn't matter to dogs. In the previous list of resources your dog craves, you might notice that missing from the list are the things human beings prize: money, fame, electronic gadgets, wardrobe, and square footage. Recently, we saw an article about a $30,000 doghouse built by Samsung, the electronics and technology company. Among the amenities the house offers are an electronic feeder, a treadmill, and a hydrotherapy pool. The living room (the house has three rooms) even comes with a tablet computer, in case, the article states, your pup wants to watch the Westminster Dog Show.*

We seriously doubt that the Samsung house, or its amenities, will make your dog any happier than providing him with a dog bed or a crate.

Dogs don't care about tablets or three-room houses. And they don't care where you live. We once had a client who had two dogs and a Park Avenue apartment in Manhattan. The client came to us because the dogs were pooping on a $100,000 Persian rug and next to a wall on which hung signed Picassos. When asked how much exercise the dogs were getting, the owner dutifully said that they were walked in the morning and evening, perhaps a total of a half hour at most. Basically, the only exercise was a walk around the block to potty. Without proper exercise, let alone any mental stimulation, the dogs took matters into their own hands and made a mess of the Park Avenue home.

---

* http://www.geek.com/news/samsung-made-a-30000-high-tech-dog-house-1617270/

Even dogs living in the middle of the city want to walk and to touch nature from time to time. Having a dog in the city almost guarantees you'll get out more and even meet more people.

When the owners told us about the dogs' defecating in the apartment, they were incredulous. "Why are they doing this?" they asked, as if the dogs should've known the price tag of the rug.

Dogs don't care about your fancy address—or your humble one. They are much more interested in the relationship you share with them wherever you live. Your dog can be just as happy living in a modest domicile as on Park Avenue—as long as he's with you. And happier yet if you're a good pack leader.

8

The Good Pack Leader: Providing Food, Water, and Toys

Dogs place such modest conditions on their happiness.

The answer to most dog behavior problems lies in controlling the resources dogs covet. This method is profoundly simple. It works in a manner that will not exhaust you, that will not place unbearable pressure on the relationship you have with your dog, and, in fact, will broaden the parameters of that relationship in ways you might not have thought possible.

In this chapter we'll discuss how to deliver to your dog the first three of these important resources.

Food

It might not come as any surprise that of all the resources your dog craves, food is the most important. Napoléon knew this when he famously said that an army marches on its stomach. But Bonaparte also understood that there was no free lunch. A dog that works for his food is happier and more compliant than a dog that expects you to serve his dinner when he rings a bell.

To control and properly provide this resource is easy. You can select from any number of jobs your dog might do to earn his supper. Require him to sit, for instance, or lie down, or enter his crate, or even give-paw for his meal. To keep your dog from becoming robotic

As pack leader, you get to decide whether you'll feed the calm or feed the frenzy. State of mind is important when feeding dogs. Here, Brother Christopher waits for the calm before giving the food.

about it, you should try to select a different job for him to do every day. We know this might sound impossible to some of you reading this, because of how highly excited your dog gets when she hears the first scoop of food hit the bowl. Even dogs that jump, bark, or spin as you prepare the meal can learn to "work" for dinner by waiting calmly. In fact, most times it's not the dog that needs to learn to do things differently. Some dogs have trained us to drop the bowl of food as fast as possible to stop the madness. This happens even to experienced dog trainers.

MARC   I'll be honest and admit that my Doberman, Diablo, had me well trained for many years. He was a very cooperative dog in most situations. But Diablo had an obsession with food. He loved food. He adored food. He would have sold his soul for a crouton. Twice a day, for much of his life, Diablo would explode with emotion and activity when I so much as touched his bowl. Spinning with excitement, he would crash into cabinets, my knees, or furniture as I made the meal. Even though I'm a dog trainer, my own dog trained me to make the meal as fast as I could and to drop the bowl as quickly as possible.

One day, nursing a bruised knee, I realized I had to do something. That night, as I began to prep Diablo's meal, and as he started to spin, I told him to sit. Frankly, I had to tell him twice. Diablo was actually a bit confused that I was changing "the deal," or the routine that we had always followed. In his mind the deal worked like this: Get hysterical and the food comes quicker. After all, that is what I inadvertently had trained him to believe.

So this one night I simply stopped preparing his dinner; in fact, I stopped moving altogether and just froze every time Diablo got up to spin. He finally sat and held still. I filled the bowl and put the food down. Then I released Diablo to his dinner.

This plan worked for a few days. In fact, by the third meal, Diablo started to offer the sit as soon as I was prepping food. This was better for my knees and the cabinets, but Diablo wasn't completely sold on "the new deal." While he was sitting, my dog was trembling with anticipation and salivating, and in the instant I released him, he would scramble from his position to the bowl so fast that he would nearly fall over.

When I first changed the deal, I thought I was doing so because I didn't want my kneecaps smashed by my overexcited Doberman that weighed just under a hundred pounds. But I also wanted Diablo to view me as a calm and stable pack leader, a good and trustworthy provider of food. His antics over meals were slightly amusing on the one hand, but on the other, my role in our relationship was much more important than any momentary entertainment I was receiving (at Diablo's expense). What I wanted to change wasn't so much the spinning but his frantic state of mind. The fact that Diablo still wasn't calm about food meant I wasn't being the clear pack leader I should have been.

So I tried a new tactic. While I prepared Diablo's meal, he sat trembling, fixated not on me but on the floor where the bowl would land. As far as Diablo was concerned, I was nothing more at this moment than a food-delivery machine that would, for some reason, work faster if he sat. But on this morning, rather than drop the bowl to a trembling, scrambling dog, I just stood there, bowl in hand, and waited. Diablo trembled, focusing intently on the exact spot on the floor where the bowl always landed. I waited. He trembled more, eyes locked on the precise floor tile where his bowl should materialize. I waited.

Within sixty seconds Diablo broke his focus on the floor and looked up at me in confusion. Confusion and excitement are two different things, and in his case, confusion was quite a bit calmer than trembling and salivating. Diablo held eye contact with me for a long moment until I put down the bowl. Miraculously, he walked the five feet to the bowl rather than flying there. No scrambling, no drama.

I realized that I had long been rewarding the wrong state of mind. I wanted my dog to be calm at feeding time. Yet I was rewarding excitement — so well, in fact, it had turned to mild anxiety. From that day on, I never again put Diablo's food on the floor until he sat *calmly*. That's how Diablo learned that if he wanted to eat he would need to turn anxiety into tranquility. I reinforced that rule, always waiting for calm eye contact. Diablo learned to give me those things gladly. For the rest of his life, Diablo approached the food bowl with great happiness, but calmly, without hurting himself or me. After all, if his pack leader preferred calm, then to please him, Diablo would deliver it.

Don't Feed the Need

Dogs that get really excited about food tend to accelerate to frantic behavior. If you feed the excitement, you get more excitement. If you feed calm, you'll get calm. Because food is so valuable to your dog, she is willing to modify her behavior if you can just show her how to do it. Marc's Doberman loved food and was very emotional around feeding time. Diablo showed Marc how easily dogs can train people, even experienced dog trainers. Being an experienced trainer, though, Marc knew how to learn from Diablo.

Now you can learn from Marc's experience: Just don't put the bowl down until you get what you want. If it sounds simple, it is. You might find it helpful to put your dog on leash for a few days until he understands "the new deal," as Marc puts it. If you ask for a sit, use the leash to help get the sit. Release your dog to the food by saying a special word such as *free*, meaning, "You can get up now." Just be sure you stick to the routine and that your dog obeys the command right before you feed him. Eye contact should be part of the deal. If you wait a few moments, eventually your dog will look at you to see what the heck you're doing. It's important that your dog understands the connection between the work and the meal. So as soon as your dog does the job, deliver the paycheck.

Free Feeding

There are some things you should never do in supplying this prized resource. When we first met Alex, a two-year-old black Lab, he weighed 110 pounds. Though not long out of adolescence, Alex labored for breath when he ran or tried to romp. When we remarked to his owners that Alex seemed "a bit portly" (a kind assessment), they replied, "He just won't stop eating. As soon as we put the food down, he eats all of it, no matter how much we give him!"

Free feeding is the practice of leaving out a bowl of food for your dog, expecting him to eat only what he needs, and then frequently refilling the bowl as you might do for a cat. Cats, however, are not pack animals and therefore do not obey canine rules of resources (or most other rules, for that matter). Often, owners like Alex's can't even tell us how much food their dogs are consuming and are equally oblivious to the effects of excessive caloric intake on the pet.

Calories are only part of the problem that stems from this practice. It's important to remember free feeding is bad for your dog even if he's skinny (and a lot of free feeders are). A large percentage of the dogs we see with behavioral problems such as ignoring commands, aggression, and anxiety are free fed. Free feeding doesn't necessarily lead to bad behavior all the time, but if your dog does have relationship issues and you free feed, you might want to reconsider the practice. In fact, we don't condone free feeding at all.

Of all the resources your dog covets, food is the most critical and is therefore the most important of all the resources you control. It's not enough just to *give* your dog his food. It's *how* you give the food that determines whether or not you get the proper credit, and behavior, from him.

The primary job of the pack leader is to keep his pack mates alive. The pack leader does this principally by leading his pack mates to food and water. A dog with an unlimited supply of these resources, which magically appear without any work on his part, may begin to feel entitled and certainly won't feel dependent on you. In the wild, a pack leader has little patience for a pack member that isn't grateful (doesn't know its place).

The old adage goes that a dog won't bite the hand that feeds him. But if the dog thinks that there is an abundant supply of food and that it will come to him without any effort on his part, even if he doesn't bite the hand that feeds him, he might do something else wrong: ignore it. There needs to be a connection, a chain of command, so to speak, between owner and dog. Free feeding prevents you from sending the right message. As pack leader, you should be the one responsible for giving your dog what he needs. When you free feed, your dog hears you saying, "You are a special and powerful puppy. You do not need a pack leader. Manna falls from heaven for you. You need to be grateful to no one." As Marc often tells his clients, be careful or you could accidentally turn your dog into a "trust fund baby."

Of course, everything would be fine if you could only show your dog receipts for the amount you've spent on his food over the years. But your dog isn't interested in the price of his meals. What interests him is who physically provides nourishment to him when he's hungry and what he has to do to obtain it. And so it is of paramount importance that you not only personally provide food to your dog but also help him learn to do at least a little something to earn it.

In Alex's case, we asked his owners a few pointed questions. Did they know that Alex's quality of life was greatly diminished by the weight he carried? Did they realize that they were significantly shortening his life by feeding him so much? Did they know how great an impact his weight had on their relationship with him? Finally, did they ever consider that free feeding Alex was a way of satisfying their own emotional needs? This happens quite a lot, and oftentimes the owner doesn't even realize it. People can be unconscious of the real motives at play concerning their behavior, because what they're most interested in is feeling good—and pampering a pet can help them do precisely that. Some dog owners use free feeding to manipulate the dog's affections, much like they do when spoiling a child. It takes intelligent self-discipline to put the long-term well-being of your pet above your own short-term needs. In the broad picture of the relationship, this is what love looks like.

It's easy to spoil your dog with a resource. Obviously, your dog needs to eat. But he doesn't need to eat constantly. Look at it this way: If your boyfriend brings you chocolates every day, we guarantee that, along with putting on considerable pounds, you're going to start to take the chocolates, and maybe even your boyfriend, for granted. We want our dogs to be fit, healthy, and also grateful to us for being their number one provider — in the appropriate measure.

In our training programs, both the monks' and Marc's, we don't free feed. We put all of our training dogs on a two-meal-per-day schedule and give them twenty minutes to finish their meal. If they ignore it, we pick it up and offer it to them again at the next meal. So long as there isn't any illness, the dog will eventually figure out that he needs to eat when we offer him his meal. Now, in Alex's case, being picky with his food was not the issue. Alex would be more apt to eat himself to death. So the first thing we did was put Alex on a diet and expand the amount of daily exercise he received. Since he was a

Chasing the toy is a good game, but all good games have rules. Mary Mazzeri taught Mia to return right away to give her the toy and earn the next throw. *(Photo by Steven Drew)*

retriever, we taught Alex fetch using a ball launcher. At the end of his formal training, we advised his owners to continue the diet and exercise in addition to taking Alex with them on daily errands. When last we checked, the clients were complying with the program and were enjoying a robust relationship with their dog.

You Are What You Eat: Nutrition and Your Dog's Diet

Other issues arise around your dog's eating habits, but before we discuss them let's first make sure what you're feeding your dog is worthy of her bowl. Dog food manufacturers don't always make it easy for you to select excellent food. They sometimes put far more money into marketing and packaging than into quality ingredients. The US Food and Drug Administration regulates all pet foods. The agency makes sure the food is processed in sanitary conditions and that the labels read truthfully. Other voluntary organizations, such as the Association of American Feed Control Officials, also keep an eye on the pet food industry by pressuring the pet food companies to label the type of meat they use, for example. So read the ingredients and do a little Internet research. There are reliable dog food consumer websites you can use to make sure you're getting the best nutrition for the best price.*

There are also many fine books on dog nutrition, including those by Wendy Volhard. How Wendy became involved in dog nutrition is a story worth telling. In the 1970s, Wendy owned a Landseer Newfoundland named Heidi that, at the age of five, was diagnosed with severe liver and kidney disease. The vets gave Heidi six months to live. By then, Wendy had read *The Complete Herbal Book for the Dog* by the renowned herbalist Juliette de Baïracli Levy. She decided to follow the book's recommendations, which included putting Heidi on a brief fast and then feeding her a diet of oats, buckwheat, honey, fresh meat, vegetables, and herbs. "Heidi never looked back and went on to live to the ripe old age of twelve and a half," Wendy writes on her website.

---

* http://www.dogfoodadvisor.com/dog-food-reviews/dry/5-star/

Wendy would go on to breed Landseer Newfoundlands. By feeding them a diet similar to the one she gave Heidi, Wendy has nearly eradicated in her dogs the hip and elbow dysplasia common in Newfies. The diet has also extended the life spans of her Newfies from the national average of seven years to up to fourteen years.

But doesn't a diet like Wendy's drive up the cost of feeding your dog significantly? Probably. But it is inevitably cheaper in the long run than the vet bills that can come with a less than standard diet. Even by just excluding dog foods that contain corn, soy, or by-products, you'll eliminate many of the worst commercial dog foods.

Does this mean you should start shopping for dog food at the high-end supermarket? Not necessarily. Some pet foods are better for your dog than others, of course, but you can avoid falling into the trap of spending money needlessly. Over and over again, we see people who spend exorbitant amounts on pet food not for the dog's well-being but for a self-serving psychological need. You should always ask yourself this simple question when it comes to spending on your dog: Am I doing it so he'll feel better, or because I will?

If you want to feel good about yourself, give some money to a worthy charity like an animal rescue organization.

The Picky Eater

There are many possible reasons for your dog's loss of appetite. Some dogs lose their appetite after receiving a vaccination. New surroundings, as on a family vacation or after a move to a new apartment, for instance, can also impact your dog's willingness to eat. If your dog is overweight, her body might be telling her that she just doesn't need the calories right now. If this is the case, you might want to ask your veterinarian for a proper weight-reduction diet.

Some dogs are picky merely because their food is so nutrient-poor that their bodies barely recognize the food as edible. Sometimes, however, the loss of appetite indicates an underlying illness. If you think this might be the case, an immediate trip to the vet is the prudent course of action. But it's been our experience that many dogs are picky eaters simply because they take the food for granted. This is not fussy eating or a medical issue — it's a behavioral problem.

To reverse picky eating, try the following: Increase your dog's overall exercise (understand that you should not exercise him thirty minutes before or after mealtime). Require him to perform a small job to earn his meal. Allow him fifteen or twenty minutes to eat and then remove the uneaten portion. Continue this process until your dog realizes that you have a "new deal" with him. In time your dog will eat the food readily and be grateful for it afterward.

Like a child holding his breath, your dog may skip a meal or two. Don't worry. There is no reason to be alarmed. Provided your dog is in good health and not very skinny or tiny, skipping a couple of meals, or eating only portions of the meals, doesn't pose a health risk as long as you keep him hydrated. (If you have a very small dog that can't afford to go on even a brief hunger strike, or a dog that skips more than two meals, sprinkle a little bit of Parmesan cheese on his food. We especially like Parmesan for this purpose because dogs love the smell, and it's impossible to pick out and eat only the cheese. Do this for just two or three meals, until your dog is successfully eating on the "new deal.") After not eating a meal or two, your dog will begin to sit quickly for his bowl, make eye contact with you, and eat with gusto. You want your dog to be thankful to you for her meals so that later, when you ask her for better behavior, she remembers how important you are and she is happy to please you. Dogs that are thankful for their food do not pick at it. They eat it readily and are usually cooperative in other aspects of life.

BROTHER CHRISTOPHER In many respects, Wisdom, a two-and-a-half-year-old male German shepherd, would have been an ideal breeding dog for us — sound temperament, good hips and elbows, and a very handsome color and type. The only difficulty was that we discovered he was sterile, unable to sire puppies. So we placed him with a retired couple who were still active and looking for the companionship of an adult dog. As we anticipated, everything went wonderfully smooth in the transition of ownership, with one exception: Wisdom wouldn't eat. For the first ten days, he skipped a number

of meals, which caused the couple to panic a bit and to begin supplementing his meals with all sorts of added inducements: steak, liver, fish...any-
thing to get him to eat. When they finally called to ask us what they should
do, my initial response was: "Next thing you know he'll have you giving him
caviar."

After making sure that there was no illness involved, we instructed the
couple to increase the level of exercise Wisdom was receiving during the day
and to begin picking up his food fifteen minutes after offering it to him.
"Trust us," we said, "he won't starve himself." We also suggested feeding
him in his crate, something he had been used to while living in the monastery. Sure enough, within two days Wisdom's eating had regularized, and he
quickly gained back the few pounds he had lost.

Although controlling food is an important part of being pack leader,
we know of some terrible methods employed to reach this goal. Do
not try to force your dog's face into the bowl. Do not poke or prod
your dog while she is eating. Do not pull the bowl away while your dog
is eating or sniffing her food, either out of punishment or in some
type of mean-spirited game. Do not deprive your dog of needed
rations for any extended period of time as a training tactic. Also,
mealtime should be solely the time for the dog to eat. Do not take the
opportunity to brush your dog or even stroke him. Don't make dramatic moves near his bowl. If you do, your dog might try to warn you
away from his food. If you don't listen, eventually he may bite you.
Please know this is not the dog's fault. As a predator and a hunter, he
believes that once he has earned his food he should have the time to
enjoy it. A good pack leader knows this.

As pack leader, you do have the right within the social order to
determine when and where your dog eats, and your dog will gladly
comply if you use the techniques we're about to lay out for you.

To Sum Up Feeding

Here are the complete steps you should take when feeding your dog:
Make your dog sit or do some other simple task, up to and including sitting calmly and making eye contact with you, to "earn" his food. When

your dog has earned his food, and you give it to him right away, remain in the area but don't hover over him. Stand eight to ten feet away. This keeps you within your dog's social space but not directly in his personal space. What this does is reinforce the notion in your dog's mind that you are in charge of his food. You may even move a little closer while he's eating, and he should permit this without objection. Just avoid hovering and staring when in your dog's personal space—for example, where your dog is resting or where she eats her food. Even good followers don't like to be stared down at mealtime. In time, and after your dog's behavior is under control, you can start to drop the formalities. At that point, you can simplify by just asking for a quick sit, then dropping the bowl and walking away. If things start to deteriorate in other aspects of your dog's behavior, you can always go back to requiring a bit more from her in return for her food. Just keep following the steps and you'll get the hang of it, and so will your dog.

Other Tidbits

You may interrupt your dog's mealtime on occasion, such as when your dog is eating something he shouldn't. In this case, your dog should permit his pack leader to reach right into his mouth to pull out what shouldn't be there. Your dog may not fully understand—after all, a dropped chicken bone smells like a pretty good treat to him. But a pack member should never question a pack leader's reasonable actions, and your first priority is to keep the pack member safe. You just don't want to constantly interfere with your dog's meals. Dogs love structure and order. It's in the absence of these that bad behavior arises. If you train your dog along with controlling his resources, you can teach him a skill called *leave it*. When you say "Leave it," a trained dog will drop whatever he has no matter how much he wants it.

You can begin to pattern the leave it command by getting your dog used to the idea that when you want to take something away from him, chances are good that you're going to trade him for something even better. Use an irresistible treat for the beginning stages when you take something away from your dog. Think chicken (or a liver treat). Imagine he has taken a sock out of the laundry basket and is reluctant to let it go, preferring to play tug-of-war instead. Stick a high-value treat right at your dog's nose and say "Leave it." Chances are he'll drop the sock to get the treat. Problem solved.

Lest you—or your dog—think he's being rewarded for stealing the sock in the first place, you won't always trade a treat for the leave it command. But the first few times, it will show your dog not only what you want but also that it's a pretty good idea to go along with you. Eventually, the command alone may work. If not, you might need to put a leash on your dog to practice a bit more control using the objects he's most likely to steal and not give back. Once your dog understands leave it for a treat, you can keep the treat in your pocket until he actually drops the item. If he fails to do so because you're no longer putting the treat to his nose, substitute an insistent tug on the leash to indicate that you really did mean leave it. Once the object is dropped, immediately reward. In this instance, you have delayed the reward. When that is working consistently, you can reward occasionally but not every time. Make rewards variable. More about that in a moment.

It's worth calling out a practice that we hear about all too frequently: sticking your hands in your dog's food bowl while he is eating. This is common Internet advice to prevent or cure food aggression. Some dogs are so tolerant that they will permit it. Others react the same way you might if someone filched too many French fries off your plate as you were trying to eat. We do not recommend thrusting your hands into your dog's food while he's eating. If you have reason to believe that you should be so personally involved with the process, then consider a different approach.

You can ask your dog to sit, eventually working him up to a calm sit and making an instant of eye contact with you. And then you can drop one handful of his food into the bowl and let him eat it unmolested. Repeat until the meal is complete. You truly will be the hand that feeds the dog.

How to "Treat" Your Dog

Of the sixty billion dollars Americans will spend on their pets this year alone, a hefty chunk of that sum will go toward dog treats. From the generic biscuits sold at big-box stores to the gourmet dog cookies and cupcakes baked by hand, our pets gobble up millions upon millions of goodies. Every major city in the country now has at least one gourmet bakery for dogs. Many of them also bake birthday cakes and host parties for their customers' pets.

Why do we give our dogs treats when clearly all they need is a proper ration of good-quality food?

Once again, it's time for us to hold up the mirror. It makes us feel good to give our dogs a treat. We like treats! And, yes, our dogs do too. So it makes the heart glad to make our dogs happy. What's the problem?

Well, the problem is twofold. First, obesity and the myriad health problems associated with obesity can strike dogs even harder than they do people. As we have already observed, obesity shortens life span, causes joint deterioration, and can lead to increased rates of cancer as well as heart disease and diabetes. This is an epidemic among certain portions of our human population in America (the poor, for instance, who can't afford good food), but our pets are also suffering in large numbers (here, though, the reason isn't poverty but excess).

The second part of the problem is that dogs don't differentiate treats from any other food. So, just as with free feeding, when a dog is constantly rewarded with treats without a reason he can understand, he may begin to feel a certain sense of entitlement, a mind-set that is never good for a pack member. Invariably, it leads to bad behavior.

Like most grandparents with their grandchildren, many of us dote on our dogs. If doting doesn't make your dog jump on people, bark in your face, or defiantly run away when you ask him to come, then, by all means, moderately dote away. When your dog starts to exhibit an air of royalty and begins to treat you and your family like a houseful of servants, you might want to think twice about lavishing attention. You might also want to think twice about overdoing the treats.

We carry and use dog treats all the time, but we use them as a food resource. You should too. Bones are a food resource. Rawhide, pig's ears, chew hooves, and bully sticks are all food resources. As pack leader, you should treat all of them accordingly. And if you're going to

You can teach your children how to be good and fair little pack leaders. Noah has learned that sometimes Maya Chojnowski will give him a reward for a job well done, like doing a sit.

buy them, make sure you stick with domestically produced products that haven't been chemically treated. This means distributing them so that every treat is a reward for a job well done: Your dog comes when you call? He walks calmly next to you? He doesn't act on his prey drive and chase the squirrel when he's on the leash? All of these may deserve a reward. You don't want to overdo it, though. In giving out treats, act more like they're fancy hors d'oeuvres than a $5.99 all-you-can-eat buffet. We suggest small, high-value treats, such as boiled chicken, liverwurst (dogs love liverwurst!), or one of your own recipes.

MARC   There are two kinds of people in the world: those who enjoy an occasional dinner of liver, and those who think the first group is crazy. Of course, among liver lovers you have subcultures such as your bacon-and-onion group. By and large, though, when it comes to liver, either you're in or you're out.

Of course, dogs like to eat all sorts of things that humans eat, but also some items that we don't. The one thing the vast majority of dogs won't turn down is liver, and they don't even need bacon or onions.

Although you don't have to make your own dog treats to find healthy choices, you might find it fun and far less expensive to do so. Here is one of our favorite recipes. It features a single ingredient. You guessed it: beef liver. This treat won't be quite as dry as beef jerky, but it won't be slimy like liver either and will be rather dry. Be prepared to dole out these treats only as a reward for good behavior. Dogs go crazy for them.

Prepare a large baking pan by spraying it with nonstick oil.

Preheat your oven to 200°F.

Slice the liver into strips, no more than 2 inches wide and 1/4 inch thick.

Arrange the strips in the baking pan so that they are close but not touching.

Bake for two hours. If your oven doesn't heat evenly, you might want to turn the pan around once or twice, but don't constantly open the oven.

After two hours, remove and allow the liver strips to cool.

Once cooled, slice into small bits, 1/4 to 1/2 inch square, depending on the size of your dog. Remember, these treats are intended to be small so that you can use them more frequently to reward good behavior such as come or sit. Also, liver is rich, so you don't want to overwhelm the digestive system.

It sounds good enough to eat, doesn't it? When your dog earns a treat, it's important that the treat is something she really looks forward to. Look at it this way, would you wash a car for a saltine cracker? Probably not. But if the car's owner told you she was going to take you out for a steak and lobster dinner, there's a better chance you'd grab the sponge. If your dog comes when you call, reward him with a pat on the head and a tiny liver treat and watch how he starts coming more often, especially if he learns this is the only way he will earn that special treat.

Keep a small handful of these homemade liver treats in a plastic bag in your pocket for use throughout the day. Some can be stored in the fridge for a week, and the balance will keep for months in the freezer.

Also consider making your grandmother's recipe for yourself. With vitamin A and a host of minerals, liver is good for both you and your dog.

In the training world that Marc and the monks inhabit, dogs are encouraged to earn their treats. Our dogs know not to nudge our pockets or bark at us for treats. They know that treats do not fall from the sky. They know this from experience. They also know that if they come and sit when they're asked, if they sit and look not at the pocket but at our face, making eye contact, the chances are at least fifty-fifty that we will reach into our magic pocket and provide that which they crave. This practice keeps your dog in a state of anticipation, which is the best mind-set for learning. Once your dog learns the skill, then you can begin to randomize the reward.

As we have said, we are not especially enamored with the Skinner model of behavioral science as it relates to living with dogs. However, Skinner did discover an interesting cognitive quirk in lab mice. The mice responded better to a variable reward schedule. Mice were taught to push a lever for a treat. Sometimes they would receive a small treat, sometimes a larger one, and sometimes none at all. Those mice pushed the lever more intensely and more regularly than mice that received the same treat every time they pushed the lever. The randomness of the reward seems to be the important factor not only to the mice but also to human beings when playing slot machines. Watching those dials whirl around provokes a sense of anticipation, releasing powerful brain chemistry that seems to tickle the pleasure centers. The same holds true for dogs. If you constantly shower your dog with treats, the treats will ultimately lose their appeal. When teaching something new, reward constantly. But as soon as your dog begins to understand, slow the treat storm down to a drizzle and watch your dog try harder to please you and earn the reward.

It's important to make eye contact with your dog when you're rewarding her because it turns the process of earning a treat from "gimme" to "please." So how do you get your dog to make eye contact if he doesn't naturally offer it? Ask your dog to sit. Show him a treat, but raise it up to your forehead. He'll probably look up at you, if for no other reason than to follow the treat with his eyes. Quickly deliver the treat after he's done that, and he'll soon get the hang of both complying with your request (to come or to sit or to leave it, etc.) and making eye contact. Also, when you deliver the treat, have it tucked in your hand and put the back of your hand toward your dog's mouth. This will prevent him from lunging for the treat and nipping you, teaching him to take it calmly. Once he is calm, turn your hand around and let him have the treat.

If your dog starts jumping at you rather than making eye contact, remove the treat altogether and put your dog on a leash held short, meaning close to the dog's collar, so you can teach him the trick a bit more calmly. Pull out the treat again and show him that jumping isn't allowed and only slows down delivery of the treat. Most food-motivated dogs will quickly calm themselves to earn the reward.

Treat training is as simple as that, and the results can be remarkable. Remember that you're not bribing your dog for good behavior but rather reinforcing it.

Out of Reach

You might consider storing your dog's treats in a high cabinet, away from his reach and sight. Over and over again, we've had clients report to us about dogs that open cabinets themselves looking for treats, or that go to the counter on which they see the jar and bark repeatedly until the owner does as commanded and delivers a treat. Do not comply. If you do, the messages you are sending your dog are:

Your wish is my command.

Bark at me and I'll do what you want.

It's your world and I just live in it.

That last slogan might be funny stitched into a doggy pillow, but in reality it can have real negative consequences.

Conversely, if you keep the treats out of your dog's mental and physical reach, then the message you send him is that you are the master of all that is yummy and that you can produce treats out of thin air in return for behaviors you request.

Will Work for Food?

Clients often ask us whether dogs must always work for treats. Isn't it okay to surprise the dog every now and then? We received the following email from a client:

This evening we prepared a meal, and there was a bit of leftover chicken breast, not quite enough to save, yet too much to throw out. Two of our dogs were close by, but not pestering for food because they never receive food by pestering. So they don't bother. I broke the piece in two and held one out to each dog. It made me smile when they both hesitated a moment, as if to say, "This is a trick, right? We only get treats for doing something." I literally said, "Go ahead," and they both enjoyed their treat. Did we do the right thing?

Everyone enjoys a freebie once in a while. After all, life's unexpected good fortune is what makes it interesting. But most of the time we, and our dogs, are better off working for what we want instead of having it fall into our laps, especially if we tend to be lazy or easily distracted in the first place. Carry tasty treats but give them as a reward only on the occasions when your dog does what you ask. If your dog doesn't like to go in his crate, for example, toss a treat in, not before as a bribe, but after he goes in as a reward. Soon you'll find that behavior that is rewarded is repeated more often.

That said, every once in a while, a little surprise couldn't hurt.

Water, Water, Everywhere...

Managing resources can be a controversial topic. One of our clients stood and left the room when we broached the subject of regulating her dog's water. She had this image of a dog crawling in the desert and us refusing him the only bowl of water for miles. We assured our client that our aim is never to deprive a dog of an element it needs to be healthy and happy. When we talk about treating water as a resource, we are not talking about dehydrating a dog. We are not suggesting that you make your dog uncomfortably thirsty in order to force him into a behavior you want from him. Our goal is simply to honor the nature of dogs by appealing to their appreciation for leadership. As we've mentioned, one of the critical assignments of the pack leader in the wild is to lead pack members to food and water.

Like any other resource, then, a good pack leader should be in charge of providing water.

How to Provide Water

Simply understand that there are times when your dog will want and need water. Key watering times are shortly after meals or after heavy exercise. Most of the time, the water bowl should remain on the floor where your dog can freely choose his moment of access. But right before key moments, such as feeding or exercise, put the bowl up on a counter. After that meal or that romp, hold the bowl, ask your dog to sit, and then wait until he does to put the bowl down. Then release your dog to the bowl. Alternatively, place your dog on a leash and, when he's thirsty, lead him to the water bowl. That's all there is to it. Obviously, water is a critical resource for your dog. You'll be his hero if he knows that you provide it for him. Conversely, if the bowl of water is always on the floor and constantly full, then your dog doesn't think that you have anything to do with providing water.

It's important to bear in mind, however, that your dog needs proper hydration. Again, the goal is never to deprive your dog of water but, rather, for him to notice that the elements of life that he wants and needs come from you.

Toyland

Does your dog live in the canine version of FAO Schwarz? We have had clients arrive at our boarding and training facility with sacks filled with toys for their dogs. We could only imagine what their homes looked and sounded like — with squeaky toys, plush toys, electronic toys, automatic treat dispensers, balls, and flying discs lying around. At the risk of sounding like the Grinch: This is a not a good thing. Invariably, what happens is the toys lose their appeal to your dog. How can the toys be special when they're lying around any time he wants them?

Toys can contribute to a happy relationship with your dog. For one, they are a great way to get your dog some exercise. Dogs that have an abundance of toys lying around tend to think that everything is a toy: your shoes, a book or magazine, socks. This may lead to all sorts of problems with destructiveness and inappropriate chewing. It is reasonable to focus your dog's attention on one toy at a time and to be the one who decides which toy is available. If you have toys lying all around the house, pick them up, put them in a box, and put the box in a closet. When you think your dog would enjoy playing with a toy, select one from the box and give it to her. What's important here is that you are making the selection, not your dog. Ask your dog to sit or lie down before giving her the toy. Then allow your dog to play with the toy, or play with the toy with her, but periodically remove it. This is a perfect opportunity to practice the leave it command. If your dog clamps down and doesn't want to release the toy, either attach a leash briefly or stick a high-value treat right in her nose for a trade, then say, "Leave it," and when the dog opens her mouth to accept the treat, praise her warmly as the toy falls to the ground. When you give the toy back, ask for a come or a sit. Remember, you're providing the toy in return for compliance with a simple request. Do this for thirty days and watch the results! Using these steps also addresses possessiveness, for instance, where a dog may protect a desired object like a toy or a bone. The steps are practice for real life.

Guarding

When your dog believes that he has dominion over the toys, he might start to guard them.

If your dog starts guarding his toys from you or from other dogs, it could be an indication of a larger problem, especially if your dog growls when you try to take a toy from him. We had a client who brought us a happy-go-lucky yellow Lab named Buddy. Buddy developed a rash while with us, and we had to bring him home before his training was complete. We told his owner that we would continue the training as soon as Buddy's skin irritation cleared up. While we were in the client's house, Buddy grabbed a plush toy. "Oh, no," the owner said, "I'll never get that back from him." Her reaction surprised us. We had had Buddy for a week and found him to be upbeat and compliant. But when we went to take the toy from him, he ran under the kitchen table. Defendable space. Not only that, when we ducked our head and looked under the table, Buddy put his paw on the toy and curled his lip with a full-tooth snarl. We picked the table up, which exposed Buddy, took him by the scruff, and firmly removed the toy. The owner was amazed and surprised, and frankly, so was Buddy. He had never been confronted over a toy before. Buddy hadn't been taught that toys are a resource and that he wasn't in charge of them.

We don't recommend that you get into a physical confrontation with your dog under such circumstances. It should never get that far. We made a judgment call in touching Buddy in the midst of that snarl. Our read on him was that he was bluffing — very, very impolitely — but bluffing nonetheless. He was.

Tug-of-War

Opinions on tug-of-war vary from dog trainer to dog trainer. Some trainers forbid their clients from playing tug with their dogs, and other trainers teach their clients how to play the game. Although we're not totally against tug, we believe it should be done in a very specific way, and here's why: It can awaken your dog's desire to compete with you on a physical and mental level. There are plenty of dogs that can play tug without making it a test of wills. Such dogs are able to relish tugging on the toy but are able to let go when the owner says "Leave it" or "Out." But tug can become a vivid illustration of the dog's willingness to acknowledge the owner's leadership. If your dog is willing to let go of the toy in the midst of a stimulating game of tug, then resume playing on your command. But if your dog is not willing to let go of the toy, we would suggest you don't play the game with him or make it a point to teach him your rules for this particular game.

Finally, remember that it's up to you to decide when playtime is over. When it is, put away all the toys. For your dog it's as though

Brother Christopher plays tug with Ella on the beach while owner and friend Kate Hartson looks on. Tug isn't a bad game, but here's a good rule to follow: your dog must allow you to call a time-out and take the toy.

you've made the toys disappear. He then knows that you hold the power to make them appear again. In time, he'll also know that he has to be a good boy for you to make that happen.

If you've read this chapter and are still feeling guilty about taking charge of your dog's food, water, and toys, then bear in mind that if you love your dogs as we love ours, they have a pretty good deal in place, complete with lifetime job security, free room and board, and a great health plan with zero deductible.

In controlling these three resources — food, water, and toys — you not only will remind your dog how good she has it but also will have gone a long way toward building the structure that allows a happy and productive relationship with your dog.

9

The Good Pack Leader: Providing Space, Activity, and Scent

Dogs are intensely curious about the world they live in, and they investigate its breadth relentlessly with all their senses.... Checking out an irresistible scent in the grass captivates them as much as gnawing at a treasured bone in the yard.

Space is both the most difficult and the easiest aspect of your dog's life to control. It is the easiest because dogs are genetically programmed to understand how to occupy space and also how to yield it. It is the most difficult because space is everywhere, and to control it, you must consistently be aware and focused on many factors that dogs think about but that humans rarely do. One thing is for certain, though: Either you will control your dog's space or he will control yours.

So what does space mean to a dog? Well, two things. First, it's the place where he puts his body. Second, it's any spot he wishes to control. Controlling space comes naturally to dogs since they, like their wolf ancestors, are territorial. They have the instinct to patrol and protect large tracts of space. Dogs are also social animals that interact in close proximity to one another and also to humans.

If you watch two dogs meet for the first time, you'll notice that most dogs do not greet each other face-to-face immediately. To walk frontally into a strange dog's space would be considered an invasion and, therefore, a challenge. So dogs will often approach each other obliquely. They tend to sniff each other's rears before going eye to eye. Partly this is because dogs relate to one another more with their sense of smell than with their vision, but also because they are negotiating their proximity to one another. They are figuring out how to share space. Dogs that are sociable need to make the introductions and then move on to the next phase of the relationship, which usually is to run and play. Dogs who are not sociable might take a little more time to interact, and some never do.

Whether you realize it or not, you are in constant spatial negotiation with your dog. Every time your dog rests his head on your lap, he is invading your body space. When you reach out to pet your dog on the head, you're invading his space. In a healthy and respectful dog-human relationship, this type of interaction is just fine — the dog feels confident enough to approach his human and also confident enough to allow his human to approach him. There is nothing wrong with permitting your dog onto your lap or on a couch so long as you con-

Dogs don't greet each other face-to-face. Initial meetings are more about scent than eye contact.

trol the invitation and so long as she gets off of you or the furniture when you want her to without any objection.

Here's a little secret. You've been successful at training your dog when (1) your dog comes when you call; (2) your dog moves away, or off, when you ask; and (3) your dog does nothing heinous in between.

But sometimes the relationship doesn't go as easily as one, two, three. Owners of dogs with behavior issues need to consider their dog's space more than other dog owners. If your dog invades your space by jumping on you, he is treating you as he would another dog he wants to wrestle with. Sure, it seems playful. But it's also devoid of the necessary respect you will need in other areas of your relationship with him. Besides, if you happen to be living with a ninety-five-pound Bernese mountain dog, the habit could get old pretty quickly.

Ideally, your dog respects your body space, permits you to move freely in your own home, and does not guard this valuable resource called space from you. If a dog misunderstands his role in the family, he may believe that he is the pack leader and that he has an obligation to determine how you use space, rather than the other way around. If he growls at you when he is on the couch, on the bed, or walking through narrow spaces, he is exercising authority over you.

Guarding is an instinctual behavior for dogs. It is useful to us when dogs warn strangers who intrude on their (and our) territory. One of the earliest benefits dog provided to man was to serve as an early warning intruder alert system. In this regard, barking is verbal territoriality. It is the dog's way of saying: "This space has value and it belongs to me and my pack." In fact, dogs guard all sorts of things, some tangible, such as food and toys, others intangible, such as space. Dogs also guard tangibles and intangibles from one another. You shouldn't expect to see a submissive dog take a highly valued bone or scrap from a more dominant dog. Should he try, he'll face a swift warning. But that's rarely necessary in the structure of a healthy dog pack, where it is clearly understood who is entitled to what and when.

But what happens when the dog doesn't have a clear understanding of what he can and cannot guard? The results can be disastrous: a dog that guards something from his owners. We use the following example in our training seminar.

We have clients with a 125-pound Rottweiler. The family has had the dog since puppyhood, and the owners, a young professional couple, have always let the dog sleep in the bed with them. One night, the husband returned home at about 10:30. So as not to awaken his wife, he came quietly into the bedroom. The Rottweiler was asleep in the bed. When the husband tried to get into the bed, his dog met him with a low, guttural — and very scary — growl. Although the husband was able to defuse the situation (he turned on the lights and awakened his wife), this scene could have ended much, much differently.

There is perhaps no more serious occurrence in the dog-human relationship than a dog attacking its owner. Unfortunately, it does happen, and it usually happens when the dog is guarding a resource he shouldn't have had dominion over in the first place.

Side note, while we're on the subject: Although we're not proponents of the practice of sharing a bed with your dog, we understand how much it means to some of our clients and how popular it's become. According to some surveys,* nearly half of American pet owners allow their dogs or cats to sleep in bed with them. Whether you do or not, however, should depend entirely on what else is happening in the relationship. If your dog is not aggressive with you or with anyone else, then, usually, no harm will come from sharing space with your dog in this way. We know many trainers who sleep with their dogs. (We don't.) But the reason they do is because the pros know how to control resources for their dogs.

For your dog, your bedroom is the most important room in the house. Your scent is strongest there because you sleep for eight hours in one place. Think of the bedroom as the throne room, and your bed as the throne. Only powerful advisors to the king and queen are permitted in the throne room. Sleeping in your bed is a way of sharing the royal chair itself. With respectful and willing dogs, it is a way of sharing intimacy and affection. Dogs with challenges, however, assume that you're ceding some (or maybe all) of your royal powers to them by letting them into the bed.

As we've written extensively in our other training books, having a

* http://pets.webmd.com/features/pets-in-your-bed

dog sleep in his own bed in your bedroom is a wonderful and low-maintenance bonding opportunity. It also inhibits behavioral problems. Of the dogs we see with behavioral problems, the majority of them sleep either marginalized outside of the bedroom or coddled in the bed.

If you decide to let your dog share your bed, it's important that you show him it's a privilege; otherwise, even well-behaved dogs can develop issues. But if your dog gets it that you're in charge of this prized resource, then, by all means, go ahead and snuggle away.

Back to the Pack

In the dog pack, if the top dog wants to walk from point A to point B, he may do it even if he has to nudge a lesser member out of his way. If the more submissive dog protests, what he is typically doing is challenging the authority of his leader by trying to guard the space he occupies. If the leader is a true pack leader, this isn't allowed to happen.

The very same dynamic occurs between humans and dogs. Say your dog helps himself to a place on the sofa. You sit down next to him or you try to remove him, either verbally or, perhaps, by the collar. If your dog growls or snaps at you, he's guarding space. Moreover, he's stating in dog language that he believes you're taking liberties reserved for the pack leader.

This may also occur when you push past your dog through a doorway, pass him in a narrow hallway, or get very close to him while he's lying in his favorite spot.

Many times, the human occupants of a home do not realize that their dog is guarding space until the dog becomes aggressive and something bad happens. One of the main reasons for this kind of bad behavior is that we fall back into the same old habits, applying human standards to canine behavior. For example, say your dog is sitting on the spot where you usually sit. You're aching to watch *America's Got Talent*, but you don't want to be impolite and ask your dog to move. Although you think you're being considerate, your dog interprets this quite differently. For him it's a conquest. *This is my space now*, he's thinking. *And while you're up, pass me the remote. I want to watch* The Real Chihuahuas of Beverly Hills.

Among our species it is impolite to pull someone out of a chair or to shoulder him aside when you want to watch your favorite television program. So if a dog growls when his owner sits near him on the couch, many people wrongly assume the dog is just being grumpy, or that he was too comfortable to be disturbed.

Clients have told us that they have actually chastised their children for being impolite by sitting close to a dog or nudging it aside. People subconsciously try to accept guarding problems as quirks of the dog. Many owners try to work around a dog defending space by not disturbing him no matter how inconvenient that may be.

In doing that, however, you're telling your dog that he is the pack leader and is therefore entitled to guard the space in question. Guarding problems can escalate and, in fact, often do. It may begin with the dog growling under very limited conditions — say, when being nudged aside on the sofa — but then it often reaches the point where the dog begins to growl as soon as you approach him.

Dogs instinctively guard with more intensity as the opportunity allows for it. For some dogs, dominance is a self-rewarding behavior. You want to remove your dog from the couch. He growls. So you back off. To your dog, his behavior worked. Eventually he might growl even when you just look at him on the couch. *They don't seem to get it*, the dog is thinking. *This is my space. I'll have to warn them earlier.*

Such behavior can become very problematic for pet owners, particularly those with young children.

MARC   Willy was a three-year-old German shorthaired pointer. His owner, Lisa, called us one day very concerned. Willy had been growling at her eleven-month-old baby every time the child approached him in his dog bed. Sometimes Willy guarded the couch in the same way: The baby would come close, Willy would growl. What made matters worse was that Willy had started growling at Lisa whenever she sat near him on the couch. Lisa was confused because Willy had never acted this way before. But it had been going on for a month now and seemed to be getting worse.

We had our suspicions about why this was happening. Lisa's baby had begun to walk a month earlier. To Willy's mind, this impudent little human was intruding on his space, and Willy believed he had higher status than the baby. After all, Willy slept in Lisa's bed, while the baby was relegated to a space (the baby's room) far away from the pack leader — a sign of lower status. In Willy's eyes, even Lisa's position as pack leader had begun to wilt. After all, she had spent an entire month showing him how dominant he could be by not addressing his space-guarding behavior. The unintended message to Willy was that he was dominant. That's why he began to guard space from Lisa, too.

Not every dog is like Willy, but when such a situation is left unaddressed, some dogs that guard space will eventually scare or even bite their owners. This can have disastrous results — the dog might be removed from the home or even put down. What makes this so tragic is that often the behavior is easily fixed.

With Willy, we had our chance: He came to stay with us for two weeks. In that time, we showed him that space was not a resource he should guard from his humans. We started this lesson with the walk.

The walk is the most important time of the day because it is when you, the pack leader, and your dog patrol your territory together. Normally, Willy pulled hard on the leash. We showed him that pulling was not effective. When Willy strained, we held the leash and briskly turned around the other way. As soon as Willy was walking by our side again, we praised him, turned around, and resumed the walk. In short order, Willy learned that walking on a loose leash and allowing us to control where he put his body meant that he could continue the pleasant journey.

In the process, Willy made an unexpected discovery. Of course, he resisted at first because he was accustomed to making his own decisions about where he walked and what space he occupied. But once he allowed us to make that determination for him, Willy found that walking alongside his pack leader felt great. He felt protected and calmer.

There are a variety of products that can help you teach your dog how to walk alongside you. Head halters and training collars are among your choices. Use any tool gently. If it's not working effectively, you may need to seek the help of a professional trainer.

Crate training was Willy's next lesson. As we've mentioned, although some owners are reluctant to place their dogs in crates, the confines of the crate are actually very healthy for the dog's state of mind. The whole idea

Some trainers dislike head halters, and others love them. This dog is walking nicely on a halter. Whatever tool you choose, learn to use it correctly.

behind crating is to have a place where you can regulate the stimuli that normally surround your dog so he can relax. Dogs are born in a calm, quiet space such as a whelping box. In the wild they were born in dens. Instinctively, dogs can learn how to enjoy this private space. A dog that calmly permits you to crate him respects your authority. To help your dog learn to enjoy the crate, never place him in it as punishment. Instead, toss a treat into the crate and allow your dog to consume it in his own master bedroom. Your dog will learn to enjoy his space even faster if you feed him his meals in the crate.

By tossing a treat into the crate, we accustomed Willy to placing his body into space we selected for him. The pack leader sometimes decides what space a dog will occupy. Eating meals in his crate helped Willy enjoy this space rather than merely tolerate it. We knew we were making important progress when we could point at the crate and Willy would enter voluntarily.

After teaching Willy to walk at our side and to enjoy his crate, we began to walk occasionally through his space, gently nudging him aside. When Willy moved out of our way, we praised him. We also called him to us and then praised and petted him, so Willy would understand we didn't want him to avoid us but merely to yield space to us when we needed it.

In the course of this training, Willy was banned from human furniture. He had developed a history of guarding furniture from humans. Dogs that have growled when guarding space on furniture should lose the privilege for at least thirty days while you work on establishing your role as pack leader. Dogs that have bitten when guarding space should permanently lose furniture privileges. This is not punishment. Rather, you want to set the dog up for success instead of failure. We want your dog to remain safely in your home, and a sofa ban is a small price to pay.

So, for Willy, we removed the furniture privilege and instead gave him jobs at which he could succeed, such as practicing and reinforcing sit stays inside the front door while a family member outside rang the doorbell. All Willy really needed to know was that he wasn't Little Lord Fauntleroy anymore but rather a treasured pet. Once Lisa walked him more regularly — while insisting on attentive leash manners and not allowing him to sniff and pull the whole way — things improved. Jobs for a dog can be quite simple, such as performing the occasional come command at opportune moments. But such moments can present themselves when the dog might prefer not to do to the job, such as when he hears a car door slam and what he really wants is to run to the window and bark. Willy's owner began to take advantage of some of these opportunities throughout the day to give her dog something to focus on other than his own desires.

Willy began to understand very quickly. Space wasn't worth guarding anymore. In fact, each time we asked Willy to give up space, he became willing to do so at once and calmly. At the conclusion of our training, we reoriented Willy to his family and his environment, and we explained the behavior modification techniques to his owner. Then we left.

Lisa called us two days later. She reported that Willy was leaving his dog bed as soon as the baby approached. We were happy with this report. At least Willy wasn't growling at the baby. But Lisa was concerned. She wanted Willy and her baby to be friends and she worried that the dog was now fleeing from the baby.

We explained that this was progress given that Willy had modified a major behavior and was now yielding space rather than guarding it. We advised her to give it some time to see whether Willy would eventually find pleasure in sharing space, time, and bonding with the baby in his new role as follower. We warned Lisa that not all dogs bond with all people, but that there was a distinct possibility Willy would. We also asked Lisa to carefully supervise all contact between her child and Willy to ensure that neither was unfair to the other.

Two weeks later Lisa called again, and she was very happy. Willy and the baby were interacting appropriately. Apparently, Willy had come to realize that while he was no longer able to guard space, there was a wonderful pleasure in sharing it.

Willy has been home for several months now, and all the reports bring good news. Here is a dog that was at severe risk for rehoming and that might possibly have injured a child. Now he is bonding with his little master.

Dogs and Babies

The trust between small children and dogs is something that grows over time and with experience. Dogs often tend to see children as peers rather than pack leaders because children are usually affectionate or rowdy with dogs, and do not control their resources. Although most of us want to trust our dogs, we must also carefully monitor the relationship and interactions between our pets and children.

A fair number of clients come to us shortly after a baby is born with concerns about the relationship between their child and their dog. It's common practice for parents-to-be to carry around a doll before the baby is born to get the dog used to the sight of a baby in her master's arms. After the birth, but before the baby is brought home, many dog owners give the baby's blanket to the dog so the dog will become familiar with the baby's scent. Although we see no harm in either of these practices, we are not sure how much they contribute to the dog's adjustment to the presence of a new baby.

The reality is that dolls don't cry, coo, or make any other baby noises. Some dogs don't give a fig for such sounds, but others are captivated for reasons that run the gamut from bonding, on the desirable side, all the way through to prey drive, on the very worrisome end of the scale. A very important *but* is that if we do all the right things, the vast majority of dogs will learn to get along just fine with our children, as they have for millennia.

Although we see no harm in the baby doll and blanket routines, allow us to add a simple idea or two to your arsenal that might be even more useful. First, recognize that once the baby comes home, your dog takes a step back in your household's hierarchy. This is hard to imagine for many people who have raised or rescued and loved a dog. In fact, we have noticed that during pregnancy, both men and women psychologically preparing for being a parent may actually increase the amount of attention paid to the family dog. Expectant parents tend to talk to and pet their dog even more than normal.

With birth, however, that changes. Quite naturally, the dog assumes a different role because the new child will occupy such a large amount of your mental and emotional focus. If you're not careful, you can take a dog that is used to a certain amount of fussing before pregnancy, get him used to even more attention during pregnancy, and then — from his perspective — suddenly draw back to what seems to him like being ignored.

As longtime breeders and trainers, we can assure you that the dog doesn't understand the situation as you do. Mother dogs do not readily present their puppies to the father dog or even female pack mates. They're naturally protective and concerned that the other dogs may confuse puppy noises for prey. The mother dog will actually discourage other dogs from approaching her nest for quite a while. Eventually, after the other dogs get accustomed to the scent, sounds, and sight of the baby dogs, momma dog will begin to permit a careful approach.

We can learn from this by making baby and dog introductions into less of a presentation and more of a non-event. Tethering your dog, and teaching your dog the go to bed command — teaching methods and skills we will cover at length in the coming chapters — can help indoctrinate your dog to the changes in the household.

It's important that your dog learn your baby falls under the gentle protection of the pack leader and that he should focus on the job you give him: sit-stay, go to bed, etc. Over the first couple of weeks, you'll notice that your dog, while interested in your baby, will get over the initial rush of excitement. That means he'll get used to the scent, sound, and sight of your little one. At that point you might start to allow your dog to approach you while you're holding the baby, but you should avoid holding the baby out to him as though presenting your dog with a new toy. Just like a mother dog, you'll be giving him time to understand that your new baby is special to the pack leader, and therefore treated accordingly. In time, you'll see your dog making correct decisions on his own about how to react to close encounters with the new arrival.

Activity: Come On, Let's Play!

"Do you want to watch *Downton Abbey* or Animal Planet?"

It is a profound and simple truth in the realm of human existence that all power lies in the hands of those who hold the TV remote. In the dog-human relationship, it's the human who should hold the remote. Within the healthy pack, decision-making is often fluid, with each party having input, but it's the pack leader who has the last word.

Although it might seem cute that your dog brings you her leash as if to say, "Come on, let's go for a walk!" or drops a ball or some other toy into your lap when she wants to play, what she is really doing is seeing how much she can get away with. We had one client whose dog would pick up his dinner bowl and drop it at her feet if he was hungry. Who says dogs are poor communicators? Adorable as the dog's actions may be, what many dogs are really saying is: "I think you're my maid. Let's have some room service. Now." It's fine sometimes to go along with what your dog is asking you to do. But if you *always* do so, if you never contradict, if you rarely have your own agenda, then you're creating layer after layer of miscommunication that tells your pet he is the decision maker, the one who determines what happens and when. This is problematic at any time, but especially so when situations change, such as when a new baby comes into the home and your priorities shift.

If your dog is clear on the chain of command — that you're the one in charge and that you make all important decisions — then change won't be so hard for him to accept. Dogs who think they have final say in the decision-making process live in a state of anticipation, which can exacerbate the anxiety that comes from change.

MARC My Scooter is a rat terrier that doesn't like to be ignored. Like most terriers, persistence has been genetically engineered into her nature. She has a method of challenging me when my choice of activity does not please her: It's her "Pet me, pleeeeeaaaasssseee" dance. She stands on her hind legs as tall as she can, extends her front feet way over her head, spreads her toes, and paws rapidly at the air. If I walk away, Scooter will dance after me. I have to admit, sometimes the dance gets to me and I have to stop and pet her.

From Scooter's point of view, her little dance is randomly and intermittently rewarded. She never knows when I will reward her with some activity — like taking her for a walk — but she believes that sooner or later I will. We understand from decades of science experiments that random, intermittent reward is the most psychologically powerful form of reward on earth.

It's how casinos make all their money. Even the most naïve gambler knows full well he's not going to win every time he pulls the lever on a slot machine. In fact, he knows he won't win on most pulls — that's why they're called one-armed bandits. But all it takes is a win once in a while to keep the gambler playing and paying. The casino programs the machines, and the percentage of winning pulls is predetermined. Of course, the odds always favor the house, and nothing is left to chance. What the casino is counting on is the player being in the powerful state of anticipation, and it's the same emotion that prompts Scooter to do her dance.

The state of anticipation can work for or against your relationship with your dog. When it leads your dog to be attentive to your guidance, to work for what he values, an attitude of anticipation is a very good thing. For example, after you teach your dog a skill, such as going to his bed when the doorbell rings, he might start anticipating the command as soon as he hears the bell ring. This is good anticipation.

A lack of patience coupled with anticipation, however, can lead to belligerent behavior. For example, if we pick up a leash and the dog jumps in anticipation of the walk, and we rush to get the dog out the door, we've reinforced the frenzy. A walk that starts with an excited, out-of-control dog, especially one that is aggressive by nature, is likely

If you start the walk with a moment of calm control, chances for a pleasant walk increase. Teach your dog that the walk starts with a sit at the door. Don't open it until she relaxes.

to end in aggression toward other dogs or people. So, instead, interrupt the frenzied behavior with a sit-stay. Make sure you don't open the door until your dog is calm. Before you know it, your dog will understand that in order for the door to open, he must be calm. Chances are, if you start the walk calmly, it will continue calmly and end calmly.

Tip: Tethering your dog will teach her patience and will counterbalance her frenzied anticipation of the walk. Although at times beneficial for the training process, anticipation can become constant excitement. Obviously, that's not what we want from our dogs. While their persistence can be entertaining, remember that you never want to reward a behavior that you don't want your dog to repeat. Instead, interrupt the behavior and guide the dog to a behavior that you can praise, such as a down-stay.

Dogs, especially active breeds such as retrievers or Jack Russells, need mental and physical outlets for their energy. Even excitable dogs can be taught to relax, but young, energetic dogs need plenty of activity. Doggy day care and less formal or impromptu playgroups for dogs are a great way to run off energy. We have a client who is lucky enough to live near the ocean on Long Island. She and about thirty other dog owners meet on the beach each morning for a pack walk. Not only has this provided a valuable outlet for her dog's energy every day, it also has created a reliable social environment with other dogs. If the ocean isn't an option, a local park or field will do fine.

It's important to remember, however, that the pack leader dictates how and for how long the dog gets to play. Allowing your dog to pull all the way to the dog run, or not teaching her to come to you when she's playing with other dogs, doesn't do your relationship with your dog any good. There must be rules, or these moments turn from play-time to work very quickly. One way to set the rules is by establishing calm on the walk to the dog run or play space. If your dog starts to pull or bark when she senses where you're headed, turn immediately around and return to the car or house. Do this until your dog gets the message that she will get what she wants by being calm.

Maybe the most important part of your dog's daily activity is your playtime with her. Nothing builds the human-dog bond better, or brings more joy to the relationship, than playing a game with your dog. Like all resources, however, you, as pack leader, have to be in charge of not only when you play but also how you play.

Even though fetch, played correctly, can bring you and your dog moments of pure bliss, too often owners allow fetch to turn into a game of keep-away: your dog coming tantalizingly close to you with the toy, then darting out of reach just as you are about to take it. The problem usually isn't that the dog doesn't like a proper game of fetch. He simply doesn't know how to play. What he does know, most likely, is that if he gets close to you with the toy, you're going to try to snatch it away. Besides, your dog finds it great fun to run circles around you and to watch you hop up and down while he gets to possess his favor-ite throw toy. Of course, this game barely resembles fetch, which, when played right, teaches all sorts of wonderful lessons, such as cooperation and impulse control. (Think about asking your dog to wait calmly in his doggy bed while the pizza delivery guy is at the door and having him comply. Is that the kind of quality you want in your dog? Everybody does.)

The following is a simple suggestion that could help you change the game from keep-away back to fetch. Put a long leash on your dog and hold the end. We prefer a twenty-foot length. Find two toys your dog really likes. Hide one toy, preferably a squeaky toy, in your pocket. Wiggle the other toy as you show it to your dog. Toss it only a few feet away, and the instant your dog goes out to it, whip the hidden toy out of your pocket, kneel down, and make it squeak. Most dogs will happily trade toys. This is how you begin the pattern in which your dog returns to you with a toy.

Play like this for several consecutive days. Once your dog's got the idea, you can begin to let go of the line and throw the toy farther. Kneel down, inviting your dog back, but this time when your dog gets to you, take hold of the line so he can't run away. Do not jerk, but rather hold the line loosely, and pet your dog and praise him for returning with the toy. Do this while your dog is holding the toy in

Fetch is a great game for both of you, but only if your dog comes back with the toy. Use a long line and a second toy to encourage a quick return.

his mouth. Pet him for a moment, then present the other toy and trade him for the toy he returned.

The next step is for you to layer on additional controls over this activity. When your dog returns to you with the retrieved object, pet him, then take the object and ask him to sit. As soon as he sits, toss the toy again. Until he is reliably returning right back to you, continue to give him encouraging body language by kneeling slightly to welcome him back. Spreading your arms open wide is another signal to the dog that you are a friendly target and he should return to you. Then stand up straight and ask for the sit. Gradually extend the duration of the sit between retrieves until your dog will wait thirty seconds between throws.

After a few days of practice, you may be able to eliminate the line altogether. If your dog takes advantage of you after the leash is gone, substitute a lighter, shorter leash until he plays the game your way. You can also take the line in hand to help your dog sit as you ask. The game of keep-away — an activity you never selected — has now become a fun play-and-learn session that you *have* selected and that you control. It consists of sit, fetch, return, give back the toy, sit, and do it all over again. This is a fun game for both of you, and best of all, you're controlling activity for your dog in a way that he'll love.

The ideal number of tosses will vary from dog to dog. The key point is to quit while your dog still wants to play. Some dogs will play this game until they drop. Others have only two or three happy play retrieves in them at a time. Always leave your dog wanting more and looking forward to the next game.

One last thought about fetch: Some dogs just won't take no for an answer. They'll drop the ball at your feet and then bark and bark and bark while they're looking at you, as if to say, "Hey! Do your job!" That barking can sometimes turn even more aggressive if you ignore the dog.

The fault here doesn't lie with the dog but with you. You're acting like a human tennis-ball launcher rather than a benevolent pack leader who sets the agenda. If your dog is overly insistent while playing fetch, or any other activity for that matter, here's a simple trick: Start to view those demands as though your dog has just volunteered for a little bit of homework. Use your sit command, or a simple trick like give-paw or down-stay. Once the task is completed, go along with your dog's original demand, but now you both can view it as a reward for a job well done.

Heaven Scent

Bloodhounds can track people who have been lost in the woods for days. Jack Shuler, a well-known bloodhound trainer, told us about one of his dogs that worked for the FBI. An agent set fire to a gallon jug of an accelerant and then traveled to a location more than a mile away. The bloodhound was brought in a full twenty-four hours later. The dog sniffed the ashes, picked up the man's scent, and was able to trail the agent to the location where he was hiding with little trouble.

All dogs are literally born to sniff. Puppies' eyes don't open until they are ten to fourteen days old. Their ear canals are sealed until shortly thereafter. But the puppy's nose works from birth, and it is far more sensitive than ours. The very first action a puppy takes is based on using his nose. Blind and deaf, he sniffs his way to his mother's nipple.

Deep inside the dog's nose reside olfactory sensors that detect scent. The dog has one of the most brilliant noses found in nature. His powers of scent observation are many times greater than our own. What we call fresh air is broken down by your dog into thousands of elements, almost to the molecular level.

Just one drop of human blood in five gallons of water? Your dog knows it's there. A rabbit hopped by sixteen hours ago? Your dog not only knows it was there but also whether it lingered or raced along. By sniffing the air or the ground repeatedly, your dog is able to concentrate the scent. The smell doesn't fade; in fact, the more effort your dog puts into smelling, the stronger the scent becomes to him.

Ned Rozell, in his article "The World According to a Dog's Nose," writes: "Lurking behind those textured, damp nostrils are sensitive membranes that allow a dog to distinguish smells — molecules of odor that emanate from every living or once-living thing — at least one thousand times better than humans."

In *The Language of Smell*, Robert Burton tells us that while humans' sensitive membranes, or olfactory receptors, are the size of a postage stamp, dogs' membranes "can be the size of a handkerchief."

Dogs sniff our luggage at airports looking for drugs. They protect our cities scenting for bombs. Of all dogs' wonderful senses, smell is the most powerful by far. It is therefore one of the most powerful resources to control.

Dogs love to use their sense of smell. In fact, they are genetic computers in sorting smells. In other words, they can't help themselves. But in the wild, if five different pack members are following five different scents, then the pack is drawn in at least five different directions. This is why only one member of the pack decides which scents to follow. That pack member, as you might have guessed, is the pack leader.

Once you control this sense, you possess the keys to your dog's heart, mind, body, and soul. Your dog was born to sniff, created to both want and need to analyze the world around him with his nose. And you'll permit him to do so...on your terms. We must always be fair to the nature of the dog. We do not suggest that you keep your dog from sniffing the air, ground, other dogs, or people—in the same way you wouldn't prohibit your children from running, playing, or investigating their world. But it should be up to us to determine when a child is to focus on schoolwork and when he may blow off steam on the playground.

You can do the same for your dog. Start during your leashed walks. Set a rule that you are the one who decides when it's okay to stop for a sniff. Many people complain that their dog constantly becomes distracted by smells, stopping at literally every tree or lamppost. This is a natural desire, of course (Marc calls it reading their peemail), but by deferring to your dog, you're ceding your power over him. Did you slow down or pause so he could partake of the smell, or did your dog just stop dead and yank you to the tree? We've seen little rat terriers stop three-hundred-pound men in their tracks because a smell caught their attention.

Sniffing interesting smells on a walk is part of being a dog, but smells are also a privilege given by the pack leader. Have your dog concentrate on the walk by not letting him sniff during the first few minutes. Then, when he's walking attentively, allow him the occasional opportunity to sniff. The point is, walking your dog means just that: You are walking the dog, not the other way around. Should your dog have to relieve himself, by all means give him the opportunity. But if he fiddles around, take charge by resuming the walk. One of the biggest complaints we get as trainers is that the dog takes too much time to relieve himself. Well, if you let the dog sniff at everything before he decides where to go, the dog figures he might as well take his time. Watch your dog. He always thinks the next place is the best place. That's part of what makes dogs great: their unbounded enthusiasm. The truth is, however, there is really not a whole lot of difference between pee places! So, please, take charge. In the very short run, your dog will not only get it and adhere to your wishes but also realize it's easier on him. He doesn't have to keep all that urine in reserve while he searches for the perfect spot that never comes.

Why is this important? Why should you deny your dog the pleasure of sniffing every leaf and every bush and every tree and every pole on your walks? It's not really about denial; it's about providing. If your dog takes the liberty to sniff everything, then you really haven't given the dog anything, have you? You've just thrown him in the candy store, where he can have any and all of it if he wants and he doesn't even have to say please.

Now, there are plenty of times when your dog should be allowed to sniff to his heart's content. That's what a walk in the park, a romp in the woods, or a turn out in the backyard is for. Your dog should be given those pleasures frequently. But not on the morning and evening walk. Think of those times more like an exercise mission, both mental and physical. Get your business done and then power walk to the best of your ability. If your dog has done a good job of it, when you get to that one bush you know he loves more than all others, by all means stop and let him have a moment. See? Now you've given him a gift, and he'll know it came from you.

Attitude

Dogs can tell from your body posture, pace, and leash handling whether you are determined to migrate purposefully through your territory or if you are indecisive and lacking willpower. Pack leaders never lack willpower. They always exhibit determination.

When walking, find your 'tude, your inner wolf, the "great champion" spoken of by Rick McIntyre. Hold your body upright, with your shoulders back and your chest out. Walk proudly, looking ahead in the direction you have chosen. You are in charge of the pace, and the best speed is one that requires your dog to trot. Normally that is a fast-paced walk for a human — it will be good exercise for both of you! The key is for you to be the pack leader with a defined agenda. Your dog must realize that you are on a mission, just as the wolf pack leader selects a quick trot during the hunt for prey, which is serious business with no time for foolishness such as random sniffing. Dogs love to walk at this pace — they think they're headed someplace special.

One of the things we continually emphasize with our clients is the pace of their walk. Too often, clients project tentativeness and indecision by walking slowly. The dog reads this immediately and often begins to forge ahead and control the pace of the walk.

A good pack leader stands upright and walks forward quickly and with purpose, looking not at her dog but in the direction she has chosen for the walk.

If you've ever spent any time in New York City, then you already know how to walk like a pack leader. People in Manhattan pour out of the subway and off buses with a focused determination. They achieve this attitude by walking at a brisk pace, their eyes set with a great certainty of purpose.

Try to emulate this position of strength and power when you walk your dog. This will keep your dog at a trot, and he simply won't have time to sniff the ground. The air contains plenty of scent, and you cannot take it away from your dog, but you can keep him moving so he doesn't have time to concentrate on it. A simple exercise we often advise in conjunction with a quicker pace is making a series of quick turns (either 90 or 180 degrees), which makes the dog focus its attention on the owner. This helps counteract the owner's initial lack of confidence and enables the owner to experience a new feeling of leadership.

Your ability to take your dog on a focused leash walk in the real world—which means your dog walks calmly next to you in spite of all distractions, with the leash having a bit of slack (this excludes, by the way, all retractable leashes)—can have perhaps the biggest impact on her overall behavior. Does this mean you always and forever have to march with your dog as though you're a drill instructor? No, but when your dog realizes who's in charge of the walk—and of what she smells along the way—then walks can become a leisurely and enjoyable stroll for both of you.

Again, controlling resources like space, scent, and activity serves the relationship you have with your dog. It doesn't make you unlikable in your dog's eyes. Your dog will not resent you. Rather, you're elevating your importance to the dog by establishing yourself as the provider of all things good.

10

The Good Pack Leader: Emotion

Dogs are creatures of the heart. Their emotions are plainly before us, as if their bodies were transparent. Is it any wonder that we treasure our connection with them?
— Bless the Dogs

Allow us, if you will, to share a little history of humankind's relationship with dogs.

There was a time when only the privileged few kept dogs as pets. We can see from hieroglyphics that as far back as ancient Egypt, members of the ruling class kept dogs for companionship. Ramses the Great (1303–1213 BC) is shown with his hunting dogs in wall paintings in his tomb. The well-to-do of the ancient world were often buried with their dogs to help guide them in the afterlife. Along with their owners, these dogs were sometimes mummified.

In the year 1000 or so, the king of the gold-rich Ghana Empire in Africa kept dogs that wore gold and silver collars. In the Middle Ages, the rich held their pet dogs in the highest regard. There is the story of the Duke of Berry, who during the Hundred Years' War was so moved by the sight of a dog that would not leave his master's grave that he arranged a lifetime pension to keep the dog well fed and cared for.

During the Renaissance, noblewomen were sometimes painted with their lapdogs. In many parts of the world then, from Europe to China, the wealthy and royalty kept dogs for a variety of recreational purposes, such as hunting and racing.

Throughout most of human history, however, dogs were not kept as pets or for companionship but rather as working helpers, in some cases more capable and always far cheaper than people. Even before the time of Jesus, dogs herded and guarded sheep. Survival for everyone meant hard work. There was game to be hunted and retrieved; livestock to be herded and brought in; fish that had floated free from nets to be retrieved. Food was difficult to come by and required backbreaking labor. So if you were going to give food scraps to a dog, you wanted a return on your investment. In other words, if your dog wanted to be part of the family, it had to work. We won't tell you what happened to the dogs that wouldn't work, but believe us, it wasn't good.

The dogs that did show an aptitude for helping humans, however, became tremendously valuable assets. Those lucky dogs were fed, cared for, and encouraged to pass along their genes.

Then came the Industrial Revolution and a fundamental change in the relationship we all had with our dogs. As manufacturing sped the production of goods, a phenomenon called leisure time developed. Though there was, and still is, a set of working dogs—in farming and security, for instance—humans generally didn't have to depend on dogs to work as much as they had in the past. This trend continued throughout the late nineteenth and twentieth centuries until companionship became the primary role of our dogs.

Today, in a digital age in which people's connection to one another is often electronic, when aging baby boomers increasingly find themselves alone, and when marriage rates are historically low, the dog has stepped into the breach and has become for millions even more than a companion. Dogs have become our children, our crying towels, our significant others.

In the appropriate measure, there is nothing wrong with sharing emotions with your dog. In fact, our emotional connection with our dogs contributes to both our mental and our physical health. An American Heart Association panel found that keeping dogs as pets lowers the risk of heart disease. Dr. Thomas Lee, co-editor of the *Harvard Heart Letter*, writes, "People who have dogs live longer than people who have cats, and the assumption has been that dogs naturally cause their owners to be more active. The emotional benefits of having an affectionate creature are also one of the theories for why dog-lovers live longer." Dogs can allow us to feel connected to another living, breathing creature, one that doesn't get too busy to see us, that doesn't just send us the occasional text or email, and that really wants to be with us.

Yes, in the right proportion, and in concert with taking the pack leader role, our emotional relationship with our dogs can be a very good thing.

MARC   Paulina had a young adult male collie named Bailey. Bailey was big and beautiful, rambunctious and filled with much more energy than Paulina could handle. A retired nurse, Paulina was seventy, very overweight, and suffering from diabetes and symptoms of early heart disease.

Paulina and Bailey's relationship had a couple of problems, not the least of which was that Bailey would wait for Paulina to sit on her couch, then would go to the far end of the house, run at Paulina full speed, and hit her right in the chest with his front paws. He also wouldn't let Paulina groom him. All Paulina had to do was hold the brush, and Bailey would begin to growl at her.

It wasn't as if Paulina was a novice with dogs. "He's the fifth collie I've had in my life," Paulina told me. "All the other ones loved to be groomed. It was our special time, and I taught all of them to fetch me the brush. This one? He won't get the brush, and when I'm holding it, he growls if I try to touch him!"

The fuel that fed Bailey's "mischief engine" comprised two parts: First, Paulina was overly emotional with him. As a breed, collies can respond well to a lot of emotional attention. Paulina's other dogs had. But not all collies do, and Bailey didn't. The second reason Bailey acted as he did was a buildup of energy with limited opportunity to work it off. With her physical ailments and a shaky leash technique, Paulina was not able to walk Bailey. She had, however, spent his entire puppyhood coddling, stroking, and chatting with him. Long story short, though Bailey was strongly bonded to his owner, he thought she was a pushover.

After training Bailey, I sent him home with instructions for Paulina to touch and praise him only when he had done something good that she had requested. I also suggested that she begin to walk Bailey. "I can only walk twenty feet before I start struggling for breath," she said.

Twenty feet is a good start, I told her.

Paulina bought a cane that opened to a stool. She began walking Bailey in short increments at first, resting when her breathing became too heavy. Then a funny thing happened. Paulina started to gain stamina. Within a few months, her walks with Bailey were extended considerably. With the longer walks, Paulina's health improved. With a healthier heart, she was able to have a procedure that helped her reduce her weight dramatically. A year later, Paulina called me and asked if I'd watch Bailey for her — she was taking a cruise with her family. When I inquired about Bailey's progress, Paulina told me her relationship with him was as strong as any of the ones she'd had with her other collies.

"He gets me the brush," she told me.

Because Paulina placed Bailey's need for exercise and leadership over her own needs, Bailey no longer jumped on her to demand attention. Paulina took the leadership role in the relationship, and Bailey began to enjoy the bonding experience of grooming. Along with his owner, Bailey became healthier and happier thanks to the walks.

Paulina and Bailey's story is inspirational and exemplifies what a good relationship with our dogs can produce. Yet for every dog owner who has seen the light like Paulina, there are far too many others who engage their dogs in an unhealthy emotional relationship.

Emotion as a Resource

Although some might call it anthropomorphism, we are not afraid to assert that both people and dogs are emotional creatures. Increasingly, scientific evidence backs up the concept that dogs experience emotions in ways similar to people's experience. Dr. Stanley Coren, a professor of psychology at the University of British Columbia, writes,

> We have now come to understand that dogs possess all of the same brain structures that produce emotions in humans. Dogs have the same hormones and undergo the same chemical changes that humans do during emotional states. Dogs even have the hormone oxytocin, which, in humans, is involved with

feeling love and affection for others. With the same neurology and chemistry that people have, it seems reasonable to suggest that dogs also have emotions that are similar to ours.*

It's no wonder we're so tempted to share our emotions with dogs. They not only respond in kind but also affect us in profoundly emotional ways.

This has good and bad aspects. Good because dogs enrich our lives, but bad because they are not equipped to handle the emotions we load onto them. Perhaps more than any of the other resources your dog covets, emotion should be given with the greatest of care. It is the caviar of resources, rich and satisfying. But, like caviar, it should be served in proper portions and only at the right moment. In fact, the emotional resource is so powerful that if your dog doesn't earn it, you are sending the message that you are not the pack leader who is to be respected, but rather a sibling to be played with.

Fortunately, you can have both emotional sharing and the required respect. You just have to take the lead. Control your emotions, dole out words, touches, and caring glances as rewards for jobs well done, and there will be many more well-done jobs coming from your dog. Most important, you're likely to see a lot less anxiety and disobedience.

The best way to show your dog you love her is by caring for her. Caring does not mean lavishing her with gifts and looks of love. Caring is seeing to her well-being, providing for her, and keeping her healthy and safe. Caring for your dog means giving her the resources she covets in moderation. It means educating her in manners that will keep her healthy and safe.

Here's our promise: If you share your emotions with your dog only in the appropriate moments and proportions, you will have a healthy emotional relationship with him. Period.

Still, it's important to remember that dogs and humans belong to different species. Although there is little doubt that dogs can love, they do

---

* Stanley Coren, PhD, FRSC, "Which Emotions Do Dogs Actually Experience?," *Psychology Today,* March 14, 2013, https://www.psychologytoday.com/blog/canine-corner/201303/which-emotions-do-dogs-actually-experience.

Sharing your emotions is natural when you feel love. Share the love calmly when your dog is in a relaxed state of mind, and you'll get more calm behavior.

not exercise that prized emotion the same way we do. A dog can love us only in the way in which he is equipped. To fully respect who dogs are, and what they need to be happy, we must understand this: Dogs are not human. Their needs are different from ours. Humans tend to express love with touch and words. So we pet our dogs constantly and talk to them throughout the day. Yet if you watch dogs that are relaxed and bonded with each other, you'll certainly see that they sometimes touch each other, and might even wrestle and vocalize some. But their play is more likely to resemble mock combat, during which they're actually working out who is stronger and who is more committed. What bonded dogs will do even more than wrestle and vocalize is spend significant time fully experiencing togetherness. They're not watching TV or reading texts. They're not fussing with each other. They are simply lying in close proximity, maybe even together, and are being together in a way from which we humans really can learn. There is an art to togetherness, and dogs are good at it. This is a high form of love: being close and needing no other distraction or entertainment as a diversion.

Sometimes dog play resembles mock combat, but much of the time bonded dogs stay close together without a lot of touching and pestering. We can learn from their example.

Yet dog owners too often fall into the trap of making dogs their emotional equals and projecting human feelings onto them. This becomes especially alarming as the size of contemporary households shrinks. Dogs are commonly used to fill a human void: the empty nest, a single lifestyle, or the departure or death of a significant other. Too many owners consign the role of child, lover, or even therapist to their dogs.

According to a recent Purina survey, 61 percent of American women tell their dog about their problems and 31 percent feel their dog is a better listener than their partner. Fourteen percent of men say they receive more affection from their dog than from their loved ones. Twenty-four percent of men use their dog to talk to a good-looking stranger in the park.

So what's the harm? Well, the harm is that none of the human behavior described above has anything to do with the dog. On the human's part, it is solely self-serving and, worse, often misinterpreted by the dog. Though dogs are keenly aware of emotional changes in their owners, they do not have the ability to fully comprehend why the changes are happening. Mostly they are disturbed in some way by the changes in emotional weather. Mind you, it's natural to feel and express emotion in the presence of your dog. And your dog can almost certainly tolerate that, and even offer you comfort. We've all had dogs that have come close and leaned on us as if to offer a literal shoulder to cry on. And that's okay, but we still must remember that just as the dog offers us her shoulder, we absolutely must give her what she needs to be happy as well. If we take comfort without giving a structured life complete with work, rest, and play, it's simply not fair to the dog.

Anthropomorphizing

However well-intentioned, humanizing a dog can quickly become a primary cause of bad dog behavior.

MARC   We had a client who owned a German pinscher named Sadie. A small- to medium-sized dog, with breeding lines that include Doberman and standard schnauzer, the German pinscher is sleek, shiny, and stream-lined, according to the American Kennel Club. These dogs are very intelligent, have a high degree of energy, and have a strong drive to work and be useful — they were first bred in Germany in the mid-1800s for farm work. Our client was far from a farmer. In fact, she took to painting Sadie's toe-nails, carrying her in her arms like a baby, and indulging Sadie's every whim, especially with human food. On the other hand, the owner rarely walked the dog, because Sadie would attack anyone within leash distance. She had brought Sadie to us because the dog had recently bitten someone who was visiting her home. The bite had drawn blood, and the owner was worried that Sadie might be taken from her.

In working with Sadie, it quickly became evident that the dog had not been allowed to learn even the most basic skills of how to be a dog. She was uncomfortable just walking on the ground, let alone at the end of a leash. She wasn't used to wearing a collar. The least little doglike activity put her into an emotional shutdown, freezing her in fear.

Our course of action was, first, to have Sadie socialize with our trained dogs. Initially, Sadie would run from the sight of other dogs and hide under a table. As the days went by, however, she became curious as she watched the other dogs at play. Slowly, Sadie began to interact. At the end of ten days, she finally began to spend significant time within the pack. When she was sur-rounded by normal dog behavior, Sadie's layers of anxiety began to fall away. We also started setting rules for her that were fair and clear: Don't bolt out the door ahead of us, don't bark at strangers, and so forth. Soon we taught her leash manners, and not too long after that, Sadie began to exhibit the characteristics of a normal, happy pet. Dogs want to normalize, and given the chance and guidance, they will.

BROTHER CHRISTOPHER I recall a couple who brought an out-of-control Cavalier King Charles spaniel named Princess for training. The owners doted on this dog, taking her for walks in a baby stroller, dressing her up in a wide variety of outfits, and bestowing a well-intentioned but suffocating amount of emotional attention upon her. Then the wife became pregnant. When the owners began treating their pet as the family dog, Princess would have none of it. She was wholly unresponsive to their attempts at training and pleas for obedience.

It doesn't take a lot of imagination to guess how we approached Princess's rehabilitation. We provided a very structured and balanced program of obedience training and integration into the pack to allow her dogness to blossom, and she responded beautifully to our program. Princess's owners also gained a new appreciation of her reality as a dog and delighted in her calm and balanced behavior.

We realize, as a practical matter, that it's very difficult to temper the emotional feelings we have for our dogs. We love our dogs. They're part of our families and, for many of us, our only close companion. But emotion is a very powerful energy. Too much emotion is hard enough for humans to process in a healthy way. For a dog it's nearly impossible.

It is not that anthropomorphizing always results in canine aggression. It doesn't necessarily. But it can bring forth a host of other problems, such as separation anxiety, excessive barking, and destructive chewing. Even if the dog's behavior is fine, what does trying to recast her as a human being say about our attitude toward the dog? Instead of honoring the dog for what she is—a dog with her own highly refined, dignified, canine nature—we parade her around as some type of shield against our shortcomings or insecurities. This is not only a gross disservice to our dog but also foolish and sad. A dog can certainly fill a void in anyone's life. But dressing the dog up in human clothing, having her eat at the dinner table, throwing birthday parties for her? All that does is deny you the greatest gift your dog can give: the beauty, grace, and dignity of being a dog.

The Spirituality of Silence

BROTHER CHRISTOPHER   Many of us live in urban settings where ambient noise is a constant. We're subjected to a cacophony of car horns, sirens, construction noise, and disconnected voices. There's probably not a real moment of silence in the city, even late at night. Add to that the omnipresent technological explosion — cell phones, iPads, headphones, etc. — which allows us to be in unending communication with one another and with other stimuli. It's not unusual at all to go to a restaurant and see people sitting together but texting on the phone to other people. When we get home, the first thing we do is turn on the television or stream a movie, filling every last space with sound. We're immersed, perhaps encased, in noise. As a society we are not only familiar with the noise surrounding us, we're comforted by it. It has become our security blanket.

The monks know this well because of how disconcerting the absence of sound is to people who come to the monastery for retreat. It takes our visitors time to get used to the silence, or near silence, of our setting. Why is silence off-putting at first? Because it forces people to keep company with themselves. The thoughts that pass through the human consciousness in everyday life are usually lost to the distractions of the surrounding noise. Take those distractions away, and you're left with just the thoughts, some of which are uncomfortable to contemplate.

Even in conversation you see this. How many times have you rushed to fill an uncomfortable silence, a pregnant pause? Often, we at the monastery are called upon to offer spiritual direction. During these conversations, some of which occur at times of struggle or pain in someone's life, even the briefest silence can become uncomfortable to the people to whom we minister. It is very hard for them to be still for even a minute or two. The instinct is to fill the silence with more thoughts and words. But we believe that words lose value in numbers — the more you use them, the less meaningful they become. Words can dilute our presence, both mentally and spiritually. In a more corporeal sense, what happens is that the words become mindless chatter, and people pay less attention to them and take them less seriously.

Same goes with our dogs.

Most people would consider talking to their dogs as the most valuable way to communicate with them. In fact, much of the communication between owner and dog is almost entirely verbal on the conscious level.

Dogs, however, don't speak English. Nor do they understand Italian, French, Farsi, or any other human language. Yes, studies* have concluded that dogs can learn upwards of 165 words, or what a two-year-old human can comprehend. But unlike the two-year-old human's intelligence, the dog's intelligence has peaked at that level. For most healthy two-year-olds, their intelligence is a platform on which their comprehension will continue to

---

* http://www.sciencedaily.com/releases/2009/08/090810025241.htm

expand. So, yes, some dogs are incredibly cogent with language, but language does not have the same depth and resonance with dogs as it does with humans. To dogs, words are merely sounds that represent actions. In fact, independent of our body language, intonation, and the emotional energy with which we infuse our conversations, it's doubtful your dog would know many of those 165 words.

Although they may be lacking in spoken language skills, dogs, as we've mentioned, are positively adept at interpreting our feelings. How many times has your dog instinctually responded to you during times of emotional upheaval, and done so without your trying to solicit his attention? Dogs are particularly skilled at reading our emotional temperature. In other words, sometimes dogs relate to us better without words.

It makes sense, then, to try to improve your nonverbal communication with your dog. One powerful way to sharpen your skills is through a kind of fast. We call it the Twenty-Four-Hour Vow of Silence Challenge. The goal of this challenge is twofold. One, you'll learn that your dog listens to you more

There can be great power and reward in nonverbal communication with your dog. If you speak less, your dog will listen more. California trainer Jen Freilich shares a quiet moment with Han Solo.

and watches you more closely when you're quieter. Two, your dog will learn that what you say in the future is probably important.

Twenty-Four-Hour Vow of Silence

Here are some points to bear in mind as you consider taking the challenge:

- Your dog might not miss the words as much as you will.
- Your dog speaks in body language, so try using gestures to communicate what you want.
- If you want your dog to come to you, try bending down slightly and holding out your arms in a welcoming manner. Most dogs will read that as an invitation to receive affection and thus respond. (You can also hold out your hand with a treat in it to make your dog even more motivated to come promptly.)
- Raise a treat in the air, just over your dog's nose, as a signal for sit. Then lower and give the treat as soon as your dog sits.
- Just for today, keep a leash on your dog and let it drag behind him while you're together. Since your dog will be used to receiving verbal commands from you, he may test limits in any number of ways until he starts paying close attention to your body. For example, should your dog hop up on the couch or bed, simply pick the leash up to remove him instead of verbally scolding him for forbidden behavior.
- You don't have to avoid speaking to people, just to your dog.
- Remember, the challenge will be over in twenty-four hours, and you can go back to speaking to your dog...when it's important.
- Don't worry if it seems hard. Habits are hard to break...even for twenty-four hours.
- If you speak less, your dog will listen more.

Some may find this challenge very hard, but the results can be dramatic. Believe us, we know a little about the importance of quiet.

Techniques like the Twenty-Four-Hour Vow of Silence can be used to deepen your connection and communication with your dog, not only on a temporal level but also in a spiritual way. The vow of silence helps you avoid throwing out arbitrary commands and verbiage, and allows you to be present and focused and truly in tune with your dog's needs. If you are really tending to your dog, the relationship will grow in ways that you wouldn't necessarily have thought possible.

Humans are sensual beings, yet we often tunnel our communicative ability into words and in doing so shortchange our other God-given talents. Conversely, when we shut down our verbal communication, it enhances our nonverbal skills — similar to the way the other four senses of a blind person are sharpened. To be self-aware is crucial in a successful relationship with your dog.

Emotional Training

In today's caffeine-fueled, not-enough-hours-in-the-day world, some people leave dogs by themselves for long stretches of time. When the owner finally returns home, she's so excited to see the dog, or feels so guilty about having been away from him, she greets him in endearing terms often delivered in a falsetto voice. She scratches, pets, and even picks the dog up and kisses him. Although the dog might appreciate the attention, he really doesn't understand why there's so much excitement all of a sudden. Look at it from the dog's point of view: He's at home, probably sleeping, maybe dreaming of squirrels, then the door opens up and all hell breaks loose. Yes, the dog's delighted reaction to the owner reinforces her expectations. And, yes, the dog is probably happy the owner is home, but the happiness should be expressed by the dog and not in some artificial or aroused way. We at New Skete call this putting the dog in emotional Disneyland. When the owner then takes the dog out for a walk, he is likely to be unfocused and unresponsive, and at worst he will begin to behave badly. Is there any wonder why?

On the other hand, say you come home from a difficult day. You throw your briefcase on the couch or kick your shoes across the room as you remove them. Your dog might run up to greet you, and maybe you'll say, "Will you just stop it?" or "Calm down!" What happens then is a vicious cycle: The owner is agitated, which agitates or frightens the dog. The dog becomes confused and might react in a number of ways, none of which is helpful, only agitating the owner more. On the tail end of it, so to speak, the owner may feel guilty and try to verbally apologize in a tone that further confuses the dog.

Many dogs owned by people who constantly talk to them just tune their owners out. You might think your dog understands you, but all the dog is hearing is *wah wah wahhh wahhh wah*, like Charlie Brown's teacher. Our words fade into the background like static. The owner then complains to us that his dog just doesn't listen.

Here's a suggestion that might alleviate the problem: Instead of making a fuss over your dog when you come home, or taking your frustration out on him, try to be calm each time you enter the house (this might contribute to your well-being, too). If you want to greet your dog, make sure the greeting is subdued: no high-pitched squeals or baby talk. You'll sometimes even want to delay the greeting for a few moments if you have a dog that is easily excitable. If you have an anxious dog, you might want to quietly get the leash, leash the dog, and then bring him into a sit. Instead of saying anything to the dog, just gently pet him and make eye contact. (We'll elaborate on the importance of eye contact below.) By entering the house with minimal drama, you've not only taken the edge off the dog's excitability but also given yourself a chance to be present and focused rather than throwing at the dog the collective noise of the day.

The Look of Love

It has been written that the eyes are the lamp of the soul, and this is true in dogs as well as humans. Consider how your dog's eyes speak to you if you only listen. From joy to fear to curiosity, mischief, and boredom — your dog's eyes reflect a broad range of inner emotion. How often have you looked into his eyes and wondered what he's thinking?

When you see softness in the eyes of your dog, it ignites a connection in your body chemistry but also deep in your soul.

Searching your dog's eyes for hints of his thought process is a pleasurable exercise, and in more ways than one. According to a recent study published in *Scientific American*, a leading journal of original scientific research, the simple act of gazing into your dog's eyes (or your dog gazing into yours) releases a chemical in the human body called oxytocin. The body's production of oxytocin — also known as the "cuddle hormone" — causes a physiological effect similar to what a mother feels toward her infant. Other interactions with your dog, like petting, playing, or even talking to him, can release additional bonding neurochemicals such as dopamine and endorphins.*

This connection, one that we'd like to think begins both in our chemistry and in our souls, might be the only connection of its kind between humans and another member of the animal kingdom. In us, the light in our dog's eyes can bring the warmth of childhood and the love a parent feels toward a child. Without a doubt, this emotional

* http://www.scientificamerican.com/article/is-the-gaze-from-those-big-puppy-eyes-the-look-of-your-doggie-s-love/

cause and reflect, so to speak, is what makes the relationship between dog and man singular.

Like any love affair, however, this intense emotional bond can also be the cause of a great deal of heartache — ask any owner who has outlived his dog. Many of us have gone through the searing pain of putting a canine friend down. We look into our dog's eyes one last time and are struck with a grief that rivals the loss of a human loved one.

In life, though, being aware of eye contact with your dog is a sure way to control emotion. Humans make eye contact reflexively, without thinking about it. It's notable primarily in its absence. We take a certain measure of eye contact as a sign of respect and interest in the other person. You would find it disquieting to talk to someone who doesn't look you in the eye. Imagine sitting at a table across from a person who only occasionally makes eye contact with you. Chances are you would think that person was odd or didn't like you. Now think about a person who stares at you constantly. Might make you a little self-conscious, no? In normal human interactions, people look at each other's faces, look at the other person's mouth as she speaks, frequently make eye contact, and then glance away.

To really feel the power of eye contact, try a simple two-part experiment. Have a conversation with a friend in which you do not look into your friend's eyes at all. You might find that it's difficult, but try your hardest and then note your friend's reaction. She will no doubt detect that something is off. In fact, she is likely to think something is wrong. Maybe she will ask you about this immediately. Maybe not. Either way, let her in on the experiment afterward and discuss.

Now try the opposite with someone else. Have a conversation and do not break eye contact. Blink as normal, but remain focused on your friend's eyes without glancing away. See what happens. Chances are your friend will try to break eye contact with you a couple of times. He might feel uncomfortable or challenged. This part of the experiment will likely end with your friend asking, "Why are you staring at me?"

For humans, the matter of eye contact involves many subtle cues that we use instinctually (though some of these cues are influenced by our culture).

The ocular connection we have with dogs, however, is a bit more complicated because it travels across species. Dogs most certainly do not eyeball one another to the same degree people do. In fact, sustained direct eye contact between two dogs most often means only one of two things is about to happen: hard play or a fight.

Mother told us it is impolite to stare, but when it comes to our dogs, we just can't seem to help ourselves. And sometimes dogs can't help themselves, either. They see you staring at them, and optimistically, they take it as an invitation to play. If you're staring into your dog's eyes while you're seated, he'll probably wind up in your lap. If you're standing, he might jump on you. Either way, this probably wasn't what you had in mind. Very few people look into their dog's eyes thinking, *Gee, I wish you'd jump and scratch me right now.*

There is a difference between the eye contact we want and spoke about earlier and staring. Eye contact is a glance from your dog to you, as if to say, "Do you need anything, boss?" But heavily sustained direct eye contact—what our mother admonished us not to do—carries a lot of emotional weight when delivered from person to dog. Your dog will have a reaction, and it might not be a nice one. Does this necessarily mean that sustained eye contact is bad or wrong? Not at all. As we've mentioned, when you're feeding your dog, it's always a good idea for the dog to focus on you rather than on the bowl or treat. If you're just gazing at your dog, he might not construe it the wrong way. But other dogs might, so it is important to help them gradually get used to it and understand your meaning. Start with shorter instances of eye contact accompanied by an affectionate word or touch, and then calmly look away. As your dog gets accustomed to this, gradually increase the length of time you gaze. Be aware that what you're saying with your eyes may very well mean one thing to you (I love you) and a very different thing to your dog (he's inviting me to jump on him right now), so start slowly and be patient. Glancing at your dog says, "Hi, what are you up to?" but staring can say, "It's on." Many people don't realize this.

At its best, eye contact is your dog's way of asking, "Do you need anything from me?" Teach extended eye contact slowly and purposefully, as Mary Mazzeri has done with Mia.

Marc   Recently, I had a client with a Lab named Holly. Holly had the usual set of behavior difficulties: pulling on the leash, coming when called only selectively, and jumping on people. Holly responded very nicely to training, and when the client came to pick Holly up, the dog's new manner both pleased and impressed him. They took a long leash walk around my farm, and Holly neither strained nor pulled. After the walk, I instructed the client to have Holly sit and to pet her without saying anything, which he did. All good so far, right? Then the client squatted in front of Holly and stared her right in the eye as if to say, "I'm so proud of you." Holly leapt at him with both paws and knocked him on his rear. "Well," the client said, dusting himself off, "I guess you weren't able to stop her from doing this."

I asked the client to have Holly sit and pet her again, but this time kneeling down and without the stare. Holly sat there as nice as can be.

*   *   *

It's especially important to remain aware of your lingering gaze when you encounter a new dog. Your urge to stare into a dog's eyes is understandable. You love dogs and want to engage. But put yourself in the dog's place for a moment: A perfect stranger walks right up to you, stares you in the eye, and then begins talking in a high-pitched voice telling you how cute you are. Weird, right? Threatening, perhaps? It might actually cause you to react in a not-so-nice way. Well, that's pretty much how the dog experiences it.

For most of this chapter, we've been discussing the emotions that travel from you to your dog. The relationship with your canine, however, is a two-way street. Dogs experience and emit all kinds of emotions, from jealousy to grief to unbridled joy and even laughter.

It was Konrad Lorenz in *Man Meets Dog* who perhaps first articulated in print the idea that dogs laugh: "An invitation to play always follows; here the slightly opened jaws which reveal the tongue, and

What dog lover would doubt that dogs get excited to play, sometimes "smile," and become so excited they start panting? Nobel Prize–winner Konrad Lorenz was convinced.

the tilted angle of the mouth which stretches almost from ear to ear give a still stronger impression of laughing. This 'laughing' is most often seen in dogs playing with an adored master and which become so excited that they soon start panting."* Lorenz would quantify the idea a bit later in the text: "Perhaps these facial movements are preliminary signs of the panting which sets in as the playing mood gains ascendancy" — but he seems to hope his theory is correct.

A half century later, the animal behaviorist Patricia Simonet recorded dogs at play in dog parks and discovered a panting sound that was of a different frequency than regular dog panting. When she imitated the sound back to dogs, it seemed to have a pleasing effect on them.

We have no doubt that dogs like to laugh and we encourage dog owners to laugh right along with them.

Without question, dogs can be medicine for our souls. Perhaps the greatest gift they give us is the opportunity to forget about the unproductive introspection in which we all too often engage. They draw us out of ourselves. Although the urge to load them with our own emotional baggage is understandable, it is patently unfair to the dogs because it disregards their reality. We can do justice to a relationship with a dog only when we honor it as it is.

Treat your dog like a dog. The mystery of that interaction alone will keep you too busy to think about yourself.

---

* Konrad Lorenz, *Man Meets Dog* (London: Methuen & Co., 1954), p. 58.

Work, Rest, and Play: How to Structure the Relationship with Your Dog

More than anything else, dogs are creatures of play, whose spontaneous interaction with life bespeaks its goodness. — Bless the Dogs

So what does a dog need other than a pack leader who dispenses certain resources and does so in a deliberate manner? In a word: structure.

"Ah, but you're taking all the fun out of the relationship," we can hear you say. True, the word *structure* connotes rigidity and scheduling, but from rigor and order, spontaneity and creativity are born.

To understand what we mean about structure, allow us a high school analogy. During our high school years, we knew exactly what time we had to wake up each weekday. Most of us knew what time we were leaving for school and how we were getting there. The day was formally divided into segments so precise that a bell marked the beginning and end of each period. We ate lunch at virtually the same time every day.

Much of the day may have seemed like drudgery, but if we listened, we learned. We also found time to have some fun, maybe in gym class or with friends at the lunch table. For others, fun was in the library or the Science Club. Still others couldn't wait for the final bell to ring so that their fun could begin.

On some level, your relationship with your dog can be compared to high school. It's a time when the dog learns the basic structure of his life: when he must be in class, when he eats, and when it's time to play. This is not drudgery for your dog. He craves a regular schedule in the same way that we sometimes pine for it—what stressed-out adult hasn't yearned for those simpler days when the only decision we had to make was which pair of jeans to wear? Part of growing up is learning how to handle freedom and to create one's own structure, but dogs don't ever quite grow up (which, by the way, is probably one of their greatest charms), so in some sense they're in high school for their whole lives.

In our boarding school programs, both at the New Skete monastery and at Marc's Little Dog Farm, a regular schedule is foundational. The most important ingredient for a happy dog is a life that makes sense to him. For dogs, structure is easy to figure out.

BROTHER CHRISTOPHER   In Marc's dog behavior program and here at New Skete we have the same end in mind when it comes to our board-and-train environment: providing a structured, predictable routine that reinforces the dog's understanding of what we expect of him. That is the key.

Recently, we trained a German shepherd for a couple who had adopted him from a friend when the dog was thirteen months old. Boris was now sixteen months old, and the owners were having all sorts of problems with him, both physical and behavioral. The previous owner made Boris live in his crate — spending more than twelve hours a day there — and because of her busy social schedule, she had spent very little time with the dog when she wasn't working. This was neglectful, and the less social contact Boris had with his owner, the wilder he became, trying to extract attention from her by heavy mouthing and nipping, jumping up, excessive barking, stealing, and being destructive. You name it, Boris was into it. He couldn't look at himself in a mirror without getting excited at the prospect of some social contact. He was hyperactive and uncontrollable whenever loose in the house. So the owner crated Boris more frequently and began to distance herself from him even further. It became a vicious circle. Boris was starved for attention, received minimal exercise, had little or no interaction with other dogs or people, and could never gain enough weight to look healthy. When the owner tried to take Boris in public he would growl, bark, and pull. Finally, the owner decided to rid herself of the problem by rehoming Boris.

Enter our clients. The new owners, while well-intentioned and aware of Boris's history of neglect, were not experienced dog handlers. They tried their best. They provided him with the best food, dropped him at doggy day care for socialization several times a week, and tried private training — which didn't work out. We were their last resort.

Here's what we did: We created a basic foundation of structure. We took Boris out for regular walks and potty breaks. We fed him at specific times. Then we instituted some fundamental obedience exercises. We also taught Boris a reliable retrieve that the owners could practice in their backyard for additional exercise. We had a blood panel done on Boris that revealed borderline but treatable pancreatic insufficiency, which helped to explain his difficulty in maintaining weight. In a span of a couple of weeks, Boris made significant progress and was well on his way to becoming the dog his new owners hoped he'd be when they adopted him. What was so apparent in this particular case was the resilience this dog demonstrated. For thirteen months, Boris had been subjected to about as much deprivation as imaginable — a total misuse of the crate and a pathetic lack of socialization and care provided by his original owner — and serious behavioral problems were the clear result. Yet when the basic needs of the dog were met in a structured, programmed way, he began to blossom, and to heal.

In our outtake interview, we offered the new owners some suggestions. Our advice was to include Boris in their lives as much as possible. In addition to daily walks and practice of the obedience exercises, for the first two weeks he should be tethered, kept on a leash at all times when he was with either owner. We advised them that Boris should sleep in their bedroom, on the floor. That he should go for drives in the car with them.

What we offered Boris's owners was a program in which they could meet his natural needs by being conscientious, responsible, and truly invested in the role of pack leader.

MARC   Here, step by step, is how we structure our dogs' lives at my Little Dog Farm.

The day begins every morning when we ask a dog politely to come out of his kennel. If the dog begins to get overexcited as we're opening the kennel

Dogs are eager to start the day's activities just like we are. An adventure that begins with a moment of calm politeness is much less likely to result in a wild dog. We ask dogs to sit before we open the kennel door. (*continued on next page*)

We attach the leash and calmly exit to start our walk under control. Try this at home when taking your dog out of the crate, or even out of the house for a walk.

door, we pause and wait until his excitement passes. Dogs, as you may already know, are usually in a hurry to get out of the house. But we don't want a dog lunging through the kennel door, knocking into us in the process, first thing in the morning. Allowing a dog to do this sets an overexcited or even anxious frame of mind for the rest of the day. The dogs in our care learn, within a matter of only a few days, that when we open the kennel or crate door, they should wait quietly for permission to exit, which we quickly grant. A dog that tries to lunge out will find us unceremoniously closing the door. Even wild and overexcited dogs quickly learn to calm themselves. And that is a critical skill for every dog to learn.

The manner in which you start an adventure is usually how you'll finish it. So if the dog's day begins in an anxious or impolite way, the dog is likely to carry the anxiety or pushiness throughout the day. Conversely, a calm start sets a very important tone.

Here's how the rest of the day unfolds:

We open the door to the kennel, keeping our body in the opening so the dog can't scoot by, and then leash the dog right away. We then walk to the exit door with the dog by our side rather than lunging ahead. We might need to make one or two abrupt about-face turns to show the dog that progress happens when he follows our lead and remains in step. The no pulling rule must be obeyed. After a few days in the program, most dogs usually catch on and happily comply. Here again, dogs enjoy structure.

At the door, we ask the dog to sit. Though this skill has already been taught, to assist or remind the dog, we might apply light but steady upward pressure on the leash, but only when necessary. A dog's head must be raised for his rear to sit on the floor. The upward pressure on the leash is relaxed the instant the dog is seated.

We manage the leash in our left hand and reach for the door with our right. The dog remains seated outside of the door's arc so he won't have to get up when the door swings open. As we open the door, newer dogs will start to get up from the sit, so we merely reapply the light upward leash pressure to ask for the sit again. We ask that the dog remain seated until the door is open and we give the verbal signal "Let's go" to let the dog know that the sit is over now and we're moving out.

We walk to the potty area and ask for reasonable leash etiquette on the short trip, even though we know most dogs will want to get there quickly and eliminate. After potty we walk back to the kennel, the dog sits at the door, and then we put the dog back in his crate until all the dogs have been taken out. Then we feed breakfast, and that makes everyone happy. But if a dog is leaping and barking for his food as we approach his kennel, we pause before opening the kennel door until he stops the behavior (and they always do). That's when we open the door and put down the food.

After breakfast, we give the dogs an hour or so of quiet time to digest.

Then it's time for a more significant walk, during which we practice a variety of training exercises such as heel, sit, come, and stay. You can learn all about those in *How to Be Your Dog's Best Friend*. But the "come out of the kennel nicely" and "sit at the door" components that precede the walk remain constant.

After the walk, we have a structured play session. The toys your dog plays with inadvertently teach him a lesson. They can teach lessons that you'd like him to learn or ones you'd rather he not learn.

Dogs tend to start off thinking that all games are a free-for-all during which they can use their superior reflexes to beat us to the punch at every turn. Although we do want a dog to enjoy playing, we'd rather that the lesson he learns is that cooperative play is the most fun. All games are more enjoyable when others are playing with you. Your dog may not know this at first, so it's your job to teach him that all good games have rules. The majority of dogs enjoy a game of fetch. But owners sometimes complain that their dog won't bring back or let go of the toy. Although there are many ways to remedy this problem, one of the easiest is to put a long leash on your dog, say twenty feet, and throw the toy fifteen feet out. Once your dog picks up the toy, pull a hidden squeaky toy out of your pocket to entice your dog back. He'll probably come right back with toy number one and trade it for toy number two.

After playtime, it's back to the kennel for a nap or to chew on a bone.

Late in the afternoon, we repeat the walk and the training period, have a bit of fun, and then it's off to the kennel for dinner.

A quick evening walk finishes the day. Then we start over again in the morning.

BROTHER CHRISTOPHER   We're continually struck by how happy dogs appear to be after spending time in our board-and train program. The dogs have worked willingly and without protest. They have learned a clear set of guidelines and structure, and their owners marvel that the dogs seem calmer and more contented than when they arrived. What happened? Like their forebears, dogs are by nature highly social and inquisitive creatures that flourish when those natural characteristics are nurtured in a relationship with a human being.

Many people assume that the dogs resent the experience of a training program. Owners often wonder, *Will it break his spirit?* It's important to realize that dogs and humans have different emotional makeups. We need to be careful not to dump our human baggage onto the dog. Often our own personal experiences of leadership and authority have been negative, and so we assume that the dog feels the same way we do. That's not necessarily so. Dogs have and are entitled to their own worldview, according to their nature. Can their experiences with authority and leadership have been abusive or neglectful? Of course. However, the answer to negative experience is not to deprive dogs of the positive effect of compassionate and benevolent leadership.

Dog after dog, year after year, we see the same pattern repeating itself over and over and over again both at the monastery and at Marc's farm. Dogs come in with frantic energy levels and anxious behaviors such as whining, pacing, failure to relax, inability to nap, and frequent vocalization, and within a few days they settle down, relax, and are able to focus on their work.

One of the benefits of a good boarding school for dogs is the carefully crafted rhythm and routine of the day: work, rest, and play, all in an orderly, predictable fashion. Within this structure, dogs thrive. They have more fun than we had in high school.

We can almost hear you say, "Well, that's all fine and good for you. Dogs are your business. But what about us regular folk with real jobs and families to take care of?"

Your life need not revolve entirely around dogs. But you must integrate work, rest, and play into your relationship with your dog, and you can by establishing certain anchor points throughout the day and then making them routine. Obviously, the first will be a good morning walk. You can schedule time for play with your dog when it's most convenient for you—for example, during a late afternoon or early evening walk—but then you need to consistently keep to that schedule. Make sure you feed your dog at the same times every day.

Throughout your daily interaction with your dog, make sure he knows that he has to accomplish small tasks to receive praise, treats, or that squeaky toy he loves so much. What you're doing then is creating for your dog the same stability that we offer at our board-and-train program. You'll find that consistency is very comforting to your dog and is an important ingredient for an overall healthy relationship with him. In short, you can achieve all the same benefits of a board-and-train program right in your own home if you invest the requisite time and mental energy in your dog.

Scheduling for Busy People

The dog evolved alongside humans who kept hours according to the rise and fall of the sun, a human animal who lived in tight tribal communities, hunting and gathering with their canine assistants in tow. As agriculture developed, so too did the dog's ability to herd the goats and bring in the cows. Everyone still lived together closely, and lives were ruled by the travel of sun through sky.

Naturally, as time has moved forward, people are no longer bound by the same circadian rhythms as in the past. Humans are more productive than ever before, able to conduct work even while in bed, tapping on little slabs of glass and circuitry, smartphones that give access to the entire body of human knowledge and that allow talking with family members, texting with colleagues, and watching funny videos.

Today, life for many people is chaotic. New data suggests that Americans are working longer hours than ever before. Singles trying to get ahead in the competitive marketplace have limited options when it comes to spending time with their pets. Empty nesters are busy, still employed beyond retirement age. Many folks are managing more than one job, but even the workload those busy moonlighters carry pales beside the task of orchestrating all the moving parts of a growing family: getting kids off to school, to and from baseball, ballet, swimming lessons, etc. Many lead lives that resemble the Energizer Bunny: We keep going, and going, and going. Our dwindling free time to spend with our dogs has led to an increased number of dogs behaving badly or dogs that are just unhappy.

Leaving your dog unsupervised for long stretches, either locked up in a small apartment or chained out in a backyard, is at the very least unfair and, if done consistently, cruel. Even when the minimum nonnegotiables are covered — daily walks, healthy diet, and socialization — the dog may still become the last item on the checklist for some busy people. Dogs don't do well as afterthoughts — and they don't deserve to be treated as such.

Ask yourself these questions:

- Does my dog eat at more or less the same times every day?
- Do I walk my dog at least twice per day — ideally, mornings and evenings — for a minimum of twenty minutes each time (supplementing these walks with a midday dog walker if the dog is alone during the day)?
- Is someone home at regular intervals to play with and provide companionship for my dog?
- Is my dog provided with additional potty breaks?

These are the minimums. The bare minimums. If you can't provide at least that much attention to a dog, then we strongly suggest you think long and hard about getting one in the first place. As we covered earlier, however, there are steps even the busiest among us can take to make sure the dog is given the proper care and structure: Doggy day care, dog walkers, delegating responsibilities — these are some viable options to lessen part of the load.

Find the Dog for You

For busy people, the first order of business is to find a breed or a dog with exercise needs that fit their schedule.

Although now and again we meet a lazy Labrador or Irish setter, hunting and herding breeds usually have the energy level appropriate for the specific job for which they have been carefully bred for thousands of generations. Labradors, while very popular family dogs, and rightly so for their generally happy outlook on life, weren't bred to retrieve a duck or two and then take a nap. They were developed to

If you select a dog that is likely to have energy levels similar to yours, chances for an easy relationship improve. Daily outings are a must for all dogs, but some will need more exercise than others.

have the precise set of drives to do a hard job, and to do it happily for many hours at a time. The Labrador's work ethic, matched with an equally high energy level, allows it to be good at the job it was bred for but also means that it has a need to expend the energy that was bred into it.

Deprive such a dog of meaningful employment and you'll wind up with stolen food, chewed couches, pilfered laundry, or, quite possibly, a stiff case of anxiety.

So, if you're the type of person who puts in long days and weekends at work, avoid bringing home a high-energy breed.

But there are breeds that need less exercise — Cavalier King Charles spaniels or basset hounds, for example — and that are a bit better at tolerating a more modest exercise schedule. They need walks and to move as well, but if you do your research you'll find that some breeds are lazier than others. Ideally, no dog would be left alone in a house or apartment for more than four or five hours. But that's not an option for many families, so just as important as limiting the time the dog is alone is making sure the time the dog spends with the family is productive. For example, we know of a business executive who jogs every morning for four or five miles with her dog. Although the dog spends most of the rest of the day by himself, when the woman returns home she takes the dog for a long walk. The woman's routine is more than sufficient to satisfy her dog's energy needs. Even if you're not a runner, there are plenty of ways to provide the right amount of exercise for your dog. For instance, hiring a caring and professional dog walker or using a reputable doggy day care facility. Just remember, although your situation might dictate that you farm out some care for your dog, dog walkers and doggy day care are not a substitute for your role as the pack leader in your dog's life. So the time you spend with your dog should be constructive, active for active dogs, and in line with the pack structure.

Finally, don't pick a dog simply based on his looks. Siberian huskies are fine dogs, but they have the misfortune of being strikingly beautiful. We say "misfortune" because that amazing coat and those blue eyes are arrestingly attractive. Yet this is a breed meant to pull sleds for hours a day. Don't be surprised when yours eats the house if you're not leading an active lifestyle and incorporating your dog right into it.

WRP

WRP is not a radio station but our acronym for work, rest, and play — three elements that every dog needs to live a happy life. So let's talk a bit more about each element, and then let's talk about what humans need from their dogs that might not be included on this list.

Work is whatever you determine to be your dog's job at a given moment. Walking on a leash is a job if there are standards for the walk that you have decided must apply. If there are no standards — meaning the dog pulls, starts, stops, sniffs, barks, or lunges — then the walk is work only for you, not for your dog. A chaotic walk does not build or reinforce the correct mind-set in your dog. Instead it merely riles him up so that he comes home in a feisty mood rather than satisfyingly tired.

Now, we're not saying that doglike behaviors are never permitted. Far from it. There is a time and a place, mostly in the play segment, for high-excitement behaviors. But you should be in charge of picking those times and places in which your dog is allowed to let loose. Children, for example, can really benefit from running and yelling and playing. But you wouldn't want them to be doing it in a classroom. That is what the playground is for.

Even adults can enjoy a good roller coaster ride now and again. It really gets the heart pumping with a jolt of adrenaline. But you wouldn't want to live in a constantly adrenalized state.

That's what often happens to anxious dogs that aren't given a decent job to do here and there, a job with standards. Dogs need and want that work and want to be held accountable for turning in a reasonable performance. In addition to spending most of the past thirty thousand years as a working partner to man, dogs, as pack animals, are genetically suited to work. A pack is a work crew after all, with each member assiduously going about the job assigned to him for the benefit of the entire group.

Wisdom has it that dogs sleep between twelve and fourteen hours a day. That amount varies from breed to breed and with the age of the dog. Larger breeds such as Newfoundlands and St. Bernards can sleep up to eighteen hours. In any event, for most dogs, rest makes up the biggest part of their day. Rest allows for recuperation of spent resources and also creates a counterbalance to the adrenaline rush that is so often driving dog behavior. Adrenaline works productively for dogs when they are performing a structured job such as herding sheep. Yet even that job is composed of many moments of focus so the dog can interpret, execute, and achieve the shepherd's goals. A well-trained sheepdog, for example, alternates between adrenalized moments and moments where she will conserve energy, all the while staying focused on the constantly changing ebb and flow of the job. At its best, rest teaches a dog how to control his impulses long enough to reduce his own adrenaline and to recover lost energy. At its worst, rest isn't really peaceful. We might think the dog knows how to rest, so we take him for a walk, turn him loose back in the house, and then hop in the car to run errands.

We'll give you some tips on how to help your dog learn to relax after his exercise needs have been met. Tethering, crate training, and a "go to bed" command are all useful in accomplishing this.

Is the dog resting calmly? Some dogs do well on their own, but many pace and whine or bark, showing anxiety symptoms rather than signs of relaxation. That's why it might be helpful to teach your dog to rest in a way that allows him to reduce stress and anxiety rather than build it up.

Let Sleeping Dogs Lie

In this section we will discuss how to teach your dog to rest, to find the calm brain wave that so many frantic dogs seem to lack.

We utilize three methods — tethering, crating, and the go to bed, or place, command — to teach rest and relaxation to your dog. Before you start, however, it's important to be fair to the dog: Make sure you begin teaching these methods when your dog actually needs to rest. Trying to get him to relax after a long sleep, for instance, will be counterproductive. It's also good to learn all three of these methods, and then you can pick the method most appropriate to use at a given moment. The wonderful part of this program is that you may well find that as he learns the ropes, your dog will begin to select his own relaxation method.

Tethering

You can teach your dog to rest by keeping him on a leash. Tethering involves nothing more than leashing your dog in the house, holding the leash, and silently requiring your dog to apply good manners as you go about your business. Essentially, the dog becomes your shadow. If you sit down to watch TV, the dog goes with you because he is leashed and you are holding the leash. When you sit, your dog may think this is one of those times where you'll sit close to each other on the couch and snuggle. But tethering is not an emotion or affection point. Instead it is what many of our mothers used to call "quiet time." So if your dog tries to climb on the couch or pokes you for attention, simply use the leash to keep him on the ground and to interrupt any behavior that is not consistent with quiet time. The idea is to be physically close, which is good for togetherness, but not touching each other, which is good for self-control — yours as well as your dog's. It doesn't matter if your dog stands up, sits, or lies down. Under no circumstances should you talk to your dog while tethering, as the point of this exercise is to teach your dog to be calm, and talking to him will only excite him. If your dog tries to leave, use the leash to stop him. If he begins to bite the leash, tug or pop the leash to stop him. You can even spray the leash with bitter apple — a taste he'll surely dislike — if you need to. Over time, your dog will get used to resting with you and will simply lie down and conserve energy when you're not in motion.

If you get up to go to the kitchen, the dog is going to go with you. After all, you're holding the leash. Wherever *you* go while tethering, the dog will go because he is physically attached to you. By not speaking to your dog and by not touching him, you are taking this opportunity to show him how to feel comfortable in his own skin. This will become a valuable skill to him, a critical skill even, when you leave to go to work, for example.

When tethering the dog, simply go about your business while holding the leash or attaching it to you. Your dog will learn the rhythms of your life and that you sometimes set the agenda.

You might find it hard not to speak or touch your dog when he's so close. Even if you find it hard at first, over time you'll be surprised how easily both you and your dog can enjoy shared quiet and calm time.

Most of us treasure the moments of relaxation we spend with another human being just listening to music or reading good books by the fire. This reserved communion can be deeply satisfying. By tethering your dog, you can teach him to treasure such moments as much as you do.

Tethering Tips

If your dog paces, take hold of the leash. When your dog moves to the end of the leash, don't give him more. Gently pull the leash so the dog is in a position where the leash is loose. Do this until your dog realizes this is the most comfortable available position.

If your dog jumps on you, use your free hand to push him off gently. If he seems to like that body contact, then switch tactics and use the leash to tug him off. Do this as many times as it takes for your dog to realize that you won't be allowing him on your lap.

If your dog licks or pokes you for attention, calmly push him a few inches away from you. Do this any time your dog makes unsolicited body contact.

If your dog barks or whines, tug his collar repeatedly and quickly to interrupt his train of thought. Do this each time he barks until he decides to remain quiet.

If your dog gets tangled up under furniture, you must patiently pull him out from under it, then shorten your leash so he doesn't wrap himself up again. As soon as your dog quits trying that move, let out a bit more leash.

If your arm gets tired because your dog is very large or very strong, you may want to lay the leash across your seat and then sit on it. This will help eliminate the fatigue factor. Just be sure your dog has enough leash to move around a little bit and to lie down without feeling a tight collar. If you need to, you can always release a bit more leash, or take some up.

If you have gone for a focused walk before tethering, most dogs will give up protest behaviors and lie down next to you within five minutes. Be prepared for this moment by allowing your dog enough leash to lie down next to you without feeling his collar tighten. Let him lie down on a loose collar. This is the exact moment for quiet. If you say anything at all, especially praise, chances are high that your dog will get up and you'll have to start all over again.

Once your dog settles by himself into a relaxed down position (or even a sit) with no command, glance at a clock and wait ten minutes. Enjoy your book or your television program. Allow your dog those ten minutes of peace and quiet by your side without speaking to or touching him. A dog in pack drive wants to share time and collaborate with the leader. "I have not selected an activity for you, but I have ruled out everything I don't want" is your unspoken message. A rational dog will ultimately select the one activity of which you approve.

And that is to lie down. This time will become very pleasant for your dog because he is calmly lying in close proximity to his pack leader. Eventually he will look forward to these privileged moments when he can quietly share space with you, allowing you to select the activity, which in this case is to settle.

At the end of ten minutes, calmly praise your dog with a very quiet tone. Get up from your position and release your dog.

Practice tethering two or three times each day. Remember, it is best to practice this when your dog can reasonably be expected to calm himself — after focused exercise, for instance.

Tethering isn't forever. Use it liberally when first solving behavioral problems and then dial it back. You can always resume a tethering routine later if needed.

Crate Training

How would *you* like to be stuck in a crate? That's how some people respond when crating comes up as a partial solution to dog behavior problems. Our answer is always the same: Maybe not…but if you stock the crate with a minibar, WiFi, and an iPad, the picture changes.

Dogs are not people. They don't have our innate distaste for small enclosed spaces. Dogs are denning animals that, by mother's choice, are born in a tightly confined area. They tend to relax thoroughly when they are confined in a comfortable area for a reasonable length of time. The dog's mind can relax precisely because there are so few decisions to be made.

Previously, we've introduced crate training as an important part of structuring your dog's life. Following are some aspects of the use of the crate that we haven't gone over.

The crate isn't just for when you leave home. If you use the crate only when you leave for an extended period of time, of course your dog will associate it with being alone and bored. As we've mentioned, the easiest way to introduce the crate to an older dog is to start feeding the dog in it. You don't even have to close the door. Just get your dog used to eating in the crate, and he'll soon look forward to hopping in whenever you unlatch the door. Shove the food bowl deeper into the crate every day until your dog is happily eating inside the crate. Then one day you can close the crate door until your dog has finished. With each subsequent day you can delay opening the door by five or ten minutes to get your dog used to staying in the crate for a longer period, up to a half hour to start with.

Lock your dog out of the crate when it's not in use. When you remove your dog from the crate, lock the door behind him. Let him watch you toss a few tasty treats in there. Then walk away. Let him spend an hour or so wishing he could get back inside the crate. Then latch your dog in the crate while you do a quick errand or take a shower. He'll be grateful you finally got around to it.

Here are some other ways to help your dog enjoy the crate:

- Remember: You're not making the crate optional. But you're willing to try to make it fun.
- Start with something enjoyable like meals in the crate, door open, food pushed deeper inside daily.
- Keep the best chews and toys inside the crate and don't let your dog remove them.
- Lock your dog out of the crate when you remove him, and after you lock it, let your dog see you toss in a treat.
- Stop talking to your dog ten minutes before and after crating. This makes the crate unemotional.
- Barking in the crate is to be discouraged. A water pistol might help you to interrupt the behavior so that the dog can relax more quickly. If you want your dog to change his behavior, you'll have to change yours first. Don't act or feel guilty when teaching any skill to your dog, even crate training. Understand that it's a tool you are using for your dog's benefit. Like training wheels for a child on a bike, the crate enables your dog to stay out of trouble until you help him learn to make good choices. Eventually, when your dog understands that he is to eliminate outside and chew only on his own toys and bones, you can phase out the crate just as you might phase out training wheels on a bike.
- Dogs that are walked twice daily accept the crate much more readily than dogs that are deprived of walks.

Because of dogs' denning instinct — a leftover from their wolf and early dog DNA — too much space can be unsettling to them. Having too much space to explore can actually provoke forms of separation anxiety. You're better off crate training the dog for his own comfort. Some dogs, specifically ones that have been constantly fussed with, unconsciously stroked, touched, and talked to, find solitude to be nerve-racking at first. Such dogs may howl or try to escape from a crate. Yet if left loose, they may scratch the doors and furniture to pieces. In these cases, we have found it very useful to employ one of our favorite tricks when crate training the anxious dog.

The Last Straw?

Indeed, straw can be a helpful tool when crating dogs that suffer from anxiety, especially dogs that balk at being crated.

MARC   Let me tell you how I came upon this trick. Once upon a time I fostered a Doberman that was fairly nutty in the crate. I noticed that she tore up any bedding — towels or blankets, for instance — that I gave her. I became afraid that she'd ingest the scraps of fabric. Without any form of bedding, however, she fussed and became agitated in the crate. I decided to invent a crate activity that would distract her from her woes but that would also yield some sort of bedding in the process. So I began to place cardboard boxes in the dog's plastic airline-type crate, and to place some kibble or treats in the boxes. The dog would spend happy hours tearing apart those boxes, finding treats, and eating them. By the time the boxes were demolished, she had a thick layer of confetti to sleep on, and she'd root around in that a bit to find the last of the kibble.

Then she'd sleep. At a certain point, I ran out of cardboard boxes and decided to try a new tactic. I shredded newspapers into long strips and filled the crate with a very thick, fluffy layer of newspaper. The dog rooted around in this equally well, tore some of it into smaller strips, and then began to relax in the crate. It seemed to me that she was exhibiting nesting behaviors, and the newspaper-filled crate was more settling to her than a bare crate. Within a few months, the dog was crate trained and didn't need anything in the crate.

Eventually, I placed this dog into a lovely forever home and promptly forgot all about this episode. Years later, a man called me after business hours and insisted that he wanted to bring me a screaming Lab puppy that same night. Over he comes with the puppy sleeping in his arms. Nine weeks old, tender, adorable. And sleeping.

"You can't crate this puppy," the fellow says, his eyes glowing red, "or he'll scream and you won't sleep. I haven't slept in four days. Good luck." He threw money at me and bolted out the door, the puppy now sleeping in *my* arms. Zonked. Out like a light.

I crept over to the crate, gently opened it. Oh so carefully I laid the sleepy baby in the crate and held my breath. Nothing. Gentle snoring. Perfect! I began to tenderly close the door, and one eye opened. The other eye opened. And then he screamed. And screamed. And screamed.

I rapped on the crate and then covered it with a blanket in a futile attempt to interrupt the behavior.

After one hour of nonstop screaming, screaming that left my hands shaking, I remembered. *Boxes! I need boxes.* I didn't have any. *Newspapers! I need newspapers!* I didn't have any of those, either. But I had a phone book. So I tore out the pages from Auto to Pizza, and I started to crumple each sheet into a tightly wadded ball. I piled a bunch of paper balls by the crate; the puppy did not break stride at all. He was screaming with all his might. But he kept an eye on me while I was piling up paper balls outside his crate, and when the pile was considerable, I opened the crate and he screamed while I shoveled in all the paper balls I'd made.

He was only toe deep in paper. And he was still screaming.

So I kept making paper balls. By the time I poured the second load into the crate, he stopped screaming. Now he was watching me quizzically. I loaded paper balls into that crate until this puppy nearly disappeared. He looked like a small puppy in one of those playground ball pits where children bury themselves in colored balls. I was out of paper, so I stopped. And I watched.

This is when the puppy turned three circles to nest into those blessed Yellow Pages balls, and he lay down. He was out like a light in ten seconds. I crept upstairs and slept. When I woke up, I ran on tiptoes down to the crate... and, oh my God, he's dead... lying belly up, tongue lolling out of his mouth.

I gasped. That's when the puppy opened an eye. He hadn't slept in four days, either. He was so sleep deprived that he really needed that night's sleep.

Anyway, he was fit as a fiddle now. Every day I pulled a handful of those balls out of the crate, and before long, he could sleep in the crate with nothing special.

The next time I had a dog with crate anxiety, I knew I had to come up with something better, and that's when I remembered the farmer up the street with the STRAW FOR SALE sign. So I tried straw and found that it worked great. I'm sure it will for you, too.

Straw crating tips:

- Use a plastic airline crate and fill it up to your dog's hip with straw.
- Use straw, not hay. Hay is dried grass, and dogs are more likely to eat it.
- Dogs don't normally eat the straw, but you can keep an eye out if you're concerned.
- You can also use long strips of newspaper if you prefer, but change the paper when it gets dusty.
- Put a sheet under the crate to make for easy cleanup. Straw is messy in the house.
- Many breeders keep puppies in some sort of organic bedding for a few weeks, so straw is like going back to the cradle.
- It is comforting to dogs to have something pressuring their body in the crate.
- Straw encourages some dogs that have a habit of peeing in the crate to be clean, but check for wet spots.
- Change the straw at least weekly. Dogs like fresh straw. It's like getting clean sheets.
- If the dog digs around and fluffs the straw, so much the better.
- Foraging in the crate is better than freaking out in the crate, so toss in some treats if you like.
- Even though straw helps rest time be more restful for many crate-anxious dogs, they might still need more exercise than they've been getting.
- Give it at least a few weeks, but then you can remove handfuls of straw each day to start the weaning process.

Go to Bed, or Place, Command

Imagine you come home from a walk or run with your dog and she immediately goes to her bed and spends a calm few minutes there. Wouldn't that be useful? Or how about when the pizza delivery guy rings the doorbell and you can send your dog across the room to her bed for a few moments? That would be nice, right? Or the kids spill Cap'n Crunch all over the living room...You get the idea. Responding to the go to bed command is a wonderful skill for your dog to learn, and it makes life much easier for both of you. A dog that can quietly remain on her bed for a reasonable period of time is a dog that won't have to get put away constantly. This command teaches your dog to associate patience and relaxation with a specific location.

A quick note about time on bed: A disturbing trend has emerged in which some trainers advocate reinforcing a go to bed command for hours at a time. Such trainers may even use uncomfortable or too-small beds, which require the dog to exert a great deal of effort to remain in place, thus tiring out the dog. Let us be clear here: We do not believe that dogs should be sent to bed in any punitive fashion or for any unreasonable length of time. We recommend that to be fair to your dog a go to bed session should last no longer than five to twenty minutes. It's not that you can't use the command occasionally for a slightly longer period, because you can. But if your goal is to tire out your dog—and you should be committed to helping your dog in that way, too—then go for a run, not an extended bed command.

How to Teach Go to Bed

Use a comfortable bed: Avoid thin dog beds or mats. It is best to use a thick dog bed that has bolsters running all or most of the way around it. The bolsters will make it very obvious to the dog when he is either on or not on the bed. Elevated platform dog beds are also ideal for this purpose.

Day 1: Holding the leash close to your dog's collar, accustom him to walking on and off the bed as you say the word *bed*. Say "Bed" as your dog is stepping onto the bed. When your dog is comfortable with walking

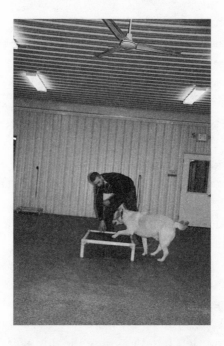

If you teach your dog a "go to bed" command, he'll have a comfortable resting place when you'd like him to hold still for a few moments.

on and off the bed, have him pause on the bed, using the leash to gently check him if he should try to get off. When the dog commits to being on the bed for a moment, you may drop a treat on the bed.

Do not allow your dog to get a foot off the bed until you release him. Release the dog by saying his name and "Let's go." Then walk your dog off the bed using the leash gently.

Days 2–4: When the dog is comfortable staying on the bed and getting off the bed when you release him, you can drop a treat on the bed when the dog isn't looking and before you send him there. Then:

- Have your dog on your left side on a six-foot leash.
- Hold the leash loop in your right hand.
- Your left hand will grip the middle of the leash and push out ahead of you to direct the dog.
- Say, "Let's go" and start walking *fast* toward the bed from ten feet away. When you're five feet away, push the leash ahead of you with your left hand to guide the dog swiftly onto the bed. After the dog's first foot is on the bed, you may continue to use the leash to guide the dog the rest of the way onto the bed if necessary.
- Place a treat on the bed sometimes, but not always. Use the treats randomly, because eventually you want the dog to execute the command without looking for a treat. Ultimately, your approval is the dog's reward, but using the occasional, unexpected treat keeps it fun for your dog.
- Vary the length of time you require your dog to remain on the bed. He may sit, lie, or stand on the bed... his choice. But he may not leave the bed until you release him by saying his name and "Let's go." While your dog is on the bed, keep the leash slack but gripped so that you're able to prevent the dog from getting far from the bed if he tries to get off. If this happens, check him firmly with the leash by tugging him back toward the position you want him to resume.
- Check your dog with a leash tug as he gets the *first foot off the bed*, and use the leash to swiftly help the dog back on. Release the leash pressure the instant the dog has four feet on the bed.

Day 5 and beyond: Bring your dog within five feet of the bed. Give the bed command and use your left hand to push your dog toward the bed. Initiate his movement by taking one step toward the bed. Allow your dog to get to the bed ahead of you, but follow him promptly. If your dog will not go without you, guide him to the bed quickly.

As you repeat this exercise, gradually increase your distance from the bed. Point at the bed, commanding, "Bed" as you take the first step forward. If the dog is going fast toward the bed, drop the leash so you don't hold him back.

You may randomly reinforce the bed as a place your dog wants to be by dropping treats on the bed when your dog is already in place, or before you issue the command. The treats become an unexpected reward for going to bed quickly.

Remember that patience and persistence are your friends. Both are required to create and keep a reliable bed command.

Tip: Practice the go to bed command for a few minutes two or three times each day to keep progressing.

Slowly add distractions over the course of several days. For example, start the process away from other pets or children, but eventually move closer to these distractions as your dog becomes more proficient. If you don't have these distractions in your environment, you can simply begin to walk around the room, occasionally passing the dog's bed. Your movement is a distraction. But remember, add distractions slowly, one at a time, and in small increments. You may find that as you introduce them, your dog will need reminders to continue performing his part. That is normal; learning is a process, so be patient as you proceed.

Play

We've spent a lot of time discussing leadership and how it contributes to a dog's well-being. Make no mistake — your leadership is imperative to the relationship. However, play also fills a critical role for dogs. It helps them blow off steam, for one thing. It lets them just be dogs, as long as they remember that we're people, not fellow dogs, and that we're unlikely to play as physically as they do. At its very best, play offers wonderful exercise and teaches teamwork—to dogs just as it does to children. As we've said, all good games have rules. We have discussed how to use toys, but what else can we do to play productively with our dogs? Especially important in difficult climates, or in cases where you can't leave the house, what alternatives are there to outdoor play?

Play can help keep your dog from going stir-crazy when you're housebound. Days of rain or bitter cold, or even unbearable heat, may require you to keep your dog inside more than usual, where there is less for him to do. On most days, outdoor activity will be possible and is important for your dog. On rainy days, use a raincoat for your daily walks and have dry towels ready by your door for when you return. But on those rare days when outdoor activity is impossible, how can you keep your dog occupied?

The first thing you need to understand is that dogs are intelligent creatures, created to fulfill a function. So imagine a healthy, intelligent eight-year-old boy or girl cooped up in the house for days on end with no computer, no books, no television, no telephone, and no exercise equipment. It's a recipe for disaster. For sure, you'll come home and find a fort built out of your best furniture, or a mosaic made out of pieces of the good china.

Intelligence combined with energy and no outlet equals trouble. No wonder dogs get harder to live with in bad weather. If you can't get out, we recommend you play productive indoor games with your dog to use up some of that brain and body power.

Remember playing hide-and-seek on rainy days? It was a great way for kids to move their bodies and exercise their brains. Play hide-and-seek with your dog, using food as the object for her to find. Here's how you start.

Begin with a hungry dog. Show her a tasty treat, something high value like a small bit of chicken, and toss it on the floor in front of her. Tell her "Find it." That won't be difficult as it's in plain sight. However, toss the next treat around a corner. Tell your dog to find it again. Slowly work your way up to hiding the treats behind curtains, under furniture, eventually in other rooms. Get your dog started by pointing her in the right direction.

If your dog is well trained, she can be on a sit-stay while you're hiding the food. If not, you may have to close her in another room for a moment. In short order, you can simply point in the general direction of the food and your dog will use her nose to find the source of that delicious smell.

Although this activity might seem less exhausting than a run in the park, the fact is that your dog will be actively using her strongest sense — smell. The olfactory center of your dog's brain expends a great deal of energy, and working scent purposefully for fifteen or twenty minutes can be quite tiring for your dog.

If you have a treadmill in your home, bad weather days offer the perfect opportunity to teach your dog to use this equipment. Make a game of it. Start with a hungry, leashed dog and another bit of chicken. Turn off the treadmill. Simply lure the dog up onto the belt and reward her with the treat. Do this multiple times, then quit without ever turning the treadmill on.

Several times per day, bring your dog near the treadmill. Be sure you use a flat buckle collar, not a slip collar. Within a couple of days, most dogs will happily hop up on the treadmill and wait for that treat. The next step is to turn the machine on with your dog near but not on the belt. Do this a few times over the course of several days to get him used to the noise. Finally comes the time to accustom your dog to walking on the machine. Be sure the belt is level, with no incline. Hold your dog's leash close to the collar, but leave it a little bit slack. Turn the machine on at its slowest speed. Encourage your dog to walk by holding the leash or collar and giving verbal encouragement.

Be prepared to turn the machine off quickly if your dog becomes frightened of the noise. If he does, just reward again a few more times while the machine is turned on, but with the dog held several feet away on leash.

In short order, your dog will hop up on the treadmill and be ready to go for his rainy-day walk. Be aware that some dogs are most comfortable at the walk speed, while others work better at a trot. Change the speed very slowly so as not to frighten your dog.

Most important, never tie your dog to the machine. You must remain nearby, holding the leash or collar, ready to hit the treadmill's emergency stop button if something goes wrong.

Last, your local pet store sells a wide variety of smart toys. These are toys that you can stuff with treats and then give to your dog, who will have work to do with the toy to extract the treat. One well-known brand is Kong, but there are others. You may find it useful to offer part of your dog's daily ration as smart-toy stuffing. Remember, dogs benefit from doing a bit of work for their food. Engaging the mind of the dog while she puzzles out a problem — such as how to get her meal out of a toy — is a valuable form of play... even more so if you ask her to sit before giving her the smart toy to work on.

Our Needs vs. a Dog's Needs

Work, rest, and play (WRP) are the primary components of a dog's life, but what about our needs?

Human beings take dogs into their homes these days primarily for emotional reasons. Just remember that although your dog will enjoy time spent sharing your love, emotion must not form the core of his daily existence. Your dog was born to share your life, yes, but he was not intended to be your teddy bear or crying towel.

Look at how you are spending the average day with your dog and compare his work, rest, and play needs with your own need to stroke and cuddle with him. There is a balance to be struck here, and each of you should be able to get what you require from the other. But if your dog suffers from anxiety, examine your relationship with him and ask yourself this question: Am I taking more than I'm giving?

Dogs are very much creatures of habit. By helping your dog to act in specific, predictable ways, by integrating WRP in his life, you can ensure that your dog will become increasingly responsive to you. Dogs look to us reflexively for guidance and tend to follow our cues easily. This allows us to provide them with more freedom, which in turn allows them to be happier and more content. Without question, providing the appropriate structure is central to a harmonious relationship with your dog.

12

Peace Without Prozac: How to Treat Anxious Dogs

Sometimes we take dogs for granted, thoughtlessly consigning them to the margins of our attention without taking into account their own needs as unique creatures.

One of the more unfortunate by-products of a lack of structure in your dog's daily life is anxiety. Like any feeling or emotion, anxiety can and often does drive behavior. Mildly nervous people might bite their fingernails, for example (so do certain dogs), but anxiety can also cause more damaging behaviors, which—for both people and dogs—can include self-destructive actions.

Hard figures on this aren't kept, but the number of dogs that suffer from separation anxiety, or that constantly act fearful, complete with whining and pacing, has increased markedly over the decades. Today, we meet all too many dogs that will chew at or lick themselves partially bald for no reason that can be medically diagnosed.

A Google search of the phrase "Prozac for dogs" returns nearly six hundred thousand hits. Prozac—or its generic, fluoxetine—is sometimes packed alongside toys and treats that owners bring for their dogs that come to our board-and-train facility. For the most part, these drugs are prescribed appropriately for dogs that have seriously abnormal behaviors, such as severe separation anxiety. Other times, however, Prozac is used instead of a steady regimen of exercise to calm dogs that have excessive pent-up energy.

That said, let's start this discussion with a couple of important statements. First and foremost, we are not veterinarians, and whether your dog should be medicated for anxiety is a conversation you'll need to have with a vet. We've seen abundant cases in which anti-depressants and anti-anxiety drugs have contributed to an enhanced quality of life for some dogs. Some veterinarians have confided to us privately, however, that they occasionally prescribe the drugs to mollify clients who are agitated about their dog's behavior.

The anxious dog may be frightened of one specific thing, such as thunderstorms. Or that particular fear may combine with others to form a more general fear of loud noises. The Fourth of July is a holiday dreaded by many dog trainers and owners. Those of us who have fireworks displays nearby tend to close windows and run air conditioners and fans along with loud music in an attempt to drown out the noise. That seems to work for some dogs but not for all.

Dogs can also become fearful of places or people that they associate with loud noises—a construction site or sanitation worker, for instance.

Some breeds, including herding breeds, seem to be predisposed to this type of anxiety. The dog learns to be anxious after experiencing trauma that he associates with the noise. Other times, medical issues such as ear infections or joint pain can trigger what appears to be anxiety.

MARC I first met Sheena in my veterinarian's office. I'd gone there to pay a final bill after having lost my beloved Doberman, Diablo, to old age. Sheena, a German shepherd, was a pile of bones with hair, lying in the corner. As I sat on the couch waiting for Dr. Deb, the dog began to creep toward me. She didn't have the strength to get up and walk, so she dragged herself to me. I put out my hand, and she laid her head in my palm, then collapsed so I had to hold her head up for her. That's when Sheena looked up at me with a pair of what appeared to be pleading eyes.

The recent loss of Diablo, and now this poor dog in my hands, was a bit much for me. I teared up and was still sniffing when Dr. Deb walked into the waiting room.

Dr. Deb Rykoff rescues dogs. This dog's owners had nearly starved the German shepherd to death and had left the poor dog outside chained to a tree in all sorts of weather, including thunderstorms. Even when the owners mowed the lawn, Sheena stayed chained to the tree. They simply ran the lawn mower around the terrified dog.

My eyes still wet, I looked up at Dr. Deb. "What's wrong with her?" I asked.

"She's had every parasite known to man, and also has heartworm that I'm treating her for," the veterinarian said. "Her name is Kate."

"No," I said, stroking the dog's head. "Her name is Sheena."

"You have to wait three days to take her," said my vet. "Because then we'll know if she'll make it."

Sheena not only lived but recovered fully, with no physical scars whatsoever. I took her home a few days after this incident and, with the doctor's help, nursed her back to health. Sheena has been with me as my constant companion for more than eleven years now. She's a people lover and gets along well with other dogs. The only sign of her ordeal is a phobia related to thunderstorms and lawn mowers. It's an understandable fear, yet many dogs get over these fears with time. Sheena did not, although now that she's an older dog and starting to lose her hearing, those particular sounds worry her a lot less than they once did.

Her anxiety isn't what we would call general. Most of the time, Sheena is content to go about the normal business of a well-adjusted dog. Her anxiety surfaces only in the presence of the trigger issue. You might call it a form of canine PTSD.

For some dogs that have experienced extreme anxiety because of traumatic situations, the best course of action is to do very little intervention. This was the case with Sheena, who, though she still paces some, is mostly fine now, as long as she is not contained in a crate during a major storm. Sheena will do some worried pacing as a storm approaches and eventually hide in a small, dark alcove at the bottom of the stairs. Any attempt to soothe her or to stop the pacing actually results in an increase in symptoms rather than the desired decrease.

In comparable circumstances, some dogs may benefit from being wrapped in a tight T-shirt. There are commercially available anxiety vests that serve a similar purpose. Sheena will simply remove such articles.

In extreme cases of phobic behavior, where the dog may harm himself, some veterinarians will prescribe a canine-appropriate form of Xanax to quickly but temporarily reduce anxiety. Xanax is not a magic fix, however. It can produce side effects, especially in improper dosage. The most common side effects are sleepiness and clumsiness, but prolonged use of Xanax can cause your dog to become addicted. In rare cases, Xanax produces an opposite result of hyperactivity. Remember never to give your dog human Xanax, which can cause serious illness and even death in dogs. Your veterinarian is the expert here.

Phobia produces anxiety. It is understandable that a dog that has spent a year chained to a tree might fear storms and lawn mowers. Yet there are dogs that feel anxiety most or all of the time even though there is no specific reason for it. Symptoms of such anxiety include excessive barking, aggression, a need to escape, and even panic attacks, and no two dogs present in the exactly the same way. Two of the more common symptoms are constant whining and obsessive licking.

Constant whining. This type of whining should not be confused with the type of complaining a dog might do at something specific — through a window at a squirrel, for instance. Rather, whining related to anxiety seems endless and is often accompanied by pacing and failure to settle down. Unlike the dog that's whining because he wants to eat (and stops as soon as the bowl hits the floor), the anxiety-ridden dog is not looking at or for anything in particular. He doesn't actually know what he wants. That's a critical distinction.

Obsessive licking. Even worse, perhaps, than pets that constantly pace and whine are pets that obsessively lick themselves or the floor. They may actually do themselves damage by abrading the tongue or by causing lick granulomas. The situation can deteriorate if the dog begins to chew at himself, which may cause significant harm.

If your dog experiences any symptoms such as the ones described above, you should certainly consult your vet. That's because undiagnosed pain can cause many if not all of the symptoms we're discussing here. Sometimes blood work, X-rays, or a thorough physical exam will uncover a heretofore undiscovered medical condition that can be treated and remedied, or at least managed with an eye to mitigating pain levels. Today, we also understand that the thyroid gland can play a critical role in the psychological well-being of dogs.

Dr. Jean Dodds is a veterinarian who has gained national prominence for establishing Hemopet, a nonprofit animal blood bank, the first of its kind in North America. Dr. Dodds currently sits on the board of directors of the American Holistic Veterinary Medical Association and has published more than 150 research papers. Her research shows that hypothyroidism in dogs has reached astounding proportions, especially in certain purebred populations.

According to her book *The Canine Thyroid Epidemic: Answers You Need for Your Dog,* the most common behavioral signs of hypothyroidism in adult dogs are aggression (unprovoked toward other animals and/or people), seizures (sudden onset in adulthood), disorientation, moodiness, erratic temperament, hyperactivity, hypo-attentiveness, depression, fearfulness and phobias, anxiety, submissiveness, passivity, compulsiveness, and irritability.

We recommend that veterinarians implement Dr. Dodds's protocols when conducting a complete thyroid profile, especially in dogs that show unusual anxiety or aggression. When this blood test yields normal results, as it often does, we can then rule out thyroid as a cause. However, thyroid problems are uncovered with surprising regularity, especially in high-risk breeds. In such cases, a daily regimen of thyroid medication usually assists in reducing unfounded anxieties.

MARC I know a woman who owned two border collies, one twelve years old and the other just one year old. The dogs appeared to be the best of friends and never fought over any of the typical high-value resources like food, space, or human affection.

However, the younger dog began to exhibit anxiety symptoms for no apparent reason. He was sufficiently exercised, well fed, and overtly healthy. Yet there were times when he couldn't seem to settle. He'd pace, whine, and seem unfocused on anything in particular. Anyone who has ever owned a border collie will tell you that they can be antsy when bored — they are not a sedentary breed. The owners of the dog were keeping him sufficiently busy, yet he was hyperactive and would periodically attack the older dog when that dog was sleeping. I recommended the complete thyroid blood panel be run on this dog. As it turned out, my suspicion was correct. The border collie had hypothyroidism. When he was treated daily with thyroid medication, his symptoms abated.

Below is a list of breeds most often afflicted with canine thyroid disorder.

- Alaskan Klee Kai
- Beagle
- Borzoi
- Boxer
- Chesapeake Bay retriever
- Cocker spaniel
- Dalmatian
- Doberman pinscher
- English setter
- Eurasier
- German wirehaired pointer
- Giant schnauzer
- Golden retriever
- Great Dane
- Havanese
- Irish setter
- Kuvasz
- Labrador retriever
- Leonberger
- Maltese
- Nova Scotia duck tolling retriever
- Old English sheepdog
- Rhodesian ridgeback
- Shetland sheepdog
- Staffordshire terrier

The Arm & Hammer Dog

Some people are more sensitive than others. There are, for example, people who feel at ease wherever they find themselves. They fall asleep easily on planes or in hotels, and don't give a second thought to the change in surroundings. Others find it difficult to relax in new locations and may carry something familiar with them when they travel, such as a favorite pillow, to ease the transition.

The same goes for dogs. We meet dogs that are happy-go-lucky regardless of what novelties are thrown at them. Put them in a new house, and quickly they're right at home. Add a family member, and they're the welcoming committee. These dogs seem to be able to handle any alteration in their environment. Other dogs? Not so much.

Trainers frequently see breakdowns in training when a new puppy is added to the household, for example, or when a grown child moves out to go to college, or when the family moves to a new home. Events such as these can cause dogs to regress to old puppy patterns of behavior, including housebreaking accidents and chewing.

Emotional shifts in a dog's environment can have an even more devastating effect than physical ones. Even emotional variations that humans might not give a second thought to can affect a dog.

When you have an argument with your boyfriend on the phone, your dog knows you're angry but doesn't know at whom and may think you're angry at her. You might compound the problem by turning your dog into a crying towel, holding and petting her. A happy-go-lucky dog can tolerate these circumstances with no ill effects, but other dogs will break under the pressure.

Over the years, we have noticed that one particular type of dog reacts more profoundly than any other to emotional changes in his environment. We call this type of dog the Arm & Hammer dog.

Although the famous brand of baking soda has many purposes, its most common use is to absorb odors in the refrigerator. Put a box of Arm & Hammer in the fridge and you can be assured it will absorb the smells of onions, garlic, cheese, and any other pungent foods to which it is exposed. A month later, the box will be redolent with undesired scents. At that point you throw the box out, because you can never rid the baking soda of those smells it has absorbed.

Unlike the box of baking soda, however, once an Arm & Hammer dog is full, it begins to exhibit a range of symptoms that may include trembling, constant whining, sudden-onset crate phobia, loss of housebreaking, destructive chewing habits, new leash aggression, glassy-eyed staring, failure to engage in normal exploring and scent-ing behaviors, and vocalizing in response to simple problems such as a foot caught in a loop of leash or the approach of another dog.

Sadly, though the results are hard to miss, the steps leading up to these breakdowns usually go unrecognized. Families under stress often punish or get rid of dogs in this condition, unable to cope with their pet's behavior. Yet we can usually cleanse the mental state of an Arm & Hammer dog, restoring him to mental health and good behavior.

BROTHER CHRISTOPHER   I will always remember Milly the Maltipoo. At the time we first saw her, she was spayed and two years old. Though she had been trained to accept her crate, and had good house manners and proper housebreaking, Milly had begun to develop separation anxiety in the crate that produced a great deal of trembling and drooling. The family felt bad for her and began to leave her out of the crate when they weren't home.

Out of the crate, Milly began to chew the house apart and to eliminate inappropriately. When we first observed Milly, we noticed that while on the leash her entire body was tense and her gait was cramped and shortened. At rest, she could not settle, alternately lying down, standing, and trembling. Her eyes were also slightly glassy. When we crated Milly, her trembling increased and she began to drool. As a test, we tossed high-value bits of food into the crate. The anxiety symptoms instantly stopped, and Milly foraged, then ate the food. As soon as the food was gone, the neurotic behaviors resumed.

This led us to believe that Milly's case was different from simple misbe-havior. The symptoms were real and dramatic. But her brain could override them in the presence of certain scents. This is not typical of anxiety caused specifically by confinement or separation. Dogs with true crate or separation anxiety will ignore treats in the crate. But as soon as the door is opened, they'll try to bring the treats out with them.

Attempting to understand where Milly's stress came from, we embarked on a delicate conversation with her owners. To understand the dog's stress, it helps to understand the family's stresses. When we asked if the family was experiencing any emotional difficulties, we learned that the mother had an advanced case of breast cancer. Both she and her adult daughter were, understandably, frightened and depressed. The father was angry that life had delivered such a blow to his family.

Milly had simply absorbed the scary emotional content in the home. We prescribed a regimen for her that included increased walks, exercise, and tethering. As we have indicated multiple times, tethering is a very effective calming exercise that can reap enormous benefits for a dog. In Milly's case, we intended it to provide structure and stability, keeping her in close proximity to her owners without overt displays of affection or attention. Tethering simply teaches a dog to be quietly present with the owner.

We also suggested that Milly be fed every meal in the crate and that she be given a raw meat bone whenever the family would be gone from the house for more than a few hours. The bone was intended to give Milly a primal, doglike activity to perform in the crate, one she could look forward to. In addition, we suggested there be a few quiet times per day, during which the family would spend time with Milly but refrain from talking, touching, or even having eye contact with her. Physical stimuli can exacerbate a dog's anxiety, and simple quiet togetherness can be healing.

As it happened, adhering to the regimen was not possible for Milly's family. And we really couldn't blame them. They had enough distress to deal with without worrying about controlling their emotions around Milly.

A couple of weeks after our consultation, the family decided to place the dog with a retired couple, who then called us for advice. We recommended a week of tethering and the other therapies mentioned earlier. A week later the couple came to see us. The change in Milly was remarkable, and we could see it from the moment she jumped out of the car. Her gait had opened up to full stride. When we all sat down at a table, Milly easily settled at her new owner's side, with no trembling. Later, we crated her with a bone and she gnawed without drooling or trembling. She looked and behaved like a completely different dog. She was no longer so affected by the emotional turmoil present within her previous family.

In consulting with owners of dogs that have telltale Arm & Hammer signs, we ask if there is trauma in the family. We are not therapists (though many dog trainers might dispute that statement), but we do need to find the root cause of the dog's problems. If we believe that emotional trauma is the problem, then we suggest a treatment of focused exercise where the owners spend time with their dog quietly and calmly. Tethering creates an emotion-free zone in which a dog can recoup lost emotional resources.

This period of decompression, as we call it, can take a while. It's kind of like when you go on a vacation and for the first few days you find it difficult to relax and almost impossible to break away from your emails and work texts. Eventually you realize you haven't even worn shoes in days, let alone checked your email.

For dogs, however, decompression can take fourteen to thirty days, depending on the case.

Exposing the Arm & Hammer dog to stable dogs—on walks, for instance—can help speed up decompression, but only if the circumstances are very controlled. Don't make it a playdate. Regular outings with a group that will allow the anxious dog to integrate and socialize in his own time frame can be very helpful. Eventually, the anxious dog will want to socialize, and you can permit this in small snippets of a few moments each until she shows that she will not panic. Then you can slowly extend the time allowed for her to socialize.

For trainers and dog owners alike, rehabilitating an Arm & Hammer dog can be very rewarding work. It requires compassion and skill rather than coddling. But the end result is a dog restored to a happy outlook on life.

For humans, stress can cause anxiety if you haven't learned good coping mechanisms such as meditation, working out, or reading and relaxing to clear the mind. But a dog has to rely on its owner to provide ways to ease her stress. Therefore, you must provide the necessary coping mechanisms for your dog. Sometimes it's as simple as being sure that she eats, potties, and sleeps at the same regular intervals every day.

Many dogs arrive at our kennel barking and whining like a jumpy bundle of nerves. They can actually disturb the peace of the dogs that have been at the kennel for some time because those dogs have absorbed the rhythm and routine of residency and have become calmer because of it. Several days later it is the dog that arrived with the jumpy nerves that is perturbed when a barky "new kid" arrives, shattering the calm.

It is wonderful to see anxiety-ridden dogs learn to relax and actually be able to focus on their work, profit from their rest, and enjoy play with their owner or with other dogs. In this regard, when you notice your dog acting nervous, you should go through a brief mental review to make sure all of his obvious energy needs have been met. *When is the last time we took a run? Played fetch? Went for a long, long walk?* More than just exercise, however, it's important to allow your dog to explore his dogness. Not allowing a positive outlet for your dog's natural tendencies will ultimately lead to some sort of neurosis.

We're reminded of Gus, Central Park Zoo's famous polar bear. Gus died a few years ago (not long after his longtime companion, Ida, died), but there was a time when Gus was the main attraction of the zoo — and not for the best of reasons. In his nondescript surroundings (think of a housing project for a polar bear), Gus exhibited neurotic behavior from the start of his stay in New York, including swimming identical figure-eight patterns for twelve hours straight and seemingly stalking children through his pool's glass wall. The press dubbed him the bi-polar bear, and his antics drew crowds of onlookers both curious and concerned. In 1994, with their star attraction garnering national negative attention, zoo officials decided to consult an animal behaviorist. The behaviorist suggested a routine of training, play, and mental tasks such as having Gus forage for his food. They also remodeled his pool. Although his city habitat never came close to resembling the polar cap, his newly renovated environs gave Gus places to explore, including an extension called the toy room, which was filled with rubber garbage cans and traffic cones.

Guess what happened? Like ice that melts in the spring, Gus's neuroses began to fall away. He never completely gave up his figure eights, by most accounts, but he lived long and more contentedly, and did so simply by being allowed to be who he was.

Like Gus, most dogs don't want or need very much. But if they are denied the simple things that keep them mentally and physically fit — exercise, shared time, and challenge — that is, if they're denied their nature, it's impossible for them to be happy.

Fear of Humans

Sadly, certain dogs are frightened of people. Some have a particular aversion to men; others fear most people regardless of gender. Such dogs often have at least one trusted human family member. Or they have more than one and may also get along fine with other dogs. But when encountering people who fall into their fear parameters (male, children, or whatever they fear), the terrified dog will attempt to flee or hide.

Under extreme circumstances, the frightened dog may bark, growl, or lunge at an unwanted person. This type of aggressive behavior differs from the aggression exhibited by a confident dog. Instead of steady forward motion, aggression by a fearful dog includes a retreat posture, in which the dog's weight is not constantly placed on her forequarters. The dog's weight is either divided between front and rear, or is solidly placed on the rear quarters, in preparation for flight.

What causes this problem? An abusive background, genetics, or poor socialization may be responsible. Whatever the cause, it is critical to treat this condition without begging (or demanding) that the fearful dog just get over it. Again, long periods of quiet tethering on a leash is your best bet for building trust. Call a professional if aggression is involved, but many fearful dogs will improve if you just take the right steps. Fight-or-flight mode is a default state of mind for these dogs, and the idea is to stop this physiological reaction. Over time, you can prevent your dog from choosing fight-or-flight mode. Here's how you can help build that trust.

- As often as possible, tether the dog and go about your business in or out of the house.
- If the dog is afraid of you, tether but *do not* talk to, make sustained eye contact with, or try to touch the dog.
- Crate the dog to stop hiding behaviors when you cannot tether on leash. Ignore the dog in the crate rather than trying to engage, which will only make her feel cornered.
- If you are the trusted family member, *do not* pet or reassure the dog when she is acting fearful.

- Use a martingale-style collar so the dog cannot back out of it while tethering.
- Ignore the dog for her own good, and require everyone else to ignore her as well until she begins to relax.
- Feed in the crate for a week, but in the second week, without talk or eye contact, try to feed by hand while tethering.
- Once the dog starts taking food this way, continue to feed by hand without looming, talking, or staring.
- Do not skip meals to make the dog hungrier, but you can motivate him more with chicken or high-value food.
- Many dogs respond positively within a week. Others take weeks or months. Be patient.

Unfortunately, there are some instances in which generalized canine anxiety has no basis in a medical condition. The dog's inability to relax and be at ease is due to either genetic or psychological issues. In these cases, we look closely at the dog's lifestyle to determine if he is receiving the right measure of what a dog needs. What he needs is a structured life with the components of work, rest, and play, a life in which he's encouraged to participate in the joy but also to respect his owner's control over his resources.

In this chapter we have revealed the various faces of anxiety found in today's dog, along with a variety of means to preemptively treat or cure these conditions. Anxiety can prevent your dog from living a full and happy life because it robs him of the simple pleasures of eating and sleeping and romping. It can also cripple his chances of forming healthy relationships with both humans and other dogs. So many of our friends and clients express one simple wish: "I just want my dog to be happy." A dog can't fix an anxiety problem by himself. Rather, you must help him build the confidence that prevents anxiety by providing a coherent structure and the trust that allows your dog to feel safe.

More Dogs to Love: The Multiple-Dog Household

Seeing playful mischief arise in one dog as it pulls a prank on another should fill us with delight. — Dogs & Devotion

We believe the precepts outlined in this book are important for all dogs, but nowhere is it more important to consider the role of the human pack leader than in the multi-dog household. Living with one dog at a time may seem complicated, but when you start adding more dogs, problems can be magnified and can take on enormous proportions. That's not to say that we don't approve of keeping multiple dogs as pets. In fact, like most dog trainers, we keep more than one dog at a time.

Marc currently lives with four dogs, all rescues of different breeds: Sheena, the German shepherd of questionable heritage; a border collie mix; a rat terrier; and a collie. Like the monks, Marc sometimes plays with one individual dog to give him or her a bit of personal attention. But most of the time, the dogs live as a pack in Marc's home and they engage in activities as a group.

At the monastery, we live with ten or twelve breeding females and two or three breeding males at a time. These dogs are not just breeding stock. They are also our pets and may join us in the dining room during dinner by doing a down-stay. You may have seen photographs of the dogs with us in church or at dinner. Although we don't often bring the dogs into the church now, we do hike with our dogs daily.

German shepherds relaxing during a meal at New Skete. Dogs that get enough exercise and learn how to behave in the home can earn the privilege of being with you even at mealtime.

Many of us play fetch with our dogs, and all our dogs sleep on dog beds in our rooms. In the evening, the dogs chew on bones and lie at our feet in the recreation room while we read or watch the news or sports on TV. (Yes, some of us monks are avid sports fans!) More often than not, however, one of us will be on his hands and knees playing with a ninety-pound dog.

That, of course, is one of the joys of living with dogs.

MARC   On my first trip to the monastery, I confess to being a bit starstruck by these monks and their dogs. After all, I grew up reading their books and held them in high esteem. I found the monks to be interesting and engaging individuals. At once, I liked all of them. But for some reason I found Brother Ambrose a little intimidating. Tall and, like all the monks, bearded, Ambrose had a rather stern demeanor. Little did I know that behind the reserved exterior was a warm person and rollicking dry wit.

One day I needed to make a phone call, and Brother Christopher suggested I go into the gift shop and ask Brother Ambrose whether I could use the phone there. Gathering my courage, I went to the gift shop and made my request. Ambrose silently pointed to the back room, where the phone sat out of sight. My call took quite a long time, and I think Ambrose forgot I was in the back room. When I hung up, from around the corner I heard baby talk but in a grown man's voice. Not quite sure what to do, I peeked around and saw Ambrose on the floor with his dog, Hoss, a one-hundred-pound German shepherd, and another dog, Lola, on a dog bed calmly relaxing. Brother Ambrose was squeaking a toy and tossing it to Hoss. They were both enjoying the game, and I hated to interrupt. Lola was unconcerned. Apparently she was used to this. So I cleared my throat loudly and emerged from the back room. Ambrose looked up at me from the floor. I think it might have occurred to him to try to come up with a reasonable explanation other than "I'm playing squeaky toy games with my dog." But he knew he was busted, so he just smiled and shrugged.

When you live with two or more dogs, they form a pack. Certain complexities can arise, and arise even more dramatically as you increase the number of dogs. That's because having multiple dogs means

Brother Christopher with California trainer and television personality Cheri Lucas, walking a pack of New Skete German shepherd dogs.

there's increased competition for resources, there are more personalities in the house, and, most important, you need to have control of not only each individual dog but the whole group. We know many people who can negotiate walking one of their dogs at a time with little difficulty. But when walking two or more dogs, things can become complicated. The dogs tangle and fuss with one another, and they're more likely to lunge at other dogs on the walk. After all, they are not alone. They have a wingman.

A quick word about control. We do not define this word to mean that your dogs and your pack will or should behave robotically. Far from it, we love to see the joie de vivre that a group of dogs displays. Moreover, if you've ever seen dogs run and play, you have no doubt sensed their delight at romping together without inhibition. The dogs show the fullness of engaging in life wholeheartedly, and the sight is deeply satisfying. What we mean by control is your ability to calmly stop your dogs from indulging in behavior that they may enjoy — such as standing at the window barking at passersby — but that you find inappropriate at that moment. The best time to add a new dog is when you have this control over the dog or dogs already living in your home. Some people buy their dog a buddy before having a sense of orderliness in the existing relationship. We can assure you that buying your dog a pal as a way of dealing with his unruliness isn't the cure.

Living with two or more dogs offers double or triple the fun and enjoyment. But multi-dog households can also present a whole new set of challenges and problems. So let's examine some of the more prevalent ones and see if we can offer you some helpful strategies for both prevention and cure.

One of the most common questions relating to multiple-dog households is how to feed several dogs safely at once. Admittedly, there can be a danger in having several dogs eating at the same time in the same room. Not all dogs eat at the same pace. When the greedy, fast eater quickly finishes his meal, he may well wander over to try to horn in on another dog's food. In that case, drama can occur. What's the best approach to avoid such problems? You can always resolve to feed your dogs in separate crates. This is what we do at the monastery.

Our dogs are quite comfortable in their crates, and the crate provides a safe place where other dogs are unable to disturb the dog while she is eating. However, sometimes owners don't like the unsightliness of multiple crates in the house.

You can in fact teach your dogs to eat safely in each other's presence, and here's how.

Imagine you have three dogs. You need first to teach each dog the meaning of go to bed, or place, and have each of the dogs able to go to his specific spot in the room. (Consult chapter 11 for detailed instructions on teaching this exercise. Note that part of the exercise is that the dog does not leave its place until it is released by its owner.) You will also need to teach each dog how to hold a sit while you place his food in front of him and to eat only after you release him. This is easily done with patience on your part: If your dog goes to eat before your release, pick up the dish quickly and induce the dog back into the sit position. Only release him when he has waited for five to ten seconds. Dogs will learn this readily with practice. Next, with your three dishes of food ready for distribution, and with each dog on his place, take one of the dishes and stand in front of the senior dog. If the other dogs break their place, use your body and voice to block them and send them back. You are the pack leader here, so be assertive and self-possessed. Then return your attention to the first dog. Place the food dish in front of him and release him to eat if he has held the sit. Then repeat the process in order of seniority. By using the place command, you can safely condition the dogs to receive their food calmly and not to interfere with their pack mates. Your goal is to feed dogs that know to remain in their corner until you release them when mealtime is over. With several dogs eating at once, we recommend you stay in the room, as a sort of traffic cop, in case any dog should decide to break the rules. Finally, once mealtime is over, collect the empty bowls and put them away. Otherwise, some of your pack might rush to the other dogs' places to see if there are leftovers. That can be a danger point because some dogs will guard their own bowls even when they're empty. Or for simplicity's sake, you may opt to feed your dogs in crates.

Typical problems in multi-dog households range from dogs that bark angrily at the door when a visitor arrives (even if they're happy to see the visitor) to dogs that fight each other in your house or yard. One common refrain we hear from clients is that their dogs distract and rile one another so often and so thoroughly that the owners feel as though the dogs don't listen to them at all — unless they start yelling, and even then any beneficial effect is only temporary.

Remember that dogs, domesticated though they may be, come pre-programmed with the instincts of predators. If your pack recognizes you as their pack leader, they will generally take their cues from you about what they can and cannot chase or hunt. Prey drive is natural to dogs. You see it every time a dog as small as a teacup-sized Chihuahua reacts to a squeaky toy by pouncing on it, biting it, shaking it back and forth, and then throwing it up in the air. To you he's playing. And he is. You call the game Squeaky Toy. He thinks of it as Kill the Mouse. This type of behavior by your dog is natural, and as pack leader, you should encourage games that your dogs enjoy. If your dogs aren't aware that you're in charge, however, then it's not a game to them at all. In a multi-dog situation, this prey drive can easily become mob rule.

One of the ways you can assert your authority over the pack is by implementing the Red Light–Green Light rule. Just as in the game from your childhood, you should be able to interrupt any roughhousing or extreme play by having your dogs give you a moment of calm — with a sit, for example — and then you can allow them to resume playing. Like any other skill, this takes practice. Begin by using the command in a firm but not excited manner: You don't want to yell or scream. You may have to step toward the dogs, or take the collar of the main offender and place him in a temporary sit. Or you may have to leash one or more of the dogs and use light but steady upward leash pressure to get the sit. Usually, if you stop the ringleader, the whole pack will settle. You'll almost never need to get loud or domineering to get your pack to take a quick time-out, but you may need to be insistent. Using calm, physical control by leashing a dog that won't stop agitating the other dogs is often very helpful and is a tactic that can eventually be phased out. Your attitude is of paramount importance here. Dogs know when you're serious, and serious to them means an unruffled, authoritative manner. Play is good. Just have control over it. Once you have this level of control, you'll have taken an important step toward ensuring the safety of your pack and other household pets.

MARC   I remember a client who called me after her dogs killed a beloved parrot. The dogs had lived with that parrot all their lives because she'd had the bird for more than twenty years. The dogs usually either ignored the bird or showed mild interest, but nothing alarming. There were four large dogs in the home and one small dog. The neighborhood was very upscale, each house on no less than five acres, most with a horse barn. I was shocked when I walked into the house. It was beautiful and stately on the outside. On the inside, it was torn to shreds. The hardwood floors were deeply gouged, the wood moldings were chewed throughout, and all the doors were scratched nearly to splinters.

I could hear the dogs raising a huge ruckus at the back of the house, barking and scratching. The client had closed them up in a few different bedrooms, most of which were empty of the furniture that the dogs had destroyed. So those rooms had essentially become kennels.

When I met the dogs they were good-natured but very rowdy. They leapt all over the owner and me. But mostly me because I was fresh meat. They vied for attention and competed for space around our feet. In other words, we were in the middle of a tornado consisting of more than three hundred pounds of wild, spinning dogs. The owner yelled vaguely at them for a few moments and then threw up her hands in defeat. "See" — she shouted to be heard — "they have no respect for me at all."

I watched the crowd for a while and noticed that all the dogs made room for one particular white dog. Even in the madness, wherever the white dog wanted to be, another dog yielded a bit of space to make room for him. And that's how I knew I had zeroed in on the pack leader. It sure wasn't my client. It was that white hound mix.

What I did next is something I do not advise you to try at home in case you have mistaken an aggressive dog for a good-natured one. If you do that, things might not turn out so well. If you're unsure, call an experienced professional trainer.

I ignored all the other dogs, made eye contact with the big white dog, and held his gaze without taking an aggressive stance. In other words, I did not square off with him the way two street fighters might as they decide who is going to throw the first punch. But I looked him square in the eye, and when he pressed into my leg, rather than backing out of his space, I stepped forward into it, bumping him out of my way. He stopped. I moved forward. He backed up. And, more or less, so did all the other dogs.

Now White Dog became calmer, wondering who the heck this person was who neither yelled nor retreated. I reached into my pocket for a treat, told White Dog to come, and then lured him into a sit by holding the treat slightly above and slightly behind his head. He sat and I gave him the treat, after which I walked through his space and deeper into the house. Without much more effort than that, I had all the dogs following me. White Dog was the first in line to accompany me. I gave out no more treats because I was after a bit of order, not a feeding frenzy. But I moved through the house, and the dogs followed like a school of fish. If one got in my way or crowded too close, I nudged into his space and he yielded it to me.

The owner was stunned and said something many clients have said to me over the years. "You can get them to do this but I can't. They don't respect me, and I guess they never will."

I responded the way I always respond to this comment. "It's not who I am. It's what I am doing. And I will teach you to do what I am doing so they will respect you, too. Once you become pack leader to these dogs, instead of leaving the job to White Dog, you'll be in a much better position to protect other family pets, such as your cat. Otherwise, she may be next."

Now, I wish I could tell you that this story had a happy ending, but I'm pretty sure it did not. I spent several hours with the owner and the dogs, working out a way for her to create structure for them rather than chaos. I talked about how to feed them. How to crate train them. How to give them work, rest, and play in a productive way. As I was leaving the house, a young woman came up to talk to me.

"I'm sorry, but I overheard your conversation. I take care of her horses. And she's not going to do any of those things you told her to do," said the woman.

I looked back toward the barn.

"Well," I said, "you can lead a horse to water but you can't make her drink."

Mob psychology is a well-known phenomenon in human behavior. Under certain conditions, such as in an agitated crowd, individuals will engage in behaviors they would not engage in alone. Violence can be one of those behaviors. The same abnormality can occur in a dog pack. Psychological and physical excitement can easily become a dogfight within the pack, or a group of dogs can gang up and behave as if the family cat has suddenly turned into a squirrel.

Mob behavior in multi-dog households usually can be thwarted before it begins by properly introducing a new dog to your existing dog or dogs. People tend to introduce a new dog by just letting all the dogs greet and sniff one another. Much of the time this method works fine, but not always. A better way, we think, is to exert greater control over the outcome.

The single best way we know to introduce two dogs is to take them on leash walks together. Two people, each with one of the dogs on leash, take the dogs out for five or six leash walks over the course of

Your dog doesn't need to stop and visit every dog he sees on a walk. But when introducing new dogs, start by taking them on a number of calm leash walks together.

several days. These should be focused leash walks, meaning you're walking fast and the dogs are not permitted to lollygag or investigate each other. After that, assuming there hasn't been growling or aggressive lunging between the dogs, the best thing to do is take them to a neutral zone, like a neighbor's yard, and drop the leashes. Holding on to the leashes merely sets the dogs up to strain and posture. A neighbor's yard is better than your own since your original dog is likely to consider your yard his personal territory.

Drop the leashes in a fenced yard and then keep moving. Don't just stand there and watch the dogs. Move! Walk around the yard—a circle will do—and it's likely that for a few moments the dogs will ignore you and get the sniffing out of the way. Eventually they will notice that you are moving, and therefore, they will move as well. By the time they get to meet, sniff, and play, the two dogs will already feel as though they know each other. Or at least that's what usually happens.

It's similar to when you meet someone you think you knew in the past.

"Weren't we in Mrs. Carter's English class together back in middle school?"

This sort of introduction is fairly low-pressure and likely to lead to a positive relationship between the dogs. There are a few considerations, though.

Be very careful what sort of collar you have on each of the dogs. Pinch collars, for instance, tend to tangle up and snag any other collar they get near. That's dangerous because the dogs can accidentally get stuck together, and if that happens, they'll fight, each thinking that the other is doing something bad to him. We know several people who have sustained serious dog bites breaking up this sort of fight. Also be sure that flat collars fit snuggly enough so that they don't dangle. One dog lover we know had a disaster when one of his dogs caught her lower jaw in the loose buckle collar of the other dog and a terrible fight ensued.

After the dogs have met, walked, played, and gotten used to each other, it's time to separate them. If they're both living in your house, then one or both of the dogs can be crated. Although you can crate them near each other, we suggest that for the time being (usually a couple of weeks or until their relationship seems solid) you block their views of each other. Dogs communicate with body language. While you're busy trying to build a good relationship between the dogs, you want to be sure they don't start throwing gang signs at each other.

Continue the daily walks followed by play sessions for a few days, and continue separating the dogs when you're not supervising them. Along with allowing the dogs to experience good times together, you'll need to observe all the nuances to make sure there is no underlying tension between them.

This procedure becomes more difficult logistically if you have more than one dog in the pack to which you are introducing a new dog. It's also more involved from the dog psychology standpoint. That's because two or more already bonded dogs may team up against the new kid who suddenly appears in the living room or backyard. It's well worth taking the time and trouble to go on controlled group walks with all of your pack. Have a friend or family member help so you can walk all the dogs at the same time, and do this multiple times over the course of a week.

If your pack is already accustomed to visiting a local dog park, then consider taking them all there a few days in a row. In the park there is room to spread out, and your dogs will likely be greeting other unfamiliar dogs as well as the family newcomer. Then, when the new guy returns to the backyard or living room, everyone will have a head start on knowing one another.

The good news is that pack animals have evolved to live and function in groups. It is natural to their species. Therefore, the vast majority of dogs can get along just fine. But we can assure you that multi-dog homes with a strong pack leader (human, not canine) experience far fewer problems than ones with tepid leadership and vague rules.

Dogfight

Perhaps the worst problem you can have in a multi-dog home is a dogfight. We're not talking about a scuffle, which usually consists of dogs making a lot of noise and jumping all over each other. A scuffle can look scary, but the difference between a scuffle and a fight is that in a scuffle both parties are trying to get out of the situation without causing or receiving serious injury. A real fight draws blood, and sometimes it's yours if you try to get in the middle of it without knowing what you're doing.

With proper introductions, you will rarely experience a dogfight among your pack. Still, it's important to be aware of how the relationships progress and develop over time. For instance, just because two dogs sleep on the same dog bed and cuddle up with each other, it doesn't mean they won't ever have a dispute, even a serious one. While sleeping in the same bed does indicate bonding, it doesn't mean they are sisters who love each other and would never fight.

So, what do bonded pack mates fight about? It all comes down to competition. There are various resources that can cause disputes among dogs within a pack.

- Space near a family member, especially a family member who is sitting and petting. Often the more dominant dog will guard his human from any intrusion by a pack mate by growling or lunging at the other.
- Food, sometimes dog food but sometimes also dropped human food.
- High-value treats such as rawhide, bully sticks, and dog bones.
- Space near doors, especially during exciting times, such as when guests arrive.
- Toys, especially if a dog is obsessed with a particular toy, such as a tennis ball.

Many owners in multiple-dog households are used to the occasional squabble, which is normal. Just like siblings who have disagreements over who gets to use the red crayon, dogs, no matter how closely bonded, can get irritated. But if, from another room, you were to overhear the children's interaction escalating toward yelling or becoming physical, likely you would quickly sort out the fray by either plucking away the red crayon or working out an equitable sharing program. Marc remembers snapping a crayon in half so that two of his children could use the same color at the same time. Dog owners should react the same way. The key point is that all dogs in the house should have practice in ceasing and desisting any internal dispute once the pack leader asserts control. Problems arise only when the owners either aren't paying close enough attention and don't see the dispute coming or haven't established a pack leader relationship with each member of the pack.

BROTHER CHRISTOPHER   A couple came to us with two female cocker spaniels and a female English bulldog. Individually, the dogs behaved appropriately. The two cockers, who were mother and daughter, were also fine when together. The younger cocker was a happy-go-lucky dog, silly, but in an endearing way. The mother dog was a bit more serious in her attitude, especially to the younger cocker, but not so much as to cause problems. We observed that if the older cocker looked hard at the younger, the daughter would avert her gaze, lick her lips in a calming signal, and avoid conflict. Both dogs were good with people, shared space and toys, and napped together on the same dog bed. They slept in the owners' bed at night, and the owners could pet both cockers one at a time, or both together in close proximity. Zero problems.

The addition of the bulldog to the dynamic, however, resulted in complete bedlam. From that statement you might surmise that the bulldog was a problem. She wasn't. Not even close. Well, she wasn't a problem until the mother cocker made her into one. But let's go back and fill in some details.

The clients were a middle-aged couple who had bred the mother cocker (from the beloved grandmother, now deceased) and also the daughter. They had a happy life with those dogs until their son, only in his early twenties, died in a tragic accident. The bulldog was his pet, and even after it was clear that the mother cocker had real issues with the bulldog, the parents — understandably — just couldn't bring themselves to part with their late son's dog.

"My son loved Beauty so much," the woman told me, "and she's all I have left of him. I'll do anything I can to keep her."

Beauty was an affectionate dog, and her instinct was to stay close to the people, perhaps to both offer and take comfort. But Beauty's urge to insert herself into the space near the owners caused the mother cocker to compete for and guard that space.

For weeks after Beauty first came into the home, the mother cocker would stare at her hard, making and sustaining direct eye contact. This is a dominant behavior, and one that the daughter cocker constantly defused by responding with submission. Unfortunately, the owners didn't realize just how unfair the mother could be. The only reason they didn't have issues was due to the submissive nature of the daughter. Nonetheless, they didn't have any problems, and would never have described themselves as pack leaders. They were content to spoil the dogs and never thought twice about it.

Over and over again, the mother cocker shot Beauty the hard stare that had always caused her daughter to yield and give up whatever resource was in contention. Beauty either didn't know what to make of the stare or didn't care. She never became aggressive toward the cocker, but she didn't yield, either. Having since gotten to know Beauty, we believe she just didn't understand the cocker's message, which, by the way, we believe to have been unfair in the first place: "I own these people and you're never allowed near them."

Eventually the mother cocker stopped staring and started attacking Beauty. Every time this happened, the daughter cocker backed up her mother. The daughter never started these fights, but she joined in on the fracas every time. And poor Beauty. Over and over and over again she would just lower her head and take the punishment, being bitten from both sides by two dogs that had started to draw blood.

One day, Beauty had enough.

The owners won't soon forget that day. Beauty stepped toward them and turned to glance at the mother cocker. The mother cocker threw a hard look at Beauty. Every other time, Beauty not only had failed to react to that challenge but also had taken the punishment handed out to her by the other dogs. The owners would pull the cockers off, but not before they were able to get a few bites in. But this time, as we said, Beauty had had enough, and when the older cocker gave her "that look," Beauty lunged and pinned her on the ground, while the younger cocker attacked Beauty from the rear.

You might think that the dogs would have sorted it out as soon as the cockers realized the bulldog not only outweighed them but was a better, if also reluctant, fighter. Sadly, you'd be wrong. In fact, Beauty learned an unfortunate lesson. She felt safest when she attacked the older cocker if that dog so much as glanced at her. Many serious dogfights ensued, and more than once, the people pulling the dogs apart were bitten.

"It's like that cocker is trying to commit suicide by bulldog," said the owner. "By now she has to know that she's going to lose this fight, but she can't stop provoking her, and now Beauty doesn't even give her a chance to start it first."

This was a very sad situation because what the family most needed was peace and tranquility in which to grieve their loss. Instead, what they were getting was constant dogfights. We took all three dogs into training at once. We made sure that they were housed near one another but not able to see one another. Remember, much of the problematic dialogue had been conducted with visual signals. It was important that we take charge of all aspects of the relationship so that we could rebuild it. Keeping the dogs close allowed them to smell one another's scent nearby but cut off any hard visual exchanges.

It turned out that by our standards none of the dogs was polite on leash. So the first order of business was to teach them to choose pack drive by walking by our side without overreacting to anything in the environment. Once the dogs had that skill well started, we began to walk the three dogs together several times per day. Among the distractions in the environment we didn't permit them to respond to was each other. Knowing that hard glares always preceded a fight, we simply didn't permit the dogs to make eye contact for more than an instant. Using a leash pop to interrupt any attempt to engage, we kept the dogs moving. After a week, all the dogs understood that they were going to be together on walks and that they had to demonstrate etiquette on leash, an important component of which was not carrying on a silent dialogue among themselves.

This was the first and most important step we took in rebuilding the relationships. We had to show each dog that a human pack leader was now making all key decisions. For the first week to ten days, the dogs were tense but compliant. After ten days, the walks became relaxed, with little if any leash popping required to interrupt inappropriate gazing.

Next we taught each dog the go to bed command. We did this individually, but as soon as the dogs were trustworthy enough to stay on their beds despite distractions, we started bringing them inside together after walks and placing each dog on a bed command. We also taught them to come on command.

Then we used this combination approach every day for several more weeks. No dog was given the opportunity to dominate another dog, let alone attack it. Beauty began to come out of constant preemptive attack mode, and the mother cocker began to understand that she was not permitted to exact discipline on either of the other dogs. The younger cocker seemed relieved that the civil war within the pack had arrived at a truce. Plus, all those now-calm leash walks meant that the dogs were finally sharing some mutually pleasant experiences. Admittedly, they weren't yet free to interact physically, but by taking control of all their resources and movements, we had stopped the violence in its tracks and had initiated the process of rebuilding trust, not only in one another but, most important, in a human pack leader who could make better decisions.

Following are the other key rules we put into effect for this trio.

- The dogs ate meals in their crates. They quickly got used to that, and it stopped all food-related aggression.
- The three dogs lost bedroom and human bed privileges. Instead, each slept comfortably on a bed in its own crate.
- High-value treats such as bones were given only as a bedtime treat in the crates and were not permitted to be removed from the crates.
- When the dogs were out of the crates, the crate doors were locked so no two dogs could accidentally run into the same crate.
- The dogs were often walked together, a minimum of twice per day, so they had ample opportunity to simultaneously drain energy and become calm in one another's presence.
- Frequent use of the bed command allowed the dogs to be out of their crates, in the same room together, but still under human control.

So this is how the sequence went: The dogs were taken for walks together. Then, when their energy was low, we would give them a five-minute bed command. Eventually we began allowing the dogs to be loose with one another after the bed command for short periods of time, but only under direct supervision. More than once we used the come command (i.e., "Beauty, come") to interrupt a hard glance that indicated one of the dogs was going to cause a problem. Generally, in such situations there is a ringleader, a specific dog that, if controlled, will permit a much speedier resolution back to balance. Beauty showed a quick willingness to stand down as soon as she realized that we would protect her. The mother cocker was far more resistant, and if we had to interrupt anyone's bad idea, it was usually hers. We'd do that by calling her if she looked ready to object to some reasonable behavior of the other two dogs. At other times we sprayed her with water from a squirt bottle to interrupt her intention, and then followed that up by reinforcing the bed command. Timing was important here. It meant anticipating the dog's bad behavior by reading her body language, giving her an interrupting squirt, and then keeping her on her bed. With consistent practice, the mother cocker got the point.

Really, the entire problem could be summed up this way: The elder cocker had been permitted to become pack leader by the human owners. Initially, it didn't much matter, because she didn't bite people, and the younger cocker never stood up to her enough to provoke a fight. So she ruled the roost with a firm hand — until Beauty came along and refused her orders, most likely because she simply didn't understand them.

Although some dogs may have the heart of a pack leader — a firm but fundamentally fair approach to resource management — there was no such dog in this house. Therefore, our course of action was to teach new rules to the dogs but also to pass along the necessary skill set to the owners. The ultimate message to the dogs was: There will be no fighting over resources in *my* house. I will manage them all, and each of you will have a share.

The tricky bit is remembering that the owners themselves were one of those resources. The dogs fought over proximity to them and their affection. Dogs only fight over humans who do not effectively prohibit it. After some weeks in rehab, we sent the dogs home with the specific protocols outlined above. Two weeks later we heard from the owners that all was well. They were happy. Of course, it took a great deal of concentration to avoid falling back into the same patterns of behavior. But once the owners changed their behavior, so too did the dogs.

One week after that first phone call, we had another. The owners had been able to break up a dogfight seconds before it turned truly serious. No one had been hurt, but the owners were shaken. They confessed that things had been going so well with the new protocols for feeding and walking, etc., that they had begun to relax the rules. As soon as they started going back to their old ways, so did the dogs. The owners agreed to stick to the plan, and all reports after that were positive.

Remember that a great pack leader is fair and makes sure each member has what he needs. It is far likelier that you will do this job better than any one of your dogs. With multiple dogs in the house you can have three times the joy or ten times the problems. Following pack leader principles will help all of you have a great life together.

Epilogue

The Dream Comes True—
An Artful Transformation

No need to remember past events,
no need to think about what was done before.
Look, I am doing something new,
now it emerges; can you not see it?   —Isa. 43:18–19

Then Jacob awoke from his sleep and said, "Truly, God is in this place
and I did not know!" He was afraid and said, "How awe-inspiring this
place is! This is nothing less than an abode of God, and this is a gate of
heaven!"   —Gen. 28:16–17

BROTHER CHRISTOPHER   Throughout this book we've spoken of how the
relationship between dogs and humans has evolved over time, and how our
current cultural circumstances present unique challenges to a relationship
that our ancestors didn't have to face in quite the same way. As we've seen,
the popularity and, hence, population of pet dogs have skyrocketed, and
sometimes the challenges of the modern world have had negative effects on
the relationship, driving us to think creatively about how to address these
challenges properly. For the conscientious dog owner, caring for a dog
requires being in step with what the dog truly needs. This means paying
attention to the true nature of the dog and taking an active role in being a
good leader. The good pack leader provides a dog with what she values and
wants. When we manage to do this, the relationship flourishes in ways that
benefit both our dog and us.

But beyond the tangible benefits the relationship brings both parties, we've learned that there is a profound connection felt by the owner who is paying attention, who is conscious of the precious ebb and flow of the now. It is a connection that helps ground us in the awareness that we are part of a vast network of creation that is filled with God's presence and that can give deep meaning and reassurance to our lives. Understanding nature as revelatory is something those of us who live the monastic life have felt from earliest times. For example, St. Antony the Great — one of the most renowned of the early Christian Desert Fathers in the third century CE — once received a visiting philosopher in his desert abode. In the course of the visit, the philosopher asked how such an educated man as his host got along in the desert without books. Abba Antony replied, "My book, O Philosopher, is the nature of created things, and as often as I have a mind to read the words of God, they are right at my hand." Such an understanding helps us see how a relationship with a dog can itself be a word of God, making us aware of God's presence in nature.

Fortunately, this insight is not reserved solely for monks. It is available to every human being by virtue of his or her humanity. It reflects a sense of connection that transcends specific religious beliefs. We have repeatedly encountered people of differing religious beliefs (even people without any formal religious affiliation) who, while they may not be able to verbalize it, intuit immediately the truth that their relationship with their dog sensitizes them to the mystery present in the broader natural world, a mystery that surrounds and encompasses each of us. There is a spiritual insight here that is well worth exploring.

Now let's acknowledge that some of our readers might find the word *spirituality*, like the even more loaded word *God*, a bit scary and off-putting. Spirituality, as we are using the term, involves the way we stay connected to reality in its most profound sense, and as such, it includes but extends well beyond formal religion. How might that be? Well, by helping us learn to see reality a bit differently than we ordinarily do. While many religious people view life dualistically as divided into sacred and secular realms — going to church, for example, as opposed to the more typical daily routine of work — what true spirituality helps us accomplish is a graceful integration of the two realms. It does this by uniting the experience of spiritual practice with our everyday lives. We become aware of an abiding presence that follows us long after we've left church and that we recognize in the most unexpected of places: like in the relationship we share with our dog.

People sometimes ask, "How did this insight into the spiritual character of the human-dog relationship develop for you?" In a way, living in a monastery naturally facilitates it. A monk dedicates himself to searching for God in all things, in all the aspects of his life.

For me, one such experience occurred after I had been training dogs for a few years. When I was first assigned to work in the training program at New Skete, I was so overwhelmed with learning how to train that I didn't really have time to think much about the spiritual nature of the relationship. I was so consumed with learning the ropes and providing instruction for our clients that anything beyond that didn't really occur to me. It was a period of intense learning. I was fortunate that after a while I discovered I had a talent for training, and since I was working every day with a variety of dogs, my technical skills grew. Yet I didn't realize that something fundamental was missing, something that went beyond technical mastery. One day I was practicing with a dog that was to be going home the following day. It was a beautiful Labrador retriever that had done well in the training program. We were practicing the routine at heel when suddenly something changed. I was no longer just engaged in a training exercise. Instead, it was as if the two of us were doing ballet, totally in sync with each other. Our attention was entirely focused on each other, and the moment seemed outside of time. There was such a sense of unity and oneness that it allowed me to sense the spiritual connection. For those precious minutes I experienced a harmony, a oneness with this dog, that was as prayerful as any I had spent in church. And then the little light went on, the aha moment that changed me forever. It helped me see how the whole of life is a piece, a sacred dance that is linked together, and how we get to continually move through its unfolding.

Integrating all the elements of life into a spiritual whole is not just a goal for monastics. It's a goal for all of us. If you're a Christian monk, naturally you'll describe this process as living consciously in God's presence, but it can also be described in any number of other ways. No matter: The reality is the same. And while the scope of this work is as broad as life itself, we've discovered that a relationship with a dog can, in a particularly poignant way, put us in direct touch with the mystery of God present in nature.

All we have to do is open our eyes. Taking a quiet walk with our

Dogs help put us in touch with nature. They never miss a scent or a sound. From them, we can learn to be more present in the moment.

dog in the woods, for example, can take us out of our anxieties and concerns, and can provide the occasion to notice the beauty that fills all creation, that continuously surrounds us even when we fail to perceive it. Simply noticing on such a walk the dog's body language, its fascination with the feast of scent, and how the dog takes in all that happens around it is a reminder to us to listen as well. Before we know it, our feelings have shifted, and we're better able to walk with equanimity and calm.

Another way dogs help keep us in touch with reality is by being a reliable source of self-knowledge. Because dogs are naturally conditioned to observe the widest range of communicative signs from their peers—from the subtleties of body language to the many different types of vocalizing—dogs tend to read reality like a book, and that includes us. They respond honestly to whatever they perceive. Dogs are guileless; they simply don't lie, and as such they are a valuable means of self-knowledge and self-awareness. They mirror back to us our emotional state directly and in ways that humans can't. By paying attention to our dogs, we can become more aware of how we're coming across to others. Who has not had the experience of being impatient with our dog and then noticing the response of sadness and hurt inscribed over his body? Such an occasion is the opportunity for us to be honest with ourselves, and to work on changing. It is not just the dog that deserves better: All with whom we come in contact deserve better as well.

Naturally, such self-discipline highlights the importance of listening to what is really going on, of discerning what is needed in a particular situation. A spiritual person is one who listens to what reality is saying and then acts on that basis. In terms of how this plays out in a relationship with a dog, it becomes our task to understand what truly serves the relationship and then to carry that out. All of the lessons of leadership we have spoken about throughout this book do precisely this. But they also help us to respond to life on a much broader and more conscious level.

Since dogs, like us, are intrinsically social creatures that thrive on relationship, that is even more the case when those bonds are faithful and strong. It is illuminating to examine the spontaneous delight dogs take in life when playing. The dog cannot hide its joy as it romps with a playmate on the beach or initiates a game of canine tag in an open field. Dogs radiate an awareness of the gift of the moment, the joy of the simplest pleasures, and that can speak meaningfully to us if we are awake. How often do we take life's simplest pleasures for granted? The dog certainly doesn't, and happy are we when we take its example to heart.

But dogs also share with us deeper moments, such as when we notice our dog gazing at us intently in shared silence, and we can read the depth of feeling that is there. What is so amazing, so mysterious, is that this comes from a creature of another species. In such a moment, perhaps we have been fortunate enough to wonder how we could ever possibly merit such love and devotion. How could it be anything other than grace? This is a wondrous thing to experience, and deeply humbling. For in spite of all our imperfections — the times with our dog that we could have handled better, when we have acted selfishly or even foolishly — the dog still loves us. The dog is able to see through all of our limitations and still desire to be with us. How can that not change us, heal us? It is when we feel something akin to this emotion that we are able to see ourselves in a new way through our dog's eyes. That sort of experience can teach us something of the very mystery of God: how God sees us, how God never gives up on us but continues to encourage us forward. And that can provide us with the inspiration to truly change, to become our best selves. We learn to live our dreams.

MARC   Gus was my first dog. He lived from the time I was eleven years old until I was nearly thirty. He was with me from the innocence of childhood all the way through high school, college, and the beginning of my adult life. I spent countless hours of my childhood — and his — training Gus. He remembered and performed his complicated obedience routine into his dotage, way after deafness and strokes, and until shortly before he died at nearly eighteen.

He was a sheltie born April 29, 1969. Now long gone, Gus came to me in a dream several years ago.

In it, he spoke to me in words that did not come out of his mouth, but which I heard. This is the exact exchange:

"Where are you?" Gus asked, intense in his longing for me.

"I'll come to you one day," I told him.

"But I have been waiting so long," he said.

"Because it's not my time yet," I told him. "But I will come."

Gus paused, but only briefly.

"I'll wait for you," he said.

"Find Bobbi and Frannie," I said. "They are greyhounds. They are mine too, and they will know you. They will wait with you."

"I will," Gus said, and he left me slowly, reluctantly, at my bidding. I woke up crying, as I cry now recounting the experience.

I have always known that dogs care about us on the deepest possible levels, but only recently did I put together my own concept of why.

I think Gus came to me that night because I was finally ready to understand the answer to my long-held question: Why do dogs care about us so much?

They care because — more than the food, shelter, and comfort we dispense — we provide them with a sense of purpose, a reason to exist, and a belief that they're not alone. When led properly, dogs consider us to be more than their pack mates or even pack leaders.

We are like their gods.

Their faith in us is absolute. It's never questioned. It's never in crisis.

When a dog is trained, he learns that he no longer has to make every decision in his life. A dog that pulls on the leash and is out of control is not a satisfied dog. Yet, if that behavior is all the dog knows, he'll do it over and over. I see this now as a cry for help, the way the dog shows his longing for leadership.

But once the dog has learned to share decision-making with a human being, a sacred bond is formed that lasts his entire life and, maybe, even endures death.

I think that's what Gus was telling me. And that feeling is as beautiful as any I've ever had.

Gus revealed to me the art of living with a dog.

Acknowledgments

Marc Goldberg
ChicagoDogTrainer.com

This book is the result of a lifetime of learning, a process that continues to this day because dogs and people always have more to learn from one another. Dogs keep us humble. They remind us to enjoy the simple things, to get out of our own heads occasionally, to smell the air, see the squirrel. Even the earthy reality of picking up after them on a walk connects us to the biology of living things.

I had many good teachers as I learned about training and artful living with dogs. Some of them were people. A number of them were dogs. Some of the most important lessons I have ever learned about dogs came as a result of making mistakes. Some of them were minor and could be easily fixed with a bit of reflection and effort. Others were more complicated, and remedied only with great effort… or not at all. Even in those instances, I have profited in a way that lets me help more people and dogs.

To every dog I have helped: I'm thankful that you allowed me to increase your quality of life and to connect you better to the family who loves you.

To any dog I have failed: You are the few I remember and think about the most. You are the reason I never want to stop learning about your species. You motivate me to be the best trainer possible and, in fact, the best person I can be.

The friendship between man and dog is very old. Some cultures mummified their dogs and buried them with their masters. Others memorialized their dogs in paintings, tapestries, and sculpture. I keep a collection of little boxes containing the ashes of my departed pack. One day I wish to be among them. That is not a morbid thought for me. Far from it. It is a happy notion that I will go to the company of my dogs.

Friendship was the starting point of this book. Not just between dogs but also between people. The love of dogs must always connect us back to people. If you think you love dogs more than people, remember dogs' high opinion of our species. Try and learn from them.

My friendship with Brother Christopher — and ultimately with all the Monks of New Skete — grew in an organic but most unexpected way. They became a second family to me. In Brother Christopher I found a kindred spirit, a sharp wit, a terrific dog man, an author, a formidable intellect, and — above all — a monk and a priest. I am deeply grateful for this friendship, which has changed my life.

Years ago I thought I might have a book in me. Brother Christopher was very encouraging and introduced me to his literary agent, Kate Hartson. Kate gave me the gift of her time, and eventually the monks and I decided to produce this volume together. Kate has been a relentless shepherd for this project. Like a border collie, she has nipped at the heels of its authors, helping us move forward and keeping us pointed in the right direction, at times through sheer force of will. She has done more for this book than we could have asked or expected.

There are always people an author wants to thank, but in this case there are also dogs. Thank-yous follow:

Brother Christopher and the Monks of New Skete, coauthors and friends

Kate Hartson, agent and shepherd

Patrick Farrell, training partner and friend, who listened to every idea about this book — twice

Wendy and Jack Volhard, who gave me great encouragement and friendship

Thanks also to Mary Mazzeri; Chad Mackin; Cheri Lucas; Heather Beck; Barney Goldberg, who gave me my love of dogs; Neshama Siner, who allowed me to grow up with a dog; Colleen Goldberg; Samantha Goldberg; Faye Goldberg; William Goldberg; Tawni McBee; Martin Deeley; Pat Trichter; and Juan Carlos Arias. Special thanks to the International Association of Canine Professionals (IACP) and to:

Gus, Sheltie
Honey, Golden mix
Bobbi, Greyhound
Franny, Greyhound
Diablo, Doberman
Lucky Laddie, Collie
Sheena, German shepherd dog
Tippy, Border collie mix
Scooter, Rat terrier

May we strive to be worthy of their love.

Brother Christopher
newskete.org

Inspiration is a mysterious thing. It is only at the end of a project such as this that one becomes conscious of just how many people played a part in helping this book come into being. Often they weren't aware of their importance, but their openness, experience, and insight have helped me to articulate some of the ideas in this book.

I am extremely grateful to my brothers and sisters here at New Skete, whose collective wisdom is deeply imprinted within these pages. They have been a steady encouragement and support throughout the birthing of this book.

It is hard to overstate the gratitude I feel to our coauthor, Marc Goldberg. The friendship that has developed between us not only has renewed my enthusiasm for all things dog but has meant even more on a personal, heartfelt level. Marc possesses more than an uncommon understanding of, and gift with, dogs — his goodness and generosity bespeak his love for people as well. Marc, it has been such a privilege to share this journey with you.

Our agent, Kate Hartson, has combined loyalty and friendship with a discerning eye that has helped guide this book to reality. What a grace to have such a trusted friend as both counselor and shepherd of this project. Also, thanks to Carl Patka, who was very helpful at a particular point in this book.

A very sincere shout-out to the many esteemed friends I've come to know in the International Association of Canine Professionals (IACP). Each year at the IACP conference I've been able to renew acquaintances, share insights and stories, and listen intently to the collective wisdom that arises from the many presentations and conversations. In particular I'd like to thank Martin Deeley, Pat Trichter, Bob Jervis, Heather Beck, Tyler Muto, Josh Moran, Mary Mazzeri, Chad Mackin, Cheri Lucas, Behesha Doan, and Tawni McBee.

Finally, to Ginger, Dunya, Deja-Vu, Natasha, Anka, Meiko, Delphi, Nino, Astro, Wisdom, Zoe, Daisy, and Raisa. You have taught me so much and helped me become a better monk and human being.

Index

About the Authors

Brother Christopher entered the Monks of New Skete in 1981 and has been director of the training program there since 1982. In addition to his responsibilities training dogs, he is the prior of the monks, a priest, an author, a teacher, and a spiritual director.

In 1969 **Marc Goldberg**'s first dog, Gus, came into his life, along with a host of dog-related problems. Gus began life as a normal sheltie puppy, but at the age of six months he was hit by a car when he would not come when called. Fortunately, his only injury was a fractured leg.

When the dog healed, Marc—who was only twelve at the time—was enrolled in dog-training school along with Gus. "Teach him so he doesn't get killed," his mother told him.

Before long, Marc became fascinated with dog behavior and training. He and Gus competed in many American Kennel Club obedience trials, winning High in Trial at their first show and, later, a Dog World Award.

As the youngest voting member of the Philadelphia Dog Training Club, Marc studied under some of the best dog trainers in the country. By the age of thirteen he was training dogs for his schoolteachers and other private clients.

Marc now runs a boarding school for dogs at his Little Dog Farm in suburban Chicago, teaches training classes, conducts private lessons, gives behavior consultations via Skype, and helps thousands of people improve their relationships with their dogs.

Marc is past president of the International Association of Canine Professionals, an inductee of the IACP Members Hall of Fame, and a recipient of the association's CDTA and PDTI titles.

Marc Goldberg's website is ChicagoDogTrainer.com.

For more information, visit LetDogsBeDogs.org.